CW01084053

THE HISTORY OF AL-ṬABARĪ

AN ANNOTATED TRANSLATION

VOLUME XII

The Battle of al-Qādisiyyah and the Conquest of Syria and Palestine

A.D. 635–637/A.H. 14–15

The preparation of this volume was made possible in part by a grant from the National Endowment for the Humanities, an independent federal agency.

Bibliotheca Persica
Edited by Ehsan Yar-Shater

The History of al-Ṭabarī
(Ta'rīkh al-rusul wa 'l-mulūk)

VOLUME XII

The Battle of al-Qādisiyyah and the Conquest of Syria and Palestine

translated and annotated
by

Yohanan Friedmann

The Hebrew University of Jerusalem

State University of New York Press

Published by
State University of New York Press, Albany

Printed in the United States of America

For information, contact State University of New York Press, Albany, NY
www.sunypress.edu

Library of Congress Cataloging in Publication Data

Ṭabarī, 838?–923.
[Ta 'rīkh al-rusul wa-al-mulūk. English. Selections]
The battle of al-Qādisiyyah and the conquest of Syria and
Palestine : A.D. 635–637/A.H. 14–15 / translated and annotated by
Yohanan Friedmann.
p. cm.—(The history of al-Ṭabarī = Ta 'rīkh al-rusul wa 'l
-mulūk ; v. 12) (Bibliotheca Persica) (SUNY series in Near Eastern
studies)
Translation of extracts from: Ta 'rīkh al-rusul wa-al-mulūk.
Includes index.
Bibliography: p.
ISBN 0–7914–0733–0 (acid-free).—ISBN 0–7914–0734–9 (pb: acid
free)
1. Islamic Empire—History—622–661. 2. Qādisīyah, Battle of,
637. 3. ʿUmar ibn al-Khaṭṭāb, Caliph, d. 644. I. Friedmann,
Yohanan. II. Title. III. Series. IV. Series: Ṭabarī, 838?–923.
Ta 'rīkh al-rusul wa-al-mulūk. English ; v. 12. V. Series:
Bibliotheca Persica (Albany, N.Y.)
DS38.2.T313 1985 vol. 12
[DS38.1]
909'.1—dc20 90-10326
CIP

For
Zafrira, Yasmin, Tamar

Preface

The History of Prophets and Kings *(Ta'rīkh al-rusul wa'l-mulūk)* by Abū Ja'far Muḥammad b. Jarīr al-Ṭabarī (839 923), here rendered as *The History of al-Ṭabarī,* is by common consent the most important universal history produced in the world of Islam. It has been translated here in its entirety for the first time for the benefit of non-Arabists, with historical and philological notes for those interested in the particulars of the text.

Al-Ṭabarī's monumental work explores the history of the ancient nations, with special emphasis on biblical peoples and prophets, the legendary and factual history of ancient Iran, and, in great detail, the rise of Islam, the life of the Prophet Muḥammad, and the history of the Islamic world down to the year 915. The first volume of this translation contains a biography of al-Ṭabarī and a discussion of the method, scope, and value of his work. It also provides information on some of the technical considerations that have guided the work of the translators.

The *History* has been divided here into 39 volumes, each of which covers about two hundred pages of the original Arabic text in the Leiden edition. An attempt has been made to draw the dividing lines between the individual volumes in such a way that each is to some degree independent and can be read as such. The page numbers of the Leiden edition appear on the margins of the translated volumes.

Al-Ṭabarī very often quotes his sources verbatim and traces the chain of transmission *(isnād)* to an original source. The chains of transmitters are, for the sake of brevity, rendered by only a dash (—) between the individual links in the chain. Thus, "According to Ibn

Ḥumayd—Salamah—Ibn Isḥāq" means that al-Ṭabarī received the report from Ibn Ḥumayd, who said that he was told by Salamah, who said that he was told by Ibn Isḥāq and so on. The numerous subtle and important differences in the original Arabic wording have been disregarded.

The table of contents at the beginning of each volume gives a brief survey of the topics dealt with in that particular volume. It also includes the headings and subheadings as they appear in al-Ṭabarī's text, as well as those occasionally introduced by the translator.

Well-known place names, such as, for instance, Mecca, Baghdad, Jerusalem, Damascus, and the Yemen, are given in their English spellings. Less common place names, which are the vast majority, are transliterated. Biblical figures appear in the accepted English spelling. Iranian names are usually transcribed according to their Arabic forms, and the presumed Iranian forms are often discussed in the footnotes.

Technical terms have been translated wherever possible, but some, such as sirham and imām, have been retained in Arabic forms. Others that cannot be translated with sufficient precision have been retained and italicized, as well as footnoted.

The annotation aims chiefly at clarifying difficult passages, identifying individuals and place names, and discussing textual difficulties. Much leeway has been left to the translators to include in the footnotes whatever they consider necessary and helpful.

The bibliographies list all the sources mentioned in the annotation.

The index in each volume contains all the names of persons and places referred to in the text, as well as those mentioned in the notes as far as they refer to the medieval period. It does not include the names of modern scholars. A general index, it is hoped, will appear after all the volumes have been published.

For further details concerning the series and acknowledgments, see Preface to Volume I.

Ehsan Yar-Shater

Contents

Preface / vii

Abbreviations / xi

Translator's Foreword / xiii

The Caliphate of ʿUmar b. al-Khaṭṭāb (cont'd)

Abbreviations

BGA	*Bibliotheca Geographorum Arabicorum*
CHI	*The Cambridge History of Iran*
EI^1	*Encylopaedia of Islam*, first edition
EI^2	*Encyclopaedia of Islam*, second edition
GAL	C. Brockelmann, *Geschichte der arabischen Litteratur*. Leiden, 1937–49.
GAS	F. Sezgin, *Geschichte des arabischen Schrifttums*. Leiden, 1967–.
IC	*Islamic Culture*
IOS	*Israel Oriental Studies*
JESHO	*Journal of the Economic and Social History of the Orient*
JSAI	*Jerusalem Studies in Arabic and Islam*
REI	*Revue des Études Islamiques*
RSO	*Rivista degli Studi Orientali*
SI	*Studia Islamica*
WI	*Die Welt des Islams*
WKAS	M. Ullmann *et al.*, *Wörterbuch der klassischen arabischen Sprache*. Wiesbaden 1957–.

Translator's Foreword*

I

Most of the present volume, which describes a part of ʿUmar b. al-Khaṭṭāb's reign, deals with the battle of al-Qādisiyyah, in which the Muslims decisively defeated the Persians. This victory heralded the downfall of the Sasanian dynasty, paved the way for the conquest of Iraq, and facilitated Islamic expansion into Persia and beyond. Al-Qādisiyyah is located to the southwest of the ancient city of al-Ḥīrah, on the border between the fertile Iraqi lowlands (*al-sawād*) and the Arabian desert. Ṭabarī's text (which records the accounts of Ibn Isḥāq, al-Wāqidī, and predominantly that of Sayf b. ʿUmar),[1] confronts the reader with manifold historical problems. Even such a basic question as the date of the battle is not easily solved: Ṭabarī's sources give the date as 14, 15, or 16/635–37.[2] Many of the places through which the troops moved on their way to the battlefield and in which the skirmishes occurred cannot be identified with sufficient precision, and it is therefore impossible to elucidate many tactical aspects of the battle.[3] The size of the armies involved in the fighting presents another baffling problem: The data for the Sasanian army vary between 30,000 and 210,000; in the early sources, the Muslims are said to have numbered between 6,000 and 12,000, but

*Unless otherwise specified, all references in the introduction are to Ṭabarī, *Ta'rīkh*, I.

1. But not of ʿAwānah b. al-Ḥakam, as suggested by L. Veccia Vaglieri in her article "al-Ḳādisiyya" in *EI*². For recent evaluations of Sayf as a historian, see A. Duri, *Historical Writing*, index; and Ella Landau-Tasseron, "Sayf Ibn ʿUmar."

2. See pp. 2377, 2349; cf. *EI*², "al-Ḳādisiyya," 386a–b.

3. Cf. Donner, *Conquests*, 204.

a later source, al-Masʿūdī, speaks of 38,000 or 88,000 Muslim warriors.[4] As far as the historicity of Ṭabarī's description is concerned, the material presently available is unlikely to yield results beyond those attained by Veccia Vaglieri, Donner, Noth,[5] and other scholars. It therefore seems advisable to refer the reader to their work and to use this introduction in order to highlight other aspects of Ṭabarī's fascinating text.

II

It seems that a considerable segment of the material included in this volume was suitable to be used by storytellers (*quṣṣāṣ*) in order to capture the attention of their listeners.[6] This is especially the case with regard to the parables related by the Persian general Rustam in order to convince the Muslims to retreat;[7] King Yazdagird's parable of the eagle and the birds;[8] the description of the magicians' contest at the court;[9] the numerous instances in which Muslims outwitted Persians in debate, deed, or combat; and the story of the bull who, while being hidden in the thicket by his owner, suddenly speaks out in order to disclose his location and enable the Muslims to lead him away, presumably to his death.[10] Descriptions of extreme personal bravery are of a different character but equally captivating, and it is noteworthy that some commanders are made to say in their exhor-

4. These rather disparate numbers constitute two versions given in the various editions of Masʿūdī's *Murūj*. The figure 38,000 appears in the first edition (Paris, 1861–67, IV, 208), as well as in the edition of C. Pellat (Beirut, 1970, III, 55). The higher figure appears in the edition published in Beirut in 1965, II, 312. The two versions are graphically fairly similar in the Arabic script, which is probably the reason for the discrepancy. See also Donner, *Conquests*, 203–5; *EI*², s.v. "al-Ḳādisiyya," 386a. G. H. A. Juynboll has recently suggested that one should divide all these numbers by a coefficient of 100 in order to arrive at a plausible description of events. See Juynboll, *Conquests*, xiii–xvi.

5. Noth, *Studien*, should be consulted particularly with regard to the historical reliability of the material, as well as with regard to the various recurrent themes in Ṭabarī's account. Noth has used numerous passages included in the present volume for his analyses. See, for instance, *Studien*, 72–73, with regard to pp. 2235 and 2251 of Ṭabarī's text.

6. See *EI*², s.v. "Ḳāṣṣ" (Ch. Pellat). See also F. Rosenthal's pertinent observation about the "colorful novelistic presentation of the events" by such traditionists as Sayf b. ʿUmar in *Muslim Historiography*, 166; and Duri, *Historical Writing*, 144–45.

7. See pp. 2281–83, 2352.

8. See p. 2248.

9. See pp. 2252–53.

10. See p. 2234.

tations to the troops that the exploits performed by the Muslims in the impending battle will be related in festivals forever and ever.[11] We may mention the harrowing story of a Muslim who, though disemboweled, continued to fight until his death;[12] the poem in which a warrior who lost his leg enjoins himself to endure and not let the lost leg divert his attention from the battle;[13] and the poem in which the hero pledges to continue using his hand in combat, though three of its fingers have just been cut off.[14] The heroism and military prowess of certain Muslims seem all the more impressive when their indomitable deeds are related and extolled by their captured enemies.[15]

Considerable space is devoted by Ṭabarī to the encounters between the Persian leaders and several Muslim delegations and individuals who were either invited to the Persian court to negotiate a solution to the conflict or sent by ʿUmar in order to invite the king to embrace Islam. In these discussions, said to have been held at the royal court or at Rustam's military headquarters, there are several recurrent themes. The Persians treat the Muslims with contempt, speak derisively about their weapons, expatiate on their poverty and primitive way of life, and assert that they do not have the military might required to take on such an empire as that of the Persians.[16] Anachronistic echoes of Shuʿūbī arguments can clearly be discerned in the speeches said to have been addressed to the successive Muslim delegations. The Persians also threaten the Muslims with death and destruction if they seek to accomplish their goals by military means.[17] At the same time, Yazdagird and Rustam make repeated attempts to dissuade the Muslims from embarking on such a course by promises of material gain if they will desist from their warlike intentions.[18] Their arguments are supported by an ostentatious display of luxury and abundance at the court.[19]

The most noticeable feature of the Muslim response to this arro-

---

11. See p. 2294, above; cf. p. 2293, above.
12. See p. 2310.
13. See pp. 2328–29.
14. See p. 2410.
15. See pp. 2263–64.
16. See pp. 2236, 2275, 2279, 2280, 2352.
17. See p. 2337.
18. See pp. 2240, 2267, 2276, 2281.
19. See pp. 2270, 2274.

gant display of opulence is studied contempt. Ignoring orders to dismount before entering into Rustam's presence, the Muslims contemptuously ride their horses on the luxurious carpets of the Persians. On other occasions they plunge their spears into the carpets and cushions, tearing them to shreds. Their rugged and shabby appearance is brought into sharp relief when contrasted with the luxury and finery of their rivals.[20]

Responding to speeches delivered by the Persians, the Muslims freely admit that the conditions in which they lived in the pre-Islamic period (*al-Jāhiliyyah*) were primitive, claiming, however, that this has lost all significance because these conditions had undergone a substantial transformation for the better with the coming of Islam.[21] The Muslim spokesmen counter the threats of the Persians with the repeatedly expressed conviction that Muslims who die on the battlefield will be rewarded in Paradise and that those who survive will prevail over their enemies.[22] The Persians are offered the three classical options: to embrace Islam, to pay the poll tax, or to be attacked and defeated.[23] None of the Persian suggestions of material support is acceptable; unlike the pre-Islamic Arabs, the Muslims do not fight for worldly possessions or in order to improve their standard of living. Their only objective is to spread the new faith of Islam.

Ṭabarī's account of the battle and of the events surrounding it contains several episodes of a symbolic nature. These are introduced at various stages in order to assure the listener or the reader that the outcome of the war will be favorable to the Muslims. In several cases these indications gain increased credibility by being associated with Persian dignitaries. It is King Yazdagird who perceives a disastrous omen in a few words used in his discussion with a Muslim delegation.[24] In another episode, Yazdagird places a load of soil on a Muslim's neck and drives him out of the capital city of al-Madā'in, together with his companions. The king's intention is to humiliate the Muslims, but Rustam's interpretation is different: He perceives

20. See pp. 2270–71, 2273.
21. See pp. 2241–42, 2268, 2283–84, 2352–53.
22. See pp. 2237, 2242.
23. See pp. 2240, 2242, 2272, 2273, 2284, but see Noth, *Studien*, 131ff.; and Crone, *Slaves*, 208–9 n. 68.
24. See p. 2239.

it as a symbol that the Muslims have taken hold of the keys to the Persian kingdom and "carried the country away."[25] Another event of symbolic nature occurs in the heat of battle. A westerly wind of gale force, which is traditionally described as having destroyed the rebellious community of ʿĀd in the legendary past, topples the sunshade from Rustam's throne. The significance is clear: God is about to destroy the infidel kingdom of Persia, as he had destroyed the sinful community of ʿĀd.[26] The Persian defeat is also indicated when Rustam dreams of an angel who seals the Persian weapons, surrenders them to ʿUmar, or takes them up to heaven.[27] Furthermore, Ṭabarī uses the astrological knowledge attributed to Rustam in order to convey to the reader the feeling that the defeat of the Persians is being predicted by the stars and is therefore inescapable.[28] Rustam is made to play a double role; on the one hand, he is loyal to his king and does his best to save the empire by trying to persuade the Arabs to desist and return to their land. When these efforts fail, he leads his army into battle. On the other hand, he is keenly aware of the fact that his efforts will be of no avail and that the Persian empire is doomed.

III

A much smaller segment of the present volume deals with battles against the Byzantines and the conquest of Syria and Palestine.[29] As in the case of al-Qādisiyyah, the chronology of these events is largely uncertain.[30] Ṭabarī describes the battles of Marj al-Rūm;[31] the conquest of the northern Syrian cities of Ḥimṣ (Emesa)[32] and Qinnasrīn;[33] the conquest of Caesarea on the Palestinian coast;[34] and the battle of Ajnādayn.[35] Following these defeats of the Byzantines, Emperor Heraclius decided to leave Syria, asserting that his departure

25. See pp. 2242–44. Cf. Yusuf, "Qadisiyya," 15.
26. See p. 2236; and *EI²*, s.v. "ʿĀd" (F. Buhl).
27. See pp. 2266, 2286.
28. See pp. 2251, 2253, 2266.
29. Cf. Donner, *Conquests*, 148–51.
30. Cf. Donner, *Conquests*, 146.
31. See pp. 2389–90.
32. See pp. 2390–92.
33. See pp. 2393–94.
34. See pp. 2397–99.
35. See p. 2400.

was final: No Byzantine would return to Syria until the end of days, except in fear.[36] Parallel to the case of al-Qādisiyyah, Ṭabarī's text reflects a sharp perception of the historical significance of these events for the expansion and durability of Islam.[37]

A chapter of special interest deals with the surrender of Jerusalem to ʿUmar b. al-Khaṭṭāb.[38] The problem of ʿUmar's visit to Jerusalem and of its historicity has been extensively discussed in two recent articles by H. Busse[39] and cannot be taken up here. Suffice it to say that in Ṭabarī's text ʿUmar's conquest of the city is predicted by a Jew, yet one of the most important actions ascribed to ʿUmar during his visit to the city reflects the disengagement of Islam from Judaism; The Muslims are enjoined to pray in the direction of Mecca alone, and the veneration of the Rock is prohibited. Fulfilling another prediction, ʿUmar cleans the rubbish with which the Byzantines are said to have covered the Temple after its destruction. In this way he restores the Temple Mount to its purity and at the same time transforms it into a sanctuary of Islam.[40] The Islamization of Jerusalem has to be considered in conjunction with other developments in Islamic ritual that had similar significance. The change of the *qiblah* from Jerusalem to Mecca[41] and the abolition of the obligatory fast of the tenth of Muḥarram, which had been established after the *hijrah* in imitation of the Jewish Day of Atonement,[42] have to be considered in this context.

IV

Some of the most important material included in this volume deals with various matters of an economic and legal nature. The conquest of the fertile lowlands of Iraq (*al-sawād*) raised the question of the legal status of the land and its inhabitants. The issue was complicated by the fact that the conquest of the area was effected in two stages. The early campaigns of Khālid b. al-Walīd — the so-called

---

36. See p. 2396.
37. For the great importance ascribed by the Arabs to the battle of al-Qādisiyyah, see p. 2364.
38. See pp. 2403–9.
39. "ʿOmar b. al-Khaṭṭāb"; "ʿOmar's Image."
40. For a critical interpretation of this episode, see Crone and Cook, *Hagarism*, 5–6.
41. See pp. 1279–81; *EI*², s.v. "Ḳibla" i. (A. J. Wensinck).
42. See p. 1281; *EI*², s.v. "ʿĀshūrāʾ" I (A. J. Wensinck).

ayyām—are estimated to have taken place in the spring or summer of 12/633.[43] In the wake of his victories, Khālid b. al-Walīd concluded treaties with the people of al-Ḥīrah and several other localities. These treaties stipulated payment of the poll tax and, in one case, obliged the inhabitants to spy on behalf of the Muslims.[44] The later battles, among which al-Qādisiyyah takes pride of place, occurred sometime between 14 and 16/635–38. The legal question was whether there should be any difference in the status of the inhabitants who made peace treaties with Khālid b. al-Walīd and who had fulfilled their obligations accordingly and those whose lands were overrun in the second stage of the conquest and who did not have any treaties with the conquering Muslims. According to the historical tradition recorded by Ṭabarī, Saʿd b. Abī Waqqāṣ, the commander of the Muslim forces in al-Qādisiyyah, implemented the treaties that Khālid b. al-Walīd had concluded earlier. With regard to the inhabitants of the *sawād* who did not have treaties, Saʿd asked ʿUmar to make a ruling. Describing the behavior of the inhabitants during the fighting, he discerned several groups among them: those who stayed in their abodes, those who left and later claimed that they had been forcibly recruited into the Persian army, those who abandoned their land without giving any explanation for their move, and those who surrendered to the Muslims without a fight.[45] The underlying assumption of his discourse is that abandoning the land at the time of the fighting is prima facie a hostile act and that an explanation is necessary in order to induce the Muslims to disregard it or to view it in a different light.[46] Saʿd made it clear that it was, nevertheless, in the best interest of the Muslims to gain the goodwill of the entire population. ʿUmar's reply made ostensible distinctions between the various groups, but its salient point was the grant to Saʿd of power to treat all inhabitants of the *sawād,* even those who had abandoned their land in order to assist the Persians, in the same way: to conclude a treaty that would allow them to keep their land and oblige them to pay the poll tax.[47] This development is best summarized in a tradition recorded by Ibn Sallām: "The people of

---

43. See Donner, *Conquests,* 178.
44. See pp. 2019–20, 2044–45, 2049–50; Balādhurī, *Futūḥ,* 244–45.
45. These groups are, of course, not mutually exclusive.
46. Cf. p. 2467.
47. See pp. 2368–71.

the *sawād* did not have a treaty. But when the poll tax was levied on them, [*ipso facto*] a treaty with them came into being" (*lam yakun li-ahl al-sawād ʿahd fa-lammā ukhidhat minhum al-jizyah ṣāra lahum ʿahd*).[48] ʿUmar resisted the demands made by some prominent Muslims—Bilāl b. Rabāḥ, the *mu'adhdhin* of the Prophet, and al-Zubayr b. al-ʿAwwām are mentioned among them—to divide the land conquered by force among the warriors. He preferred that the original inhabitants retain possession of the land, so that the taxes imposed upon them would serve as a perennial source of income for the Muslim community.[49] Only the property of the royal family and of its active supporters and some areas in public use (such as the properties of the Zoroastrian fire temples) became *fay'*, "solid booty," and were to be divided among the Muslims. It was, however, impractical to put this division into effect because the areas in question were scattered over the entire *sawād*. They were therefore administered collectively on behalf of those who were entitled to shares in them (*ahl al-fay'*).[50]

These were, in broad terms, the economic and legal arrangements that are said to have been concluded with the original population of the conquered Iraqi lowlands.[51] Ṭabarī's historical tradition speaks also about the economic arrangements made within the Muslim community. These are subsumed under the heading of the pay system (*ʿaṭā'*) and the military register (*dīwān*).[52] Seniority in Islam was in most instances the criterion according to which the amount of pay was determined. Those who embraced Islam early enough to participate in the battle of Badr in 2/624 received five thousand dirhams. Those who joined the Prophet between Badr and al-Ḥudaybiyyah (6/628) received four thousand each. With each successive stage of conversion the amount decreased: The lowest payment was determined for those who joined Islam and the Muslim army at various times after the battles of Yarmūk and al-Qādisiyyah. Muslims who acquitted themselves exceptionally well (*ahl al-balā'*) received

48. Ibn Sallām, *Amwāl*, 140 § 379. Cf. Noth, "Zum Verhältnis," 157.

49. See Abū Yūsuf, *Kharāj*, 67–73, 86–87; Ibn Sallām, *Amwāl*, 57–59; Sarakhsī, *Sharḥ al-siyar*, III, 1039–40; Duri, "Taxation," 139–40; Forand, "Status."

50. See pp. 2371–72, 2468–69; Shaban, *History*, 49–50.

51. For a discussion of the emergence of these traditions in the Umayyad period, rather than at the time of the conquest, see Noth, "Zum Verhältnis," 162. See also Schmucker, *Untersuchungen*, 96ff.

52. See pp. 2411–14.

higher pay. Several significant exceptions were made: The Prophet's uncle al-ʿAbbās b. ʿAbd al-Muṭṭalib received the highest sum mentioned. This tradition seems to be an element in the glorification of al-ʿAbbās common to ʿAbbāsid historians.[53] The Prophet's two grandsons, Ḥasan and Ḥusayn; Abū Dharr al-Ghifārī; and Salmān al-Fārisī received sums equal to that awarded to the participants in the battle of Badr, though none of them belonged to this group. A similar exception was made for the wives and the concubines of the Prophet.

Distribution of booty also looms large in Ṭabarī's narrative. One of the principles followed by Saʿd b. Abī Waqqāṣ was to award to every warrior the spoils of his slain enemy. ʿUmar considered this course of action to be conducive to the morale of the troops, and he confirmed it even when Muslims had killed Persian notables and acquired spoils of reportedly enormous value.[54] In several instances these Muslims are said to have sold their valuable spoils for large sums of money.[55]

V

In preparing this volume, I have attempted to make the annotation meaningful to students of Arabic and Islam as well as to non-Arabists. Wherever possible, I have prepared short biographies of persons who play significant roles in the narrative but are not included in such standard reference works as *Encyclopaedia of Islam*. I have also tried to highlight the ideas that are, in my opinion, implied in the text. In some cases I found it possible to elucidate obscurities of Ṭabarī's text by reference to parallel Arabic sources. I trust that Islamicists will bear with me for including in this introduction and in the notes material that they may deem superfluous and that non-Arabists will not be taken aback by the philological nature of certain notes intended primarily for the benefit of their Arabist colleagues.

Finally, I should like to thank Professor M. J. Kister for being generous as usual with his time, advice, and unrivaled erudition. Thanks are due also to Professor A. Arazi, with whom I discussed several poems included in this volume. Dr. A. Elʿad read the pas-

53. See *EI*², s.v. "al-ʿAbbās b. ʿAbd al-Muṭṭalib" (W. M. Watt).
54. See pp. 2340, 2342–43.
55. See pp. 2324, 2337, 2340.

sages on the conquest of Jerusalem and shared with me some of his insights. I am also indebted to Professor C. E. Bosworth and to Dr. E. Whelan for their painstaking editorial work. Needless to say, the responsibility for any imperfections, errors of judgment, or infelicities of style is mine alone.

Yohanan Friedmann

The Caliphate of ʿUmar b. al-Khaṭṭāb (cont'd)

The Events of the Year [2212]

14

(FEBRUARY 25, 635–FEBRUARY 13, 636)

According to al-Sarī — Shuʿayb — Sayf — Muḥammad, Ṭalḥah, and Ziyād: ʿUmar set out on the first day of the month of Muḥarram of the year 14 (635) and halted near a spring called Ṣirār.[1] He established a camp there as the people did not know whether he wanted to go farther or to stay.

(When they wanted to ask ʿUmar something, they sent to him ʿUthmān or ʿAbd al-Raḥmān b. ʿAwf. During ʿUmar's reign, ʿUthmān was called a *radīf*. They[2] have said: In the language of the Bedouins the *radīf* is a man (who rides) behind another man (on the back of the same mount); and the Arabs use the word for a [2213]
person whom they want (to rule them) after (the death of) their ruler.[3] And, if ʿUthmān and ʿAbd al-Raḥmān b. ʿAwf[4] could not get the in-

---

1. A place situated three miles from Medina, on the way to Iraq. See Yāqūt, *Muʿjam*, III, 377.

2. The pronoun stands for either the Arab philologists or the Bedouins; both groups were renowned for their knowledge of classical Arabic.

3. For *ridf* (a variant of *radīf*) as a deputy and aid to the kings of al-Ḥīrah, see Ibn Manẓūr, *Lisān al-ʿArab*, s.v. *r-d-f*; Jawharī, *Tāj al-lugha*, IV, 1363–64; Azharī, *Tahdhīb*, XIV, 96–98.

4. ʿAbd al-Raḥmān b. ʿAwf was one of the earliest converts to Islam and an influ-

formation that they wanted, they directed the question for the third time to al-ʿAbbās.)[5]

ʿUthmān said to ʿUmar: "What has come to your knowledge? What is it that you want to do?" ʿUmar gave the call for a congregational prayer, the people gathered around him, and he passed the information to them. Then he considered what the people had to say. The troops (*al-ʿāmmah*) said: "Set out and take us with you." [Outwardly] he agreed with their view and did not want to dissociate himself from them without gently changing their opinion [first], and he said: "Prepare yourself and prepare your provisions and equipment, for I am about to set out unless an idea better than that comes up." Then he sent for the men of sound judgment (*ahl al-raʾy*). Prominent companions of the Prophet and Arab notables gathered around him. He said: "Let me have your opinion, for I am about to set out." All of them assembled and unanimously decided that he should stay, send out a man from the companions of the Prophet, and provide him with troops. If the desired victory should be attained, then this is what all of them wanted; if not, he would recall the man and recruit another army. This would enrage the enemy; the Muslims would regain their strength,[6] and God's victory would come through the fulfillment of God's promises.

ʿUmar called for congregational prayer, and the people gathered around him. He sent for ʿAlī, whom he had appointed to be his deputy in Medina, and ʿAlī came to him; and he also sent for Ṭalḥah, whom he had sent to command the vanguard, and he returned to him [as well]. On the two wings of the army he appointed al-Zubayr[7] and ʿAbd al-Raḥmān b. ʿAwf. ʿUmar stood up [to address] the people and said:

> Almighty God has united the people of Islam, reconciled their hearts, and made them brethren. In all matters con-

---

ential personality in early Islamic history. See *EI²*, s.v. "ʿAbd al-Raḥmān b. ʿAwf" (M. Th. Houtsma and W. M. Watt), and the sources quoted there.

5. This parenthetical passage explains why it was ʿUthmān who asked ʿUmar about his plans.

6. *Irʿawā* means "he returned to the proper condition." The classical dictionaries do not mention the sense in which the word is used here, but de Goeje seems to have been correct in his suggestion, which I have followed. See *Glossary*, CCLXV.

7. Al-Zubayr b. al-ʿAwwām was one of the earliest converts to Islam and a trusted Companion of the Prophet. See *EI¹*, s.v. "Al-Zubayr b. al-ʿAwwām" (A. J. Wensinck), and the sources quoted there.

cerning them, the Muslims are like on body; no part of it remains unaffected by something that afflicts another part.[8] Furthermore, it behoves the Muslims that their matters be decided in consultation among them,[9] or, rather, among the wise men among them (*dhawū al-ra'y*). The people are subordinate to those who undertake this command. What the latter agree upon and are satisfied with is incumbent upon the people, and the people are subordinate to them in it. And those who undertake this command are subordinate to the wise men: Whatever the latter deem appropriate and are satisfied with concerning battle strategy, the commanders are subordinate to them. O people! I am like one of you, so that the wise men from among you prevented me from setting out, and I saw fit to stay and to send another person [instead of me]. I have summoned for consultation on this matter the commander of the vanguard and the person whom I have left as my deputy in Medina. [2214]

[ʿAlī was ʿUmar's deputy in Medina, and Ṭalḥah commanded the vanguard of the army in al-Aʿwaṣ.[10] ʿUmar called both of them (for consultation)].

According to al-Sarī — Shuʿayb — Sayf — Muḥammad b. Isḥāq — Ṣāliḥ b. Kaysān — ʿUmar b. ʿAbd al-ʿAzīz: When ʿUmar came to know that Abū ʿUbayd b. Masʿūd[11] had been killed and that the people of Persia had rallied around someone from the family of Kisrā,[12] he called the Emigrants and the Helpers and set out for Ṣirār. He ordered Ṭalḥah b. ʿUbaydallāh to move forward to Aʿwaṣ. He appointed ʿAbd al-Raḥmān b. ʿAwf to command his right wing and al-

8. For a famous *ḥadīth* expressing the idea of Muslim solidarity in a similar way, see Muslim, *Ṣaḥīḥ*, IV, 2000 (*kitāb al-birr wa al-ṣilah wa al-adab, bāb* 17): "The Muslims are like one person: If his eye has a reason for complaint, his entire body complains . . . (*al-muslimūn ka-rajulin wāḥid: idhā ishtakā ʿaynuhu, ishtakā kulluhu . . .*).

9. Cf. Qur'ān 42:38.

10. A place situated a few miles from Medina; see Yāqūt, *Muʿjam*, I, 317.

11. Abū ʿUbayd b. Masʿūd al-Thaqafī, the father of the famous al-Mukhtār b. Abī ʿUbayd, embraced Islam during the lifetime of the Prophet. He was killed in Iraq in the battle of the Bridge, which preceded the battle of al-Qādisiyyah. See (ʿI.) Ibn al-Athīr, *Usd*, V, 248–49; Ibn Ḥajar, *Iṣābah*, VII, 267–68.

12. Kisrā is the Arabic form of Khusraw and was used by the Arabs as a title for all Sasanian kings. See *EI²*, s.v. "Kisrā" (M. Morony).

Zubayr b. ʿAwwām the left wing, and he appointed ʿAlī to be his deputy in charge of Medina. He consulted the troops, and all of them advised him to set out for Persia. He had not engaged in consultation about what happened until he reached Ṣirār and Ṭalḥah returned, so he then consulted the people of sound judgment. Ṭalḥah was one of those who followed the view of the troops, and ʿAbd al-Raḥmān was among those who advised ʿUmar against it. ʿAbd al-Raḥmān said:

> I have never said, and I shall never say, to anyone after the Prophet: "May my father and mother be your ransom!" [Still] I say: "May my father and mother be your ransom!"[13] Let me bear the responsibility for the outcome of this matter.[14] Stay and send an army. In the past, you have seen God's
> [2215] decree concerning you in your soldiers, and you will see it also in the future. If your army is defeated, it is not the same as if you [yourself] were defeated. If you are killed or defeated at the outset, I am afraid that no Muslims will remain in existence."[15]

While ʿUmar was in search of a man [to command an expedition against the Persians], a letter from Saʿd (b. Abī Waqqāṣ), who was in charge of collecting alms in Najd, arrived in the wake of their consultations. ʿUmar said: "Suggest a man." ʿAbd al-Raḥmān said: "You have found him." ʿUmar said: "Who is he?" ʿAbd al-Raḥmān said: "Saʿd b. Mālik[16] (b. Abī Waqqāṣ), whose claws are like a lion's." The men of judgment went along with this suggestion.

According to al-Sarī — Shuʿayb — Sayf — Khulayd b. Zufar — his

---

13. Meaning: "I do not hold anyone in such a high regard as I hold you."

14. The expression *ijʿal ʿajuzahā bī* is difficult. For *ʿajuz* (pl. *aʿjāz*) in the sense of "outcome, result" (*ʿawāqib*), see (M.) Ibn al-Athīr, *Gharīb al-ḥadīth*, III, 185. *Pace* de Goeje, who, *Addenda et Emendanda*, (DCXV), vocalizes *ʿajz* and suggests understanding it as "impotentia."

15. The text reads: "I am afraid that Muslims will not say 'God is the greatest' and 'There is no god except Allāh.'" Cf. Masʿūdī, *Murūj*, IV, 203: "... if you are defeated or killed, the Muslims will apostatize and will never attest that there is no god except Allāh..." (*... innaka in tuhzam aw tuqtal yakfur al-muslimūn wa lā yashhadūna an lā ilāh illā Allāh abadan...*).

16. Mālik and Abū Waqqāṣ are one and the same person. Saʿd b. Abī Waqqāṣ was one of the first converts and supporters of the Prophet. He played an important role in the battles of nascent Islam. He considered himself "the first person to shoot an arrow in the way of God." See *EI*[1], s.v. "Saʿd b. Abī Waqqāṣ" (K. V. Zetterstéen); Ibn Saʿd, *Ṭabaqāt*, III/i, 97ff.

father: Al-Muthannā[17] wrote to ʿUmar that the Persians had rallied around Yazdagird, and he informed him about their military expeditions and about the situation of the *ahl al-dhimmah*. ʿUmar wrote to him: "Move to the desert, call upon (the tribes) adjacent to you, and stay close to the Persians on the border between your land and their land until you receive my orders." The Persians attacked the Muslims first, their troops fought them, and the *ahl al-dhimmah* rose against them. Al-Muthannā set out with his men, went to Iraq, and dispersed them all over the country. They established garrisons between Ghudayy[18] and Quṭquṭānah;[19] the garrisons of Kisrā and his forward outposts withdrew, and the situation in Persia settled down. The Persians were stricken with awe and fear. The Muslims set out against them in large numbers and attacked them fiercely, like a lion who struggles with his prey and attacks time and again. The Arab commanders had to hold them back, so that they might wait for ʿUmar's instructions and reinforcements.

According to al-Sarī b. Yaḥyā — Shuʿayb b. Ibrāhīm — Sayf b. ʿUmar — Sahl b. Yūsuf — al-Qāsim b. Muḥammad: Abū Bakr had appointed Saʿd (b. Abī Waqqāṣ) to collect the alms of Hawāzin[20] in Najd, and ʿUmar confirmed his appointment. When ʿUmar was recruiting the people, he wrote to Saʿd [as he did to the other governors] and asked him to choose horsemen and [other] armed fighting men, people with sound judgment and valor. Saʿd replied by letter, in which he listed the men whom he was able to gather, with God's help. Saʿd's letter reached ʿUmar after he had consulted the people [in an attempt to select] a man [to command the expedition], and, when Saʿd's name came up, they suggested appointing him. [2216]

---

17. Al-Muthannā b. Ḥārithah al-Shaybānī embraced Islam in the year 9 or 10/630–2 and fought in Iraq under Abū Bakr and ʿUmar. Because of the initiatives that he took in the Iraq campaigns, ʿUmar used to say that al-Muthannā "made himself an amīr." He is said to have encouraged the Muslims to wage war against Persia and predicted that it would be an easy one. See (ʿI.) Ibn al-Athīr, *Usd*, IV, 299–300; Ibn Ḥajar, *Iṣābah*, V, 766–67.

18. For Ghuḍayy, see Yāqūt, *Muʿjam*, III, 806–7. Ṭabarī, I, 2211, locates it "opposite al-Baṣrah" (*ḥiyāl al-Baṣrah*).

19. Al-Quṭquṭānah was a spring situated west of the site where al-Kūfah was later founded. See Yāqūt, *Muʿjam*, IV, 137; III, 539, s.v. "Ṭaff"; Morony, *Iraq*, 151; Ṣ. A. ʿAlī, "Minṭaqat al-Kūfah" 246–47.

20. Hawāzin was a large northern Arabian tribe, subdued by the Prophet in the battle of Ḥunayn (Shawwāl 8/January–February 630). See *EI²*, s.v. "Hawāzin" (W. M. Watt), "Ḥunayn" (H. Lammens).

According to al-Sarī—Shuʿayb—Sayf—Muḥammad and Ṭalḥah: Saʿd b. Abī Waqqāṣ was in charge of collecting the alms of Hawāzin. ʿUmar instructed him, as he instructed others, to choose men of sound judgment and valor, possessing weapons or horses. He received Saʿd's reply, saying: "I have chosen for you one thousand armed horsemen. All are distinguished by valor, sound judgment, and prudence; they are [well known for] protecting the families and the inviolable property of their tribes. They epitomize their people's virtues, and their views are highly respected. They are at your disposal." Saʿd's letter arrived when ʿUmar was consulting the people. They said: "You have found the man." He asked: "Who is he?" They said: "A charging lion." He asked [again]: "Who is he?" They said: "Saʿd." ʿUmar accepted their advice and sent for Saʿd. When Saʿd came, ʿUmar put him in charge of the war in Iraq and admonished him, saying:

> O Saʿd, Saʿd of Banū Wuhayb![21] You must not allow yourself to be deluded into deviation from [the way of] God if it is said: [This is] the uncle of the Messenger of God [and that is] one of his Companions.[22] God will not eradicate one bad thing by means of another but will rather eradicate a bad thing with a good one. For there is no relationship between God and any human being except obedience. In the eyes of God[23] people are equal, regardless of rank; God is their Mas-
> [2217] ter, and they are His servants. They differ from each other in their well-being, and they achieve God's favor by observing [His commandments]. Ponder the way in which the Prophet behaved since the beginning of his mission and until his death; stick to it, because this is the proper behavior. This is my admonition to you! If you disregard it and turn away from it, your endeavor will fail, and you will be one of the losers.[24]

When ʿUmar was about to send Saʿd off, he called him back once again and said:

---

21. Wuhayb was Saʿd's grandfather; see Ibn Saʿd, *Ṭabaqāt*, III/i, 97 l. 8.
22. That is to say, do not grant favors to anyone, regardless of his kinship or companionship with the Prophet and his consequent standing in Islam.
23. The original reads: *fi dhāt Allāh*.
24. Alluding to Qur'ān 5:7.

I have appointed you to wage war in Iraq. Remember my admonition because you are about to engage in a difficult and hateful matter. None but God will keep [you] safe from [the dangers involved in] it. Make virtue the habit of yourself and of your associates, and seek divine help by means of it. Know that every habit has its requisites, and the requisite of virtue is endurance. You must therefore endure what afflicts you, or afflicts you repeatedly, and fear God. Know that fear of God consists of two things: being obedient to Him and avoiding rebellion against Him. One obeys Him by hating this world and loving the hereafter; one hates Him by loving this world and hating the hereafter. In people's hearts there are realities (*ḥaqāʾiq*), which God creates. Two of these are what is secret (*sirr*) and what is publicly proclaimed (*ʿalaniyyah*). The latter means that [in the eyes of an upright person][25] people who praise him and people who blame him are equal when he acts for the sake of the truth (*an yakūna ḥāmiduhu wa dhāmmuhu fī al-ḥaqq sawāʾ*).[26] As for what is secret, it becomes known by the appearance of wisdom from his heart on his tongue and by the love of the people. Therefore do not refrain from making yourself loved, for the prophets sought people's love. When God loves someone, He makes him loved; if He hates someone, He makes him hated. Regard your standing in the eyes of the people who joined you in this affair as an indication of your standing in the eyes of God.[27]

25. De Goeje suggests in a note to this passage that the person intended here is the *amīr*.

26. Equanimity with regard to people's blame or praise is a frequently mentioned characteristic of the ideal Muslim and particularly of the *zāhid*. See, e.g., Ibn Ḥanbal, *Zuhd*, 158; Ibn al-Mubārak, *Zuhd*, 52 (separate pagination at the end of the book). A similar idea is expressed in the oath of allegiance taken by the early Muslims. They promised to the Prophet "... to speak the truth wherever we are and not to fear anyone's blame, [when acting] for the sake of God (... *an naqūla bi-ʾl-ḥaqq haythu-mā kunnā wa-lā nakhāfa fī Allāh lawmata lāʾimin*). See Bukhārī, *Ṣaḥīḥ*, IV, 401–2 (*kitāb al-aḥkām*, 43). For further occurrences of this tradition, see Wensinck *et al.*, *Concordance*, s.v. *lawmah*. The same attitude of disregarding blame should be taken by those who apply the punishments prescribed in the Qurʾān (*ḥudūd*); see Ibn Mājah, *Sunan*, II, 849 (*kitāb al-ḥudūd*, *bāb* 3). See also Kūfī, *Futūḥ*, I, 233.

27. Muslim tradition maintains that, if God loves someone, He instructs Gabriel and the people of heaven to love him as well; such a person also gains acceptance on

Then ʿUmar sent him out with the warriors who had joined him in Medina. Saʿd b. Abī Waqqāṣ set out from Medina in the direction
[2218] of Iraq with four thousand men. Three thousand came from the Yemen and al-Sarāt.[28] The people of the Sarawāt were led by Ḥumaydah b. al-Nuʿmān b. Ḥumaydah al-Bāriqī,[29] and they [belonged to the clans of] Bāriq, Almaʿ, Ghāmid, and the rest of their brethren. The people of al-Sarāt were seven hundred, and the people of Yemen were two thousand and three hundred [fighting men]. Among them was al-Nakhaʿ b. ʿAmr. All of them numbered [in total] four thousand people, including the fighting men, their children, and their wives. ʿUmar came to see them in their camp and wanted all of them to proceed to Iraq, but they insisted on going to Syria. ʿUmar insisted on Iraq; eventually half of the people complied, and he sent them to Iraq, and he sent the other half to Syria.

According to al-Sarī—Shuʿayb—Sayf—Ḥanash al-Nakhaʿī—his father and others: ʿUmar came to see them in their camp and said: "Honor is abundant among you, O people of Nakhaʿ. Proceed with Saʿd." They wanted to go to Syria. He insisted on Iraq, and they insisted on Syria. So he sent half of them to Syria and the other half to Iraq.

According to al-Sarī—Shuʿayb—Sayf—Muḥammad, Ṭalḥah, al-Munstanīr, and Ḥanash: Six hundred of the fighters were from Ḥaḍramawt and al-Ṣadif,[30] commanded by Shaddād b. Ḍamʿaj. One thousand and three hundred were from Madhḥij,[31] commanded by
[2219] three chieftains: Banū Munabbih under ʿAmr b. Maʿdīkarib;[32] the

---

earth. Accordingly, ʿUmar b. ʿAbd al-ʿAzīz is said to have been loved by God, in view of the affection that the people displayed toward him. See Muslim, *Ṣaḥīḥ*, IV, 2030–31 (*kitāb al-birr wa-al-ṣilah wa-al-adab, bāb* 48).

28. A mountain range parallel to the southwestern coast of the Arabian peninsula. See *EI²*, s.vv. "al-ʿArab, Djazīrat" (G. Rentz), 536a, "ʿAsīr" (R. Headley et al.), 707b; Yāqūt, *Muʿjam*, III, 65.

29. See Ibn Ḥajar, *Iṣābah*, II, 130 no. 1850.

30. A region in the Yemen. See Yāqūt, *Muʿjam*, III, 375.

31. For this tribe of Yemeni extraction, see *EI²*, s.v. "Madhḥidj" (G. R. Smith—C. E. Bosworth).

32. ʿAmr b. Maʿdīkarib was a famous warrior and *mukhaḍram* poet of Yemeni extraction. He converted to Islam in 10/631 but after the Prophet's death took part in the *riddah* of al-Aswad al-ʿAnsī, the Yemeni claimant to prophethood. After the suppression of the rebellion he joined the Muslims again and distinguished himself in the battles of al-Qādisiyyah and al-Yarmūk. His poetry and other materials concerning him have been collected in Ṭaʿʿān, *Dīwān*; and in Tarābīshī, *Shiʿr ʿAmr*. Some of ʿAmr's poems reflect his displeasure at the treatment he received from Saʿd

Juʿfī, the brothers of Jazʾ allied with the Juʿfī, the Zubayd, the Anas Allāh, and those connected with them under Abū Sabra b. Dhuʾayb; and three hundred men from Ṣudāʾ, Janb, and Musliyah under Yazīd b. al-Ḥārith al-Ṣudāʾī. These are the people of Madhḥij who participated in [the battle of] al-Qādisiyyah, together with those who set out from Medina with Saʿd. One thousand men from Qays ʿAylān [also] set out with him, commanded by Bishr b. ʿAbdallāh al-Hilālī.[33]

According to al-Sarī—Shuʿayb—Sayf—ʿUbaydah—Ibrāhīm: The people [who were about to participate in the battle] of al-Qādisiyyah[34] set out from Medina and were four thousand: three thousand from the people of Yemen and one thousand from the rest [of the Arabs].

According to al-Sarī—Shuʿayb—Sayf—Muḥammad, Ṭalḥah, and Sahl — al-Qāsim: ʿUmar accompanied the troops from Ṣirār to al-Aʿwaṣ. Then he stood up to address them and said:

> God has made for you similitudes and clarified for you the words in order to infuse new life into the hearts, because the hearts are dead in their chests until God revives them. Whoever knows something, let him benefit from it. Justice has its signs (*amārāt*) and indications (*tabāshīr*), and these signs are diffidence, generosity, and gentleness. The indication of justice is mercy. God has provided for everything a door and for every door a key; the door of justice is reflection, and its key is piety (*zuhd*). Reflection is remembering death [2220] by keeping in mind those who have died and preparing oneself for it by performing the commandments. Piety is taking what is due from everybody who owes it and giving what is due to everybody who has a right to it.[35] Do not grant favor

b. Abī Waqqāṣ; see Ṭaʿʿān, 99, 108. See also Ibn Ḥajar, *Iṣābah*, IV, 686–93; *EI*², s.v. "ʿAmr b. Maʿdīkarib" (Ch. Pellat).

33. See Ibn Ḥajar, *Iṣābah*, I, 299–300 no. 655.

34. For a description of the battle of al-Qādisiyyah and for an analysis of the historiographical and other problems connected with it, see *EI*², s.v. "al-Ḳādisiyya" (L. Veccia Vaglieri), and the sources mentioned there. See also Yusuf, "Qadisiyya."

35. Recent studies have shown that *zuhd* encompasses not only asceticism but also upright behavior, piety, and integrity in the more general sense. The *zuhd* of a ruler is, according to this passage, upholding justice in society. For a somewhat similar definition of *zuhd*, see Makkī, *Qūt al-qulūb*, II, 199: "... taking a thing from where it is and putting it where it should be" (... *al-zuhd fī al-dunyā huwa* ... *akh-*

to anyone in this matter. Do not give more than bare livelihood; a person who is not satisfied with this, nothing will make him content. I am between you and God, and nobody is between me and Him. God has obliged me to prevent [your] petitions from reaching Him; bring your complaints therefore to us.[36] Whoever is not able to do this, let him hand the complaint over to someone who can bring it to us; we shall willingly take whatever is due to him on his behalf [and hand it over to him].

Then he ordered Saʿd to begin the march and said: "When you reach Zarūd[37] halt in it, and spread your men in the area around it. Call upon the local people and choose from them men who possess courage, judgment, power, and weapons."

According to al-Sarī—Shuʿayb—Sayf—Muḥammad b. Sūqah—a man: Four hundred Sakūnīs passed by with the vanguard of the tribe of Kindah, with Ḥuṣayn b. Numayr al-Sakūnī[38] and Muʿāwiyah b. Ḥudayj, and ʿUmar encountered them. Among them, with Muʿāwiyah b. Ḥudayj,[39] were young men of black complexion and straight hair. ʿUmar turned his face away from them several times until it was said to him: "Do you have anything against these people?" He said: "I am perplexed with regard to them. No Arab tribe more hateful to me than these has ever passed by me." He then let them go, but he frequently mentioned them with hatred, and people were puzzled by ʿUmar's view. Among the Sakūnīs was a per-
[2221] son called Sūdān b. Ḥumrān, who killed ʿUthmān b. ʿAffān.[40]

dhu al-shay'i min wajhihi wa-waḍʿuhu fī ḥaqqihi). Returning things to their rightful owners is mentioned also in descriptions of the Last Judgment, and the language is similar. See, e.g., Ibn al-Mubārak, *Zuhd*, 497–98 no. 1416. On *zuhd* in general, see also Ibn Abī al-Dunyā, *Dhamm al-dunyā*, 20–22; Kinberg, "Zuhd." For a translation and discussion of this passage, see Noth, *Studien*, 83–84.

36. The plural pronoun here and in the next two sentences refers to ʿUmar himself.

37. Zarūd was located on the pilgrims' road leading from al-Kūfah to the Ḥijāz. See Yāqūt, *Muʿjam*, II, 928; Thilo, *Ortsnamen*, 116.

38. Ḥuṣayn b. Numayr al-Sakūnī became governor of Ḥimṣ under the Umayyad caliph Yazīd b. Muʿāwiyah and participated in the war against ʿAbdallāh b. al-Zubayr in Mecca. See Ibn Saʿd, *Ṭabaqāt*, index; Ibn Ḥajar, *Tahdhīb*, II, 392 no. 683; *EI*², s.v. "al-Ḥuṣayn b. Numayr" (H. Lammens—[V. Cremonesi]); Crone, *Slaves*, 97.

39. Muʿāwiyah b. Ḥudayj al-Sakūnī later participated in the conquest of North Afrika and acquired a position of influence in Egypt. See (ʿI.) Ibn al-Athīr, *Usd*, IV, 383–84. See also note 42, below.

40. See Ṭabarī, I, 3001, 3018, 3021; Ibn Saʿd, *Ṭabaqāt*, III/i, 51.

One of their confederates was Khālid b. Muljam,[41] who killed ʿAlī b. Abī Ṭālib. One of them was Muʿāwiyah b. Ḥudayj,[42] who, together with others, pursued the assassins of ʿUthmān, in order to kill them. Among them were also people who provided shelter and hospitality to the assassins of ʿUthmān.[43]

According to al-Sarī—Shuʿayb—Sayf—Muḥammad and Ṭalḥah—Māhān and Ziyād: ʿUmar reinforced Saʿd, after he had left Medina, with two thousand Yemenis and two thousand armed Najdīs from Ghaṭafān[44] and other tribes of Qays.[45] Saʿd reached Zarūd at the onset of winter and halted there, and the soldiers spread out around the place, in the watering places (*amwāh*) of Tamīm and Asad. He waited for the [fighting] men to gather there and for the instructions of ʿUmar. He chose four thousand warriors from Tamīm and al-Ribāb: three thousand from Tamīm and one thousand from al-Ribāb. He [also] chose three thousand from Asad and ordered them to camp on the border of their land, between al-Ḥazn[46] and al-Basīṭah.[47] They stayed there, between the armies of Saʿd b. Abī Waqqāṣ and al-Muthannā b. al-Ḥārithah. Al-Muthannā's army consisted of eight thousand men from Rabīʿah: six thousand from Bakr b. Wāʾil and two thousand from the rest of Rabīʿah. He chose four thousand of them after the departure of Khālid (b. al-Walīd); the other four thousand were those who survived the battle of the Bridge. Also with him were two thousand Yemenis of Bajīlah and two thousand from Quḍāʿah and Ṭayyiʾ. These were chosen in addition to

---

41. See *EI²*, s.v. "Ibn Muldjam" (L. Veccia Vaglieri). The name of ʿAlī's assassin is usually given as ʿAbd al-Raḥmān b. ʿAmr; see Ṭabarī, I, 3468, and cited article for the various *nisbahs* of Ibn Muljam, including Sakūnī.

42. See Ṭabarī, I, 3392.

43. These details are given in order to explain ʿUmar's negative attitude toward the Sakūnīs: He had a premonition of their future misdeeds.

44. Ghaṭafān is a northern Arabian tribe, belonging to the Qays ʿAylān. See *EI²*, "Ghaṭafān" (J. M. Fück).

45. Qays ʿAylān is a large northern Arabian tribe, represented in the genealogies as one of the two subdivisions of Muḍar. See *EI²*, s.v. "Ḳays ʿAylān" (W. M. Watt).

46. Several areas in Iraq and the Arabian peninsula were known as al-Ḥazn, or "rough terrain" (*al-ghalīẓ min al-arḍ*). The one intended here is probably Ḥazn Yarbūʿ, in the vicinity of al-Kūfah. See Yāqūt, *Muʿjam*, II, 260–62.

47. Yāqūt defines *basīṭah* as "flat land, covered with well-formed pebbles, without water or pasture, land of God most remote from population" (*arḍ mustawiyah fīhā ḥaṣan manqūsh aḥsan mā yakūn wa-laysa bihā māʾun wa-lā marʿan abʿadu arḍ Allāh min sukkān*). The place intended here lies between al-Kūfah and Ḥazn Yarbūʿ. See Yāqūt *Muʿjam*, I, 626–27.

those who had been with him before. The Ṭayyiʾ were commanded by ʿAdī b. Ḥātim;[48] the Quḍāʿah by ʿAmr b. Wabarah;[49] and the Bajīlah by Jarīr b. ʿAbdallāh.[50] This being the situation, Saʿd wanted al-Muthannā to come to him, and al-Muthannā wanted Saʿd to come
[2222] to him. Al-Muthannā died from injuries that he had suffered in the battle of the Bridge and that had failed to heal. He had appointed Bashīr b. al-Khaṣāṣiyyah[51] to take over his command. Saʿd was at that time in Zarūd. Some notables of Iraq were [at the time] with Bashīr. With Saʿd were a few people from Iraq who had gone as a delegation to ʿUmar. Among them were Furāt b. Ḥayyān al-ʿIjlī[52] and ʿUtaybah, whom ʿUmar had sent [back to Iraq] with Saʿd.

According to al-Sarī—Shuʿayb—Sayf—Muḥammad and Ziyād—Māhān: This is the reason why opinions differ regarding the number of people [who fought in the battle] of al-Qādisiyyah. Whoever says that they were four thousand means [only] those who had been with Saʿd when he set out from Medina. Whoever says that they were eight thousand means those who gathered at Zarūd. Whoever says that they were nine thousand means [also] the Qaysīs [who joined the army]. Whoever says that they were twelve thousand includes also the three thousand Asadīs from the upper part of al-Ḥazn.

ʿUmar then ordered Saʿd to march forward. He headed in the direction of Iraq while the army concentrated in Sharāf.[53] When ʿUmar

48. See *EI²*, s.v. "ʿAdī b. Ḥātim" (A. Schaade).

49. See Ibn Ḥajar, *Iṣābah*, V, 156 no. 6523.

50. Jarīr b. ʿAbdallāh, a chieftain of the tribe of Bajīlah, embraced Islam in Ramaḍān 10/December 631 in Medina, together with 150 members of his tribe. ʿUmar entrusted him with keeping together the disunited factions of his tribe. He is said to have been a handsome man and to have received the nickname "the Joseph of this community" (*Yūsuf hādhihi al-ummah*). See Ibn Saʿd, *Ṭabaqāt*, I/ii, 77–8; Ṭabarī, I, 1763; (ʿI.) Ibn al-Athīr, *Usd*, I, 279–80; Ibn Ḥajar, *Iṣābah*, I, 475–76 no. 1138; Ibn Kathīr, *Bidāyah*, V, 77–79; Crone, *Slaves*, 114–15.

51. See (ʿI.) Ibn al-Athīr, *Usd*, I, 193–94; Ibn Ḥajar, *Iṣābah*, I, 311 no. 691, 314–15 no. 705; Ibn Ḥajar, *Tahdhīb*, I, 463 no. 854, 467–68 no. 866.

52. Furāt b. Ḥayyān al-ʿIjlī was a member of the tribe of Quraysh who served as spy and scout in Abū Sufyān's wars. He was taken prisoner in one of the early skirmishes between the Muslims and the Meccans (or in the battle of the Ditch). The Prophet spared his life after he embraced Islam. Later he participated in the suppression of the *riddah* in Baḥrayn and settled in al-Kūfah. See Ibn Saʿd, *Ṭabaqāt*, II/i, 25; IV/ii, 78; VI, 25; and index. See also (ʿI.) Ibn al-Athīr, *Usd*, IV, 175–6; Ibn Ḥajar, *Tahdhīb*, VIII, 258 no. 478; Ibn Ḥabīb, *Muḥabbar*, 329–30.

53. Sharāf is an oasis situated 8 miles from al-Aḥsāʾ, in the northeastern part of the Arabian peninsula. See Yāqūt, *Muʿjam*, III, 270.

reached Sharāf, al-Ashʿath b. Qays[54] joined him with one thousand and seven hundred Yemenis.

The number of those who participated in the battle of al-Qādisiyyah was thirty odd thousand. The number of those who received shares from the spoils of al-Qādisiyyah was approximately thirty thousand.

According to al-Sarī—Shuʿayb—Sayf—ʿAbd al-Malik b. ʿUmayr—Ziyād—Jarīr: The Yemenis had inclinations toward Syria and the Muḍarīs toward Iraq. ʿUmar said to the Yemenis: "Are your family relationships moore deeply rooted than ours? Why do the Muḍarīs not remember their Syrian ancestors?"

According to al-Sarī — Shuʿayb — Sayf — Abū Saʿd b. al-Marzubān — a person who informed him — Muḥammad b. Ḥudhayfah b. al-Yamān: No Arab tribe was more courageous in the war against the Persians than Rabīʿah; the Muslims used to call them "Rabīʿah of the Lion" in addition to the epithet "Rabīʿah of the Horse."[55] The Arabs in the pre-Islamic period used to call the Persians and the Byzantines "Lion."[56] [2223]

According to al-Sarī—Shuʿayb—Sayf—Ṭalḥah—Māhān: ʿUmar said: "By God, I shall indeed defeat the kings of the Persians by the kings of the Arabs!" He did not fail to send against them any chieftain, any man of judgment, any nobleman, any man of rank, any orator, or any poet — and sent against them the most noble and illustrious people.

According to al-Sarī—Shuʿayb—Sayf—ʿAmr—al-Shaʿbī: ʿUmar wrote to Saʿd when he was about to leave Zarūd: "Send someone you trust to [al-Ubullah, known as] 'the opening for India' (*farj al-Hind*).[57] He will stay in front of it and protect you from any [danger]

---

54. See *EI*², s.v. "al-Ashʿath" (H. Reckendorf); Ibn Al-Athīr, *Usd*, I, 97–99; Ibn Ḥajar, *Iṣābah*, I, 87–89 no. 205; Ibn Ḥajar, *Tahdhīb*, I, 359.

55. The tribe of Rabīʿah had been given the epithet "Rabīʿah of the Horse" because, when Nizār, the father of Muḍar and Rabīʿah, distributed their inheritance, he gave the gold to Muḍar and the horses to Rabīʿah. See Ibn Saʿd, *Ṭabaqāt*, I/i, 30 l. 17; Ṭabarī, I, 1109, 1110; Jawharī, *Tāj al-lughah*, s.vv. "Muḍar," "Rabīʿah"; Ibn Munabbih, *Tījān*, 212–13; Caskel and Strenziok, *Ǧamharat*, II, 481a. Because of their bravery in the wars against the Persians, Rabīʿah acquired the additional epithet "Rabīʿah of the Lion."

56. Cf. Ṭabarī, I, 2046.

57. *Farj* means literally "an opening." It is used for an area that gives access to a country or a city. It also came to mean a frontier from which Muslims could stage commercial or military expeditions to areas beyond their control. Thus Sind and

that may emerge from there." Saʿd sent al-Mughīrah b. Shuʿbah[58] with five hundred men. He was opposite al-Ubullah, in Arab land; he then went to Ghuḍayy and camped with Jarīr (b. ʿAbd Allāh al-Bajalī), who was there at the time.[59]

When Saʿd established his camp at Sharāf he informed ʿUmar of his location and of the locations of his men between Ghuḍayy and al-Jabbānah.[60] ʿUmar wrote to him:

> When you receive this letter of mine, organize the people in groups of ten, and appoint a leader for each group; appoint amīrs for the military units, and arrange them in battle or-
> [2224] der.[61] Order the Muslim chieftains to come to you, evaluate them in their presence, and then send them to their men, and instruct them to meet at al-Qādisiyyah; and take with you al-Mughīrah b. al-Shuʿbah, together with his horsemen. Then inform me in writing about the situation of the troops.

Saʿd sent for al-Mughīrah and the tribal chieftains. They came to him, and he evaluated the troops and arranged them in battle order in Sharāf. He appointed commanders for the military units and appointed group leaders for every group of ten, as was the custom during the lifetime of the Prophet. These units remained in existence until the military payment system (*ʿaṭāʾ*) was introduced.[62]

Khurāsān, or Sijistān and Khurāsān, came to be known as *al-farjāni*, "the two openings" (see Ibn Manẓūr, *Lisān al-ʿArab*, s.v. *farj*). The city of Multān in Sind came to be known as *farj bayt al-dhahab*, "the opening for the house of gold," i.e., the place where Muslims gained access to the rich temple of Multān (see Balādhurī, *Futūḥ*, 440). *Farj al-Hind* means, therefore, an area from which an expedition to India may be staged. Al-Ubullah, situated on the Tigris near the head of the Persian Gulf, was known by this and similar epithets; see Ṭabarī, I, 2016, 2021, 2380. See also Balādhurī, *Futūḥ*, 341, where al-Ubullah is described as *furḍat al-Baḥrayn wa-ʿUmān wa-al-Hind wa-al-Ṣīn*, i.e., a harbor from which ships sail to the places mentioned. See also *EI*[1], s.v. "al-Obolla" (J. H. Kramers); *Glossary*, s.v. *farj*.

58. See *EI*[1], s.v. "al-Mughīra b. Shuʿba" (H. Lammens).

59. See Ṭabarī, I, 2211.

60. A number of places in the vicinity of al-Kūfah were known by this name. See Yāqūt, *Muʿjam*, ii, 16–17.

61. For an explanation of the term *taʿbiyah*, "battle order," see Ibn Khaldūn, *Muqaddimah*, 272 (tr. F. Rosenthal, II, 76); Fries, *Heereswesen*, 69ff. Because of its traditional division into five parts, the army was also called *al-khamīs*; see Ibn Manẓūr, *Lisān al-ʿArab*, s.v. *kh-m-s*. For a description of the battle order in various armies, see Mubārak Shāh, *Ādāb al-ḥarb*, 322–27 and *passim*.

62. See *EI*[2], s. vv. "ʿAṭāʾ" (Cl. Cahen), "*Dīwān*. i" (A. A. Duri).

Saʿd entrusted the banners to people who were the first to embrace Islam. He divided the people into groups of ten and appointed people of standing in Islam to lead them. He appointed men to be leaders in war and commanders for the vanguard, for the wings, for the rear guard, for the light cavalry (*mujarradāt*),[63] for the scouts, for the footmen and the horsemen. He always moved in battle order and did not deviate from it, except in accordance with ʿUmar's written orders and his permission.

As for the commanders of the flanks (*umarāʾ al-taʿbiyah*), he appointed Zuhrah b. ʿAbdallāh b. Qatādah b. al-Ḥawiyyah b. Marthad b. Muʿāwiyah b. Maʿn b. Mālik b. Irthim b. Jusham b. al-Ḥārith al-Aʿraj[64] to command the vanguard. In the pre-Islamic period the king of Hajar[65] had made him a tribal chieftain (*sayyid*) and sent him to the Prophet. Having received permission, Zuhrah marched with the vanguard from Sharāf and arrived at al-ʿUdhayb.[66]

Saʿd appointed ʿAbdallāh b. al-Muʿtamm[67] to command the right wing. ʿAbdallāh was a Companion of the Prophet and was one of [2225] nine persons who came to the Prophet; Ṭalhah b. ʿUbaydallāh completed their group, which was then numbered at ten persons. They constituted an *ʿirāfah*.[68] He appointed Shuraḥbīl b. al-Simṭ b. Shuraḥbīl al-Kindī[69] to command the left wing. Shuraḥbīl was a young man who had fought the people of the *riddah*, acquitted himself

63. The cavalry mentioned here seems to be "light" in the sense that it is unarmored. See Fries, *Heereswesen*, 42–3, 71. One should also consider the possibility of another meaning: a unit of cavalry that travels without heavy luggage and is not accompanied (and encumbered) by foot soldiers. For this meaning, *jarīdah* or *jarīdat al-khayl* is used. See Lane, *Lexicon*, s.v. *jarīdah*; Dozy, *Supplément*, s.v.; de Goeje's *Glossary* to the text; Ṭabarī, I, 2060, ll. 13–14.

64. See (ʿI.) Ibn al-Athīr, *Usd*, II, 206; Ibn Ḥajar, *Iṣābah*, II, 571–72.

65. Hajar was a town in Baḥrayn. See *EI*¹, s.v. "Hadjar" (Fr. Buhl); *EI*², s.v. "al-Ḥasā" (F. S. Vidal).

66. See note 92, below.

67. In addition to his participation in the battle of al-Qādisiyyah and in the conquest of al-Madāʾin, ʿAbdallāh b. al-Muʿtamm fought in al-Mawṣil and Takrīt. He belonged to the tribe of ʿAbs. See Ibn Ḥajar, *Iṣābah*, IV, 240–41 no. 4969.

68. *ʿIrāfah* was a group of ten to fifteen persons; see Balādhurī, *Futūḥ*, 187; Fries, *Heereswesen*, 17–18. For the story of the *ʿirāfah* of nine people that was completed by Ṭalḥah, see Ibn Saʿd, *Ṭabaqāt*, III/i, 156 ll. 6–10.

69. Shuraḥbīl b. al-Simṭ participated in the battle of al-Qādisiyyah and in the conquest of Ḥimṣ. He then became governor of Ḥimṣ on behalf of Muʿāwiyah and died there between 36/656–57 and 42/662–63. See Ibn Saʿd, *Ṭabaqāt*, VII/i, 155; (ʿI.) Ibn al-Athīr, *Usd*, II, 391; Ibn Ḥajar, *Iṣābah*, III, 329–30 no. 3874; Ibn Ḥajar, *Tahdhīb*, IV, 322–23 no. 554.

well, and received recognition for it. In honor he surpassed al-Ashʿath (b. Qays al-Kindī) in Medina, until al-Kūfah was established (*qad ghalaba al-Ashʿath ʿalā al-sharaf fīmā bayna al-Madīnah ilā an ukhtuṭṭat al-Kūfah*).[70] His father had gone to Syria with Abū ʿUbaydah b. al-Jarrāḥ.

Saʿd appointed Khālid b. ʿUrfuṭah[71] as his deputy. ʿĀṣim b. ʿAmr al-Tamīmī al-ʿAmrī[72] was put in command of the rearguard, and Sawād b. Mālik al-Tamīmī commanded the scouts, Salmān b. Rabīʿah al-Bāhilī[73] the light cavalry, Ḥammāl b. Mālik al-Asadī[74] the infantrymen, and ʿAbdallāh b. Dhī al-Sahmayn al-Khathʿamī the horsemen. The commanders of the flanks (*umarāʾ al-taʿbiyah*) were subordinate to the amīr, the group commanders (*umarāʾ al-aʿshār*) to the commanders of the flanks; those entrusted with the flags (*aṣḥāb al-rāyāt*) to the group commanders, the tribal chiefs (*ruʾūs al-qabāʾil*) to the commanders (*quwwād*)[75] and to those entrusted with the flags.

All [transmitters of these traditions] have said: Abū Bakr did not seek help from the apostates in the wars of the *riddah* or in the wars against the Persians.[76] ʿUmar [on the other hand], recruited them but did not appoint any of them to a position of authority.[77]

70. The text of this passage is dubious, and the translation far from certain. In particular, the phrase *fīmā bayna al-Madīnah ilā an ukhtuṭṭat al-Kūfah* is problematic and could not be translated literally. Balādhurī (*Futūḥ*, 138) says that Shuraḥbīl vied with al-Ashʿath for supremacy in al-Kūfah; then he was transferred to Ḥimṣ at the request of his father. In (ʿI.) Ibn al-Athīr (*Usd*, II, 392) we read: *wa-qad taqaddama nasabuhu fī (!) al-Ashʿath b. Qays al-Kindī*. Ibn Ḥajar (*Iṣābah*, III, 330) has only *ghalaba al-Ashʿath ʿalā al-sharq* (read *al-sharaf*). We can say, however, in general, that the passage reflects the rivalry between the former apostates—to whom al-Ashʿath belonged—and the Muslims who had not taken part in the *riddah* rebellion.

71. Khālid b. ʿUrfuṭah, a member of Quḍāʿah and an ally of the Banū Zuhrah in Mecca, settled in al-Kūfah and later participated in the wars against the Khawārij. He died in 60/679–80, 61/680–81, or "after 64/683–84." See Ibn Saʿd, *Ṭabaqāt*, VI, 12; (ʿI.) Ibn al-Athīr, *Usd*, II, 95–96; Ibn Ḥajar, *Iṣābah*, II, 244–5 no. 184; Ibn Ḥajar, *Tahdhīb*, III, 106–7 no. 198.

72. See Ibn Ḥajar, *Iṣābah*, III, 574 no. 4359.

73. Salmān b. Rabīʿah al-Bāhilī was a Companion of the Prophet and participated in the conquest of Syria and Iraq. He was known as "Salmān of the horses" (*Salmān al-khayl*) because he was responsible for the cavalry during the time of ʿUmar. Later he became judge in al-Kūfah. See (ʿI.) Ibn al-Athīr, *Usd*, II, 327; Ibn Ḥajar, *Tahdhīb*, IV, 136–37 no. 229; Ibn Abī Ḥātim, *Jarḥ*, II, 297.

74. See Ibn Ḥajar, *Iṣābah*, II, 119 no. 1818.

75. This rank of command has not been mentioned before.

76. Cf. Ṭabarī, I, 1984.

77. But see Ṭabarī, I, 2457; according to a tradition mentioned there, ʿUmar was willing to appoint former apostates to command small units of the army, not exceed-

According to al-Sarī — Shuʿayb — Sayf — Mujālid and ʿAmr and Saʿīd b. al-Marzubān: ʿUmar dispatched the physicians [with the army]. He appointed ʿAbd al-Raḥmān b. Rabīʿah al-Bāhilī, known as Dhū al-Nūr ("the man of light"),[78] to be the judge and entrusted him also with supervising the spoils and dividing them. He made [2226] Salmān al-Fārisī[79] responsible for the call to prayers and also ordered him to be the scout.[80]

According to al-Sarī — Shuʿayb — Sayf — Abū ʿAmr — Abū ʿUthmān al-Nahdī: The translator [of the army] was Hilāl al-Hajarī and the secretary Ziyād b. Abī Sufyān.[81] When Saʿd completed the organization of the army and appointed reliable and responsible commanders to take care of every matter, he sent a letter to ʿUmar describing what he had done.

Al-Muʿannā b. Ḥārithah[82] and Salmā bint Khaṣafah al-Taymiyyah (of the clan of Taym al-Lāt)[83] came to Saʿd after he had written to ʿUmar about the way in which he organized his troops but before he received ʿUmar's reply and left Sharāf, heading for al-Qādisiyyah. They brought to him the last will (*waṣiyyah*) of al-Muthannā (b. Ḥārithah); he ordered them to rush it to Saʿd while he was still in Zarūd, but they were not able to accomplish this in time because they had been preoccupied by [the affair] of Qābūs b. Qābūs b. al-Mundhir.

The reason for this was that Āzādmard b. Āzādbih[84] sent Qābūs to al-Qādisiyyah, saying to him: "Call upon the Arabs and you will rule those who respond to you, in the tradition of your forefathers."

---

ing ten men (*nafar*) each. On the difference between Abū Bakr and ʿUmar in their attitudes to the former apostates, see Shaban, *History*, I, 26ff.

78. See (ʿI.) Ibn al-Athīr, *Usd*, III, 292.

79. Salmān al-Fārisī was a Companion of the Prophet who embraced Islam in Medina after the hijrah. As a prototype of the converted Persians, he occupies a prominent place in the Islamic tradition. See *EI*[1], "Salmān al-Fārisī" (G. Levi della Vida).

80. *Al-rāʾid* is the person who marches ahead of the tribe, or the troops, in search of water, good halting places, etc. A classical Arabic proverb says. "The scout does not mislead his people" (*al-rāʾid lā yakdhibu qawmahu*). See Maydānī, *Amthāl*, III, 188.

81. For Ziyād b. Abī Sufyān, also known as Ziyād b. Abīhi, see *EI*[1], s.v. "Ziyād b. Abīhi" (H. Lammens).

82. Al-Muʿannā b. Ḥārithah was the brother of al-Muthannā, for whom see note 17, above.

83. Salmā was the widow of al-Muthannā b. Ḥārithah. See note 17, above; and 2227, below.

84. Āzādbih was the Persian governor of al-Ḥīrah. See Ṭabarī, I, 2037, 2191; Morony, *Iraq*, 187; Donner, *Conquests*, 180.

Qābūs went to al-Qādisiyyah and wrote to [the tribe of] Bakr b. Wāʾil in the manner of al-Nuʿmān (b. Mundhir Abū Qābūs),[85] cajoling and threatening them. When this came to al-Muʿannā's knowledge, he set out from Dhū Qār,[86] attacked Qābūs at night, and killed him, together with his associates.[87] Then he returned to Dhū Qār, went together with Salmā to Saʿd, and brought to him the will, which included the views of al-Muthannā b. Ḥārithah. They reached Saʿd while he was at Sharāf.

In his last will al-Muthannā advised Saʿd not to fight his enemy, and the enemy of the Persians who embraced Islam deep in their land, when their full force was gathered; he should rather fight them
[2227] on their border, the border between the desert of the Arabs and the cultivated land of the Persians. If God should give victory to the Muslims, the land behind the enemy would be theirs. Should the outcome be different, they would fall back to a rear echelon[88] and would find their way more easily; their spirits would be higher in their own land, until God should give them another opportunity to attack.

When the will including the advice of al-Muthannā reached Saʿd, he invoked God's mercy upon him, appointed al-Muʿannā to al-Mu-

---

85. Al-Nuʿmān b. Mundhir Abū Qābūs was the last king of al-Ḥīrah, who died at the hands of Khusraw II in, or around, 602. See *EI*¹, s.v. "al-Nuʿmān b. al-Mundhir" (A. Moberg); *CHI*, IV, 3.

86. Dhū Qār was situated near the place where al-Kūfah was later founded. It became famous because it had been the site of a battle in which pre-Islamic Arabs had for the first time gained the upper hand against the Persians. See *EI*², s.v. "Dhū Ḳār" (L. Veccia Vaglieri); Yāqūt, *Muʿjam*, IV, 10–12.

87. Al-Muʿannā's decisive action seems to have been caused by his apprehension that Qābūs was making an attempt to revive the power of the kingdom of al-Ḥīrah. Qābūs b. Qābūs b. al-Mundhir was the grandson of the last king of al-Ḥīrah and thus a natural candidate to revive its erstwhile power.

88. For *fiʾah* in this sense, see Lane, *Lexicon*, s.v.; Rowson, *Marwānid Restoration*, 9 (= Ṭabarī, II, 861). See also Ṭabarī, I, 2176, 2180, where ʿUmar describes himself as *fiʾatu kulli muslimin*, i.e., the safe place behind the front to which every Muslim can repair when in danger; and Kūfī, *Futūḥ*, I, 192.

In the preceding sentence, Wellhausen (*Skizzen*, 152) suggested emending *fa-lahum mā warāʾahum* to *lahā mā warāʾahā*, with the translation "this victory will be decisive." As this passage explains why the Muslims should fight near their border rather than deep in the Persian territory, I tend to agree with de Goeje, who rejected Wellhausen's emendation (*Addenda et Emendanda*, DCXVI). Al-Muthannā seems to be saying that, if the Muslims win, the Persian territory will be theirs in any case; if they lose, they will be in a better situation militarily if the battle has taken place near their own land.

thannā's position, and bade his people well. He asked for Salmā's hand, married her, and consummated the marriage.

In the units of the army there were seventy odd men who had participated in the battle of Badr, around three hundred and ten men who were the Prophet's Companions since the Pledge of Good Pleasure (*bayʿat al-riḍwān*),[89] three hundred men who participated in the conquest of Mecca (*fatḥ*), and seven hundred sons of Companions, from all the Arab tribes.

While Saʿd was in Sharāf, he received ʿUmar's letter, expressing an opinion similar to that of al-Muthannā. At the same time ʿUmar wrote also to Abū ʿUbaydah (b. al-Jarrāḥ), and the letters were transmitted to both of them. In the letter to Abū ʿUbaydah ʿUmar ordered him to send six thousand Iraqis and all those who desired to go with them [to join Saʿd's army]. The text of his letter to Saʿd was as follows:

> After the preliminaries (*ammā baʿdu*): Set out from Sharāf in the direction of Persia, together with all the Muslims who are with you. Put your reliance in God and seek His help in all your affairs. Concerning the task in front of you, be aware that you are about to take on a nation that has great numbers and superior equipment. Their courage is great, and they live in a well-defended country. Though it is flat, it is hard of access because of its crevices, flood plains, and torrents,[90] except if you happen to arrive when the water is low. When you encounter the Persians or one of them, attack them first, and beware of waiting until their armies gather. Let them not deceive you, because they are deceitful and crafty, unlike you; you must exert full effort in the struggle against them. [2228]
>
> Al-Qādisiyyah was in the pre-Islamic period a gateway to Persia, in which they kept most of their provisions and essential [supplies] that they desired.[91] It is a spacious, fertile,

89. See Watt, *Muḥammad at Medina*, 50.

90. *Daʾdaʾah*, pl. *daʾādiʾ*, means "sound of stones falling into a stream" (*ṣawtu waqʿi al-ḥijārah fī al-masīl*). See Azharī, *Tahdhīb*, XIV, 237.

91. *Li-mā yurīdūna min tilka al-āṣul* is difficult. De Goeje suggests (*Glossary*, s.v. *a-ṣ-l*) that *āṣul* is to be understood as "war materials." Although this may not be far from the intended meaning, the word *aṣl* does not carry this connotation.

and fortified place, and in front of it are bridges and canals that are difficult to ford. When you arrive there, let your garrisons be near the points of entry. Let your people be on the border between the desert and the cultivated land, on the sandy tracks in between; then stay in your place, and do not move from it. When they find out that you are there, they will be perturbed. They will send against you their infantrymen, horsemen, and all. If you stand firm against your enemy, seek God's reward for fighting him, and intend to be faithful to your trust, then I hope that you will be granted victory and never again will enemies like these assemble against you. And, even if they do, they will do it in disheartened state.

If you lose the battle, the desert will be behind you. You will retreat from the edge of their cultivated land to the edge of your desert; there you will have more courage and will know the terrain better. Your enemies, on the other hand, will be fearful and ignorant of the terrain. Eventually, God will grant you victory over them and provide you with another opportunity to attack.

ʿUmar also wrote to Saʿd a letter stating the date on which he should move from Sharāf: "On such-and-such a day, move out with
[2229] your men and halt between ʿUdhayb al-Hijānāt and ʿUdhayb al-Qawādis.[92] Spread the people eastwards and westwards." Then he received a response from ʿUmar, saying:

Now renew your commitment,[93] admonish your soldiers, and speak to them about [the necessity to have the right] intention and about seeking God's reward. Whoever becomes heedless about these two matters, let him revive them [in his heart]. Stand firm! Help will come from God according

92. ʿUdhayb was a spring situated 4 miles from al-Qādisiyyah. Yāqūt (*Muʿjam*, III, 626) mentions this letter from ʿUmar as a proof that there were two places bearing this name. For an attempt to identify the exact location of these two places, see Musil, *Middle Euphrates*, 111 n. 62. See also Qudāmah b. Jaʿfar, *Kharāj*, 185–86, where ʿUdhayb is described as a garrison (*maslaḥah*) on the border of the desert between the land of the Arabs and the land of the Persians, 6 miles from al-Qādisiyyah. It was a port of entry into the Persian empire for travelers from the Ḥijāz. See Christensen, *Sassanides*, 415; Ibn Khurradādhbih, *Masālik*, 173.

93. Literally: "renew the pledge to your heart."

to the [purity of] intention, and reward will come according to what you sought.[94] Be cautious with those who are under your command and with the mission entrusted to you. Ask God to grant you well-being, and say frequently "There is no power and no strength except in God!" (*lā ḥawla wa-lā quwwata illā bi-Allāh*). Inform me in writing about the place where their army confronted you and who is the commander in charge of fighting you. The fact that I do not know what are you up against and what is the situation of your enemy has prevented me from writing to you certain things which I wanted to write, so describe for me the positions of the Muslims and the area between you and al-Madā'in, and let the description be as [precise as] if I were looking at the place myself. Keep me well informed of your affairs! Fear God, hope for Him, and do not be haughty! Know that God has made a promise to you, has taken this matter upon Himself, and will not break His promise. Be careful not to turn Him away from you, lest He put someone else in your place.

Sa'd wrote to 'Umar describing the area:

Al-Qādisiyyah is situated between the moat-canal (*al-khandaq*)[95] and al-'Atīq.[96] In the area to the left of it there is a dark body of water in a deep valley with entangled vegetation. It extends as far as al-Ḥīrah and runs between two
roads. One is on high ground; the other is on the bank of a [2230]
canal called al-Ḥuḍūḍ. Whoever follows it is able to see the

94. The idea is that a Muslim will receive from God reward for his deeds if he has performed them with a pure intention and with the desire to be rewarded. This desire is called *ḥisbah* or *iḥtisāb*. See Bukhārī, *Ṣaḥīḥ*, I, 22–23 (*Kitāb al-īmān*, 41) "... the deeds are judged by the intention and the reward sought; every man will be rewarded according to what he intended" (... *inna al-a'māl bi-al-niyyah wa-al-ḥisbah wa-li-kulli 'mri'in mā nawā*). A tradition attributed to 'Umar and expressing an idea similar to that in our text reads: "O people, seek reward for your deeds. Whoever seeks reward for his deed will be rewarded for [both] his deed and his desire" (*ayyuhā al-nās iḥtasibū a'mālakum fa-inna man iḥtasaba 'amalahu kutiba lahu ajru 'amalihi wa-ajru ḥisbatihi*). See Ibn Manẓūr, *Lisān al-'Arab*, s.v. *h-s-b*.

95. This canal, or system of canals, ran on the edge of the desert from Hīt on the Euphrates to the head of the Persian Gulf. Its construction is attributed to the Sasanian king Shāpūr II in the fourth century. See Le Strange, *Lands*, 65; Morony, *Iraq*, 152–53; and the sources mentioned there.

96. For an attempt to identify the exact location of this canal, see Musil, *Middle Euphrates*, p. 111 n. 62.

area between al-Khawarnaq[97] and al-Ḥīrah. To the left of al-Qādisiyyah, as far as al-Walajah,[98] there is a flood plain.

All the *ahl al-sawād* who had concluded peace with the Muslims before me now support the Persians, are obedient to them, and are ready to fight us. The person whom they designated to fight against us is Rustam, and other Persians like him. They try to make us act heedlessly and to throw us off balance, and we try to do the same and [also] try to draw them into the open field. God's command will soon be put into effect; His decree will deliver us to the fate that He determines, whether it be for good or for evil. We ask God to decree in our favor and keep us well.

ʿUmar wrote to Saʿd: "I have received your letter and have understood it. Stay where you are until God throws your enemy off balance, and know that other [battles] will follow.[99] If God grants you victory over them, do not stop the pursuit until you force your way into al-Madāʾin. God willing, this will be the destruction of the city." ʿUmar started to pray especially for Saʿd. Others prayed with him for Saʿd and for the Muslims in general.

Saʿd sent Zuhrah (b. al-Ḥawiyyah) forward to camp at ʿUdhayb al-Hijānāt. Then he followed on his tracks and stayed with him there.

---

97. Al-Khawarnaq was a castle situated 1 mile east of al-Najaf. According to the Arab tradition, it was built for al-Nuʿmān b. Imriʾ al-Qays, the king of al-Ḥīrah (A.D. 405–33), on the orders of the Sasanian king. The castle became famous in Arab lore because al-Nuʿmān killed Sinnimār, the architect of the castle, in order to prevent the construction of a similarly sumptuous building for someone else. The story gave rise to the proverbial "reward of Sinnimār" *jazāʾ Sinnimār*). See Maydānī, *Amthāl*, I, 283. See also *EI²* s.v. "al-Khawarnaḳ" (L. Massignon), Yāqūt, *Muʿjam*, II, 490–94. For a description of the ruins of al-Khawarnaq, see Musil, *Middle Euphrates*, 104–6.

98. See Yāqūt, *Muʿjam*, IV, 939; Donner, *Conquests*, 329 and index.

99. This translation of *iʿlam anna lahā mā baʿdahā* is tentative. It seems to be supported by similar passages, such as *inna hādha yawmun lahu mā baʿdahu min al-ayyām* (Ṭabarī, I, 2611 l. 15, 2613, l. 2). See also I, 2092, ll. 11–12: "This is a day [of battle], which will be followed [by other days]; if we throw them back to their trenches today, we shall keep on throwing them back. But, if they defeat us, we shall not succeed in the future" (*wa hādha yawmun lahu mā baʿdahu. in radadnāhum ilā khandaqihim al-yawm, lam nazal narudduhum: wa-in hazamūnā, lam nufliḥ baʿdahā*).

A. Noth, who has collected and analyzed these passages (*Studien*, 118), agrees with Wellhausen (cf. note 88, above) in suggesting that these expressions indicate the decisiveness of the battle. Although this meaning is implied here, it does not seem to be the primary meaning of the expressions quoted above.

Later he sent him on farther to camp in al-Qādisiyyah, between al-ʿAtīq and the moat-canal, opposite the bridge. Qudays was at that time one mile downstream from the bridge.

According to al-Sarī—Shuʿayb—Sayf—al-Qaʿqāʿ: ʿUmar wrote to Saʿd:

> I have been given the feeling that you will defeat the enemy when you encounter him. Therefore cast your doubts away and choose firm faith[100] instead. Should any one of you joke [2231] with a Persian about safe-conduct (*amān*) or approach him with a hint, or say to him a word that the Persian will not understand and will construe as a safe-conduct, then act as if he had been given one. Beware of frivolity. Be faithful, because mistaken faithfulness is virtue,[101] but mistaken betrayal [entails] perdition; it will be a source of your weakness and of your enemies' strength. You will lose your predominance, and they will gain ascendance.[102] I am warning you not to be a disgrace to the Muslims and a cause of their humiliation.

According to al-Sarī—Shuʿayb—Sayf—ʿAbdallāh b. Muslim al-ʿUklī and al-Miqdām b. Abī al-Miqdām—his father—Karib b. Abī Karib al-ʿUklī, who was in the vanguard in the battle days of al-Qādisiyyah: Saʿd sent us forward from Sharāf, and we camped in ʿUdhayb al-Hijānāt. Then he went forth. When he was with us at ʿUdhayb al-Hijānāt, that being at dawn, Zuhrah b. al-Ḥawiyyah set out with the vanguard. When we were able to see ʿUdhayb, which was one of the Persian garrisons, we perceived people on its towers. Wherever we looked, on a tower or between two battlements, we saw a man. We were with the advance horsemen, so we halted until [more of] the troops joined us. We thought that [Persian] horsemen were in ʿUdhayb. We then set out in the direction of ʿUdhayb, and, when we drew near, a man rushed out, running in the direction of al-Qādisiyyah. We finally reached ʿUdhayb, entered it, and found that it had been abandoned. That was the man who appeared to us on the [2232]

100. Translating *al-yaqīn*, a variant mentioned in the notes, rather than *taqiyyah* of the text.

101. For *baqiyyah* in this sense, see Spitaler, "Baqīja."

102. For *dhahāb rīḥihim*, see Qurʾān 8:46.

towers and between the battlements as a ruse and then hurried to inform the Persians of our arrival. We went out in pursuit but failed to seize him. Zuhrah heard about it and rushed out himself, pursuing him,[103] saying: "If the scout escapes, they will receive the information!" He caught up with him at the moat, stabbed him, and threw him into the moat. The people who participated in the battle of al-Qādisiyyah admired the courage of this man and his military knowledge; there has never been a spy, in any nation, who stood his ground better or was more resolute than this Persian. If he had not had to run such a great distance, Zuhrah would not have caught up with him and would not have killed him.

The Muslims found in ʿUdhayb spears, arrows, leather baskets (*asfāṭ*), and other useful things.

[Saʿd][104] then dispatched raiding parties and ordered them to attack al-Ḥīrah at night. He placed them under the command of Bukayr b. ʿAbdallāh al-Laythī. Among the warriors was the Qaysī poet al-Shammākh[105] with thirty men well known for bravery and courage. They marched at night, passed Saylaḥūn,[106] and crossed a nearby bridge in the direction of al-Ḥīrah. [There] they heard a loud noise, halted their advance, and lay in ambush to examine the situation. They lay there until a group of horsemen who went ahead of that noise passed by on their way to al-Ṣinnīn.[107] The horsemen did
[2233] not perceive the Muslims; they were merely expecting the [above-mentioned] spy, did not look for the Muslims, and did not pay any attention to them. Their sole aim was to reach Ṣinnīn. The sister of Āzādmard b. Āzādbih, the governor of al-Ḥīrah, was being married to the ruler of Ṣinnīn, a Persian nobleman. The bride was accompanied by an escort, fearful of a lesser [danger] than that which they

---

103. The text reads: "... Zuhrah heard about it, followed us, reached us, left us behind, and pursued him."

104. The text is silent with regard to the commander intended.

105. Al-Shammākh, also known as Maʿqil b. Ḍirār, was a *mukhaḍram* poet who belonged to the tribe of Ghaṭafān and is said to have excelled in his descriptions of the bow and the wild ass. See Ibn Qutaybah, *Shiʿr,* 177–79; Jumaḥī, *Ṭabaqāt,* 29; *GAL,* I, 37.

106. A considerable part of Yāqūt's entry on Saylaḥūn discusses the morphology of the word. There are also some verses in which the place is mentioned, and it is clear from them that it was in the neighborhood of al-Qādisiyyah. No other significant details can be ascertained from this material. See Yāqūt, *Muʿjam,* III, 218–19; cf. Musil, *Middle Euphrates,* 108, note and index.

107. See Yāqūt, *Muʿjam,* III, 430; Morony, *Iraq,* index. For a modern attempt to identify Sinnīn, see Musil, *Middle Euphrates,* 117–18.

actually encountered.[108] The Muslims were lying in ambush between the palm trees. When a gap opened between the horsemen and the women who accompanied the bride, and the luggage of the party passed by, Bukayr fell upon Shīrzād b. Āzādbih [who was between the luggage and the horses] and broke his back. The horses panicked and dispersed; the Muslims captured the luggage, the daughter of Āzādbih with thirty women of the Persian landowners (*dahāqīn*), and one hundred attendants. The Persians had with them property of unknown value, as well as ivory, all of which Bukayr carried away. In the morning he brought the booty that God had given to the Muslims to Saʿd in ʿUdhayb al-Hijānāt. The Muslims proclaimed loudly: "God is most great!" Saʿd said: "By God, you have exclaimed 'God is most great' like people in whom I perceive glory and strength." Then he distributed the booty among the Muslims, liberally distributing the fifth[109] and giving all the rest to the warriors. They were extremely pleased. Saʿd stationed in ʿUdhayb some horsemen to guard the women, and the guardians of all the womenfolk joined them. He appointed Ghālib b. ʿAbdallāh al-Laythī as their commander.[110]

Saʿd halted in al-Qādisiyyah and camped at al-Qudays.[111] Zuhrah camped opposite the bridge of al-ʿAtīq, which is the present location of al-Qādisiyyah. Saʿd informed [ʿUmar] of Bukayr's expedition and of his camping in al-Qudays. He stayed there for a month. Then he wrote to ʿUmar: [2234]

> The Persians[112] did not send anyone to confront us and did not entrust anyone we know with waging war against us. As

108. This is to say that the escort was not strong enough to take on the Muslim raiding party.

109. For the commander's right to receive one-fifth of the booty, based on Qur'ān 8:41 ("Know that whatever booty you take, the fifth is God's and the Messenger's . . . "), see *EI²*, s.v. "*Fay*'" (F. Løkkegaard). Saʿd's decision to distribute the fifth, which he was entitled to retain, is an indication of his selfless generosity. See also Ibn Manẓūr, *Lisān al-ʿarab*, s.v. *n-f-l* (XI, 671b).

110. Ghālib b. ʿAbdallāh al-Laythī led several expeditions against Bedouin tribes during the lifetime of the Prophet. See Ibn Saʿd, *Ṭabaqāt*, II/i, 86, 87–91; Ibn Ḥabīb, *Muḥabbar*, 117, 119, 120; Ṭabarī, index.

111. Yāqūt's entry (*Muʿjam*, IV, 42–43) says only that Qudays is situated in the vicinity of al-Qādisiyyah, quoting the passage from our text together with a verse in which Qudays is mentioned in connection with the battle of al-Qādisiyyah. See also Musil, *Middle Euphrates*, 110–11.

112. The text has *al-qawm*. It is noteworthy that in numerous passages translated in this volume *qawm* is used for the enemies, while *nās* is used for the group to

soon as we receive this information, we shall write to you. I am asking God's help. We are near a low-lying stream, wide and winding, beyond which a fearful fight [awaits us]. That we shall be summoned [to engage in this fight] has already been said: "You shall be called against a people possessed of great might."[113]

During his stay in [al-Qudays] Saʿd sent ʿĀṣim b. ʿAmr to the lower Euphrates. He went to Maysān,[114] looking for sheep and cattle, but was not able to obtain any. The people in the castles (*al-afdān*)[115] kept themselves protected from him and went deep into the thicket. He followed them, encountered a man on the edge of the thicket, and asked him where the cattle and the sheep were, but the man swore that he did not know. It became clear, however, that he himself was the shepherd of the flock in that thicket. A bull exclaimed: "By God, he is lying! Here we are." ʿĀṣim went in, led the bulls away, and brought them to the camp. Saʿd distributed them among the people, and they had ample provisions for a period of time.

This episode came to the knowledge of al-Ḥajjāj during his lifetime, and he sent for a few people who had witnessed it. Nadhīr b. ʿAmr, al-Walīd b. ʿAbd Shams, and Zāhir were among them.[116] Al-Ḥajjāj asked them about it. They said: "Yes, we heard it, saw it, and led the bulls away." He said: "You are lying." They said: "We would react similarly if you had been a witness to it and we had been absent." Al-Ḥajjāj said: "You have spoken the truth. And what did the

---

which the speaker or the traditionist belong. In most cases, therefore, *qawm* denotes the Persians or the Byzantines, while *nās* is used for the Muslims. The following passages contain the best examples of this usage: pp. 2314, ll. 1–4; 2327 ll. 10–11, 17; 2339 ll. 4, 10; 2344 ll. 7, 14; 2345 l. 11; 2348 l. 13; 2351 ll. 7–10; 2389 l. 13; 2391 l. 8. See also p. 2395 l. 10, where Heraclius uses *qawm* in speaking about the Muslims; so does Arṭabūn on p. 2399 l. 15. Not all instances collected so far fall into this pattern (e.g., p. 2283 l. 12), and I do not claim general validity for this observation. Nevertheless, if used with due circumspection it can be helpful in understanding the exact meaning of *nās* and *qawm*, which can at times be crucial to the interpretation of a whole passage.

113. Qur'ān 48:16 (Arberry's translation).

114. A city and district on the lower Tigris. See Le Strange, *Lands*, 43, 80; Yāqūt, *Muʿjam*, IV, 714–15; Morony, *Iraq*, 162 and index.

115. The reference is probably to the watchtowers and barracks that the Persians built as garrisons along the *khandaq* on the border between the desert and the cultivated land of Iraq. See Morony, *Iraq*, 153.

116. The grammar is irregular here; the text reads *aḥaduhum*, which is followed by the three names.

people say about it?" They said: ["The people considered it] a good sign, indicating that God was satisfied [with us] and that we shall defeat our enemy." Al-Ḥajjāj said: "By God, such things do not happen except when the people are pious and God-fearing." They said: "By God, we do not know what was hidden in their hearts. As for what we saw, we have never seen people who shunned this world and [2235] despised it more than these. None of them was noted[117] on that day for cowardice, betrayal, or plunder."[118] This was "the Day of the Bulls" (*yawm al-abāqir*).

Saʿd then dispatched raiding parties to the region between Kaskar[119] and al-Anbār.[120] They obtained provisions sufficient for a period of time. He also sent spies to the people of al-Ḥīrah and to Ṣalūba,[121] in order to obtain information about the affairs of the Persians. The spies returned with a report that the king had appointed Rustam b. Farrukhzād al-Armanī to lead the fight against Saʿd and had ordered him to organize an army. Saʿd wrote about it to ʿUmar. ʿUmar replied:

> Do not be perturbed by the information that you receive about them nor by [the army] that they will muster against you. Ask God's help and put your reliance on Him. Send [to the Persian king] people of [impressive] appearance, sound judgment, and endurance, in order to invite him to embrace Islam. God will render this invitation a cause of weakness and defeat for them. Write to me daily!

When Rustam camped in Sābāṭ,[122] they wrote to ʿUmar about it.

---

117. For *uʿtudda ʿalā* in a sense close to this, see Dozy, *Supplément*, s.v. ʿ-*d-d*.

118. *Ghulūl* is understood as a reference to someone who appropriates spoils that are not lawfully his. See Qurʾān 3:161: "... whoever defrauds, will bring the fruits of his fraud on the Day of Resurrection." Expanding on the verse, tradition maintains that the plunder will hang on the plunderer's neck on the Day of Judgment as a concrete evidence of his transgression. See Ṭabarī, *Tafsīr*, IV, 104–7.

119. Kaskar was a district on the Tigris, in the region of Fam al-Ṣilḥ and, later, of al-Wāsiṭ. See Morony, *Iraq*, 155–8; Yāqūt, *Muʿjam*, IV, 274–75.

120. Al-Anbār is a city on the Euphrates, to the west of Baghdad. See *EI*², s.v. "al-Anbār" (M. Streck [A. A. Duri]); Yāqūt, *Muʿjam*, I, 367–69; Morony, *Iraq*, 145 and index.

121. The text is phrased as if this were a place name, but it is not to be found in the standard geographical literature as such. In an earlier passage, Ṭabarī (*Taʾrīkh*, I, 2061) speaks of Banū Ṣalūbā and identifies them as "the people of al-Ḥīrah." Cf. Morony, *Iraq*, 174 n. 30.

122. Sābāṭ was one of the seven cities that together constituted al-Madāʾin ("the

According to al-Sarī—Shuʿayb—Sayf—Abū Ḍamrah—Ibn Sīrīn and Ismāʿīl b. Abī Khālid—Qays b. Abī Ḥāzim: When Saʿd learned of Rustam's departure for Sābāṭ, he stayed in his camp waiting for his army to assemble. Ismāʿīl said: Saʿd wrote to ʿUmar: Rustam has established his camp at Sābāṭ, near al-Madāʾin, and has marched toward us.

Abū Ḍamrah said: Saʿd wrote to ʿUmar:

> Rustam has established his campt at Sābāṭ and has marched toward us with horses, elephants, and a large number of Persians. Nothing is more important to me, nor do I remember anything more often than the way in which you wanted me to behave; we ask God's help and put our reliance on Him. I have sent so-and-so [to the king]; they have the qualities that you described.

[2236] According to al-Sarī — Shuʿayb — Sayf — ʿAmr, al-Mujālid, and Saʿīd b. al-Marzubān: When Saʿd b. Abī Waqqāṣ received ʿUmar's command with regard to the Persians, he assembled a group of men of pure lineage and sound judgment and another group who had [impressive] appearance, were awe-inspiring, and had sound judgment. The persons of pure lineage, sound judgment, and power of reasoning (*ijtihād*) were al-Nuʿmān b. Muqarrin,[123] Busr b. Abī Ruhm, Ḥamalah b. Juwayyah al-Kinānī,[124] Ḥanẓalah b. al-Rabīʿ al-Tamīmī,[125] Furāt b. Ḥayyān al-ʿIjlī, ʿAdī b. Suhayl, and al-Mughīrah b. Zurārah b. al-Nabbāsh b. Ḥabīb. Those who had [impressive] bodily

---

Cities"). It was situated on the west bank of the Tigris, south of Veh-Ardashir. See *EI*², s.v. "al-Madāʾin" (M. Streck [M. Morony]), with extensive bibliography; Le Strange, *Lands*, 34–35; Yāqūt, *Muʿjam*, III, 3; Christensen, *Sassanides*, 388; Ṣ. A. ʿAlī, "Madāʾin," 61–62; Oppenheimer *et al.*, *Babylonia*, index.

123. Al-Nuʿmān b. Muqarrin was a member of the tribe of Muzaynah and embraced Islam in the year 5/626–27. In addition to the battle of al-Qādisiyyah, he participated in the conquest of Persia and was killed in the battle of Nihāwand in 21/641–42. See Ibn Saʿd, *Ṭabaqāt*, I/ii, 38; (ʿI.) Ibn al-Athīr, *Usd*, V, 30–31; Ibn Ḥajar, *Tahdhīb*, X, 456 no. 826.

124. For Ḥamalah b. Juwayyah, see Ibn Ḥajar, *Iṣābah*, II, 181 no. 2003, where he is listed as Ḥamalah b. Abī Muʿāwiyah al-Kinānī.

125. Ḥanẓalah b. al-Rabīʿ al-Tamīmī is said to have been one of the scribes who recorded the revelations of the Prophet and was therefore known as *al-kātib*. He settled in al-Kūfah and moved later to Qarqīsiyā. He died during the reign of Muʿāwiyah. See (ʿI.) Ibn al-Athīr, *Usd*, II, 66–67; Ibn Ḥajar, *Iṣābah*, II, 134–35 no. 1861; Ibn Ḥajar, *Tahdhīb*, III, 60 no. 109.

appearance, were awe-inspiring, and had sound judgment were ʿUṭārid b. Ḥājib,[126] al-Ashʿath b. Qays, al-Ḥārith b. Ḥassān, ʿĀṣim b. ʿAmr, ʿAmr b. Maʿdīkarib, al-Mughīrah b. Shuʿbah, and al-Muʿannā b. Ḥārithah. Saʿd sent them to invite the king to embrace Islam.

According to Muḥammad b. ʿAbdallāh b. Ṣafwān al-Thaqafī — Umayyah b. Khālid — Abū ʿAwānah — Ḥuṣayn b. ʿAbd al-Raḥmān — Abū Wāʾil: Saʿd came to camp at al-Qādisiyyah with the army. He said:

> I do not know, perhaps we are not more than seven thousand men, roughly, and the polytheists are approximately thirty thousand. They said to us: "You have no might or power or weapons. What has brought you here? Turn back!" We replied: "We shall not turn back. We are not the kind of people who turn back." They were laughing at our arrows, saying *dūk dūk*[127] and comparing them with spindles. When we refused to turn back, they said: "Send to us a wise man who will explain to us what brought you here." Al-Mughīrah b. Shuʿbah said: "I am the man."

He crossed over to them and sat with Rustam on the throne. They were snorting and shouting. Al-Mughīrah said: "This will not increase my honor, nor will it detract from that of your leader." Rustam [2237] said: "You are right. What has brought you here?" Al-Mughīrah said:

> We were a people living in gross error. God sent to us a prophet, guided us through him to the straight path, and gave us sustenance. Among the things He gave us was a seed that grows, so it was claimed, in this country.[128] When we ate it and gave it to our families to eat, they said, "We cannot

126. ʿUṭārid b. Ḥājib was a chieftain of the tribe of Tamīm. Having embraced Islam in the year 9/630–31 (or 10/631–32), he was entrusted with collecting the poor tax (*ṣadaqah*) of his tribe. After the death of the Prophet he joined the rebellion of Sajāḥ, the Tamīmī woman who claimed prophethood. Like numerous other apostates, he reverted to Islam after the suppression of the *riddah*. See Ibn Saʿd, *Ṭabaqāt*, I/ii, 40; II/i, 116; (ʿI.) Ibn al-Athīr, *Usd*, III, 411; Ibn Ḥajar, *Iṣābah*, IV, 507–9.

127. Meaning "spindle" in Persian. The Persians ridiculed the Arab arrows because theirs must have been much thicker. Cf. Schwarzlose, *Waffen*, 281.

128. Persia.

endure without having this seed. Let us live in this country, so that we can eat from it."

Rustam said: "This being so, we shall kill you!" Al-Mughīrah said: "If you kill us, we shall enter Paradise; if we kill you, you shall enter the Fire; or (alternatively) hand over the poll tax." When al-Mughīrah said: "or hand over the poll tax," they snorted and shouted and said: "There will be no peace between us." Al-Mughīrah said: "Will you cross over to us, or shall we cross over to you [in order to fight]?" Rustam said: "Nay, we shall cross over to you!" The Muslims waited until some Persians crossed over, attacked them, and defeated them.

Ḥuṣayn[129] said: A person from our tribe, named ʿUbayd b. Jaḥsh al-Sulamī, said:

> I observed that we have trampled upon the backs of men who were not touched by weapons but killed by each other.[130] [Then]—as I observed—we found a bag of camphor and thought that it was salt. We had no doubt about it, so we cooked some meat and sprinkled the camphor into the pot. A Christian (*ʿibādī*)[131] who had a shirt with him passed near by and said: "O Arabs, do not spoil your food! The salt of this country is worthless. Would you like to take this shirt in exchange for it?"

We took the shirt from him and gave it to one of our people to wear. We started to walk around him and to admire him, but, when we became acquainted with the clothing [of this country], it became clear that the shirt was worth [only] two dirhams."[132]

[ʿUbayd b. Jaḥsh] said: "I found myself coming close to a man who

129. Identified by de Goeje as Ḥusayn b. ʿAbd al-Raḥmān *al-rāwī*, on whom see Bukhārī, *Taʾrīkh*, II, 8 no. 25.

130. The sentence describes the confusion of battle, in which men kill each other by trampling or in a similar way.

131. For *al-ʿibād*, the Nestorian Christian community of al-Ḥīrah, see Bosworth, "Iran and the Arabs," 598–99.

132. The Muslims felt that they had been deceived when they eventually found out that camphor was an extremely expensive substance, while the shirt was of minimal value. For camphor and its price, see *EI*², s.v. "Kāfūr" (A. Dietrich); Heyd, *Commerce*, II, 594; Ashtor, *Prix et salaires*, 140, 337, 421–22 (no data for Iraq at the time of the Muslim conquest).

had two golden bracelets in addition to his weapon. He came at me; without saying a word to him, I broke his neck." (Then he said:)

> The Persians were defeated and retreated to al-Ṣarāt;[133] we pursued them and they retreated to al-Madā'in. The Muslims were at Kūthā,[134] and the polytheists had a garrison in Dayr al-Mislākh.[135] The Muslims marched toward them, the polytheists were defeated in the ensuing battle and retreated to the bank of the Tigris. Some of them crossed [the Tigris] at Kalwādhā,[136] others below al-Madā'in. The Muslims besieged them so that they did not have anything to eat except their dogs and cats. They slipped out at night and reached Jalūlā'. The Muslims, with Hāshim b. ʿUtbah[137] commanding Saʿd's vanguard, caught up with them. The place at which the battle was joined was at some distance from Jalūlā'.[138] [2238]

Abū Wā'il said: ʿUmar b. al-Khaṭṭāb sent Ḥudhayfah b. al-Yamān to lead the people of al-Kūfah and Mujāshiʿ b. Masʿūd to lead the people of al-Baṣrah.

According to al-Sarī — Shuʿayb — Sayf — ʿAmr b. Muḥammad — al-Shaʿbī and Ṭalḥah — al-Mughīrah: They[139] went out of the Muslim camp and went to al-Madā'in in order to engage Yazdagird in debate and invite him to embrace Islam. They passed by Rustam and

---

133. Al-Ṣarāt was one of the canals connecting the Euphrates and the Tigris, flowing east of al-Anbār. See Yāqūt, *Muʿjam*, III, 377–78; Le Strange, *Lands*, 66; Morony, *Iraq*, 145.

134. An important city in the *sawād*, to the southwest of al-Madā'in. See Le Strange, *Lands*, 68–69; Yāqūt, *Muʿjam*, IV, 317–18; Morony, *Iraq*, index; Oppenheimer *et al.*, *Babylonia*, 175–78.

135. I was not able to identify this locality. Ṣ. A. ʿAlī ("Madā'in," 63) places it between Kūthā and Sābāṭ, evidently on the strength of this passage.

136. A city on the eastern bank of the Tigris, not far from the site where Baghdad was later built. See Le Strange, *Lands*, 32.

137. Hāshim b. ʿUtbah b. Abī Waqqāṣ of Quraysh embraced Islam after the conquest of Mecca. He lost an eye in the battle of Yarmūk, participated in the battles against the Persians, and was killed in the battle of Ṣiffīn in 37/657–58. See Ibn Ḥabīb, *Muḥabbar*, 261, 269; (ʿI.) Ibn al-Athīr, *Usd*, V, 49–50.

138. Jalūlā' is situated to the northeast of Baghdad. Ṭabarī gives a much more detailed description of this battle in I, 2456ff. See also Yāqūt, *Muʿjam*, II, 107.

139. Apparently the members of the Muslim delegation appointed by Saʿd to invite Yazdagird to embrace Islam; see p. 2236, above.

reached the gate of Yazdagird ['s residence]. Riding on noble horses, they halted. They had with them horses without riders (*janāʾib*),[140] and all were neighing.[141] They asked permission to enter but had to wait. Yazdagird [meanwhile] consulted his ministers and the nobles of his country as to what to do with the Muslims and what to tell them. The Persians heard about their coming and came to look at them. The Muslims wore short garments (*muqaṭṭaʿāt*) and cloaks (*burūd*, sg. *burd*). They held thin whips in their hands and wore sandals (*niʿāl*, sg. *naʿl*) on their feet.[142] When the Persians made up their minds, the Muslims were allowed to enter into the king's presence.

According to al-Sarī—Shuʿayb—Sayf—Ṭalḥah—Bint Kaysān al-Ḍabbiyyah—a person who was taken prisoner at the battle of al-Qādisiyyah, became a virtuous Muslim, and was present when the [2239] Muslim delegation came: The Persians gathered around the Muslims and looked at them. I have never seen ten men who equaled, in their appearance, a thousand others;[143] their horses were striking [the ground with their feet] and made threatening noises at each other. The Persians were vexed by the condition of the Muslims and of their horses.

When they entered into the presence of Yazdagird, he ordered them to sit down. He was a man of bad manners. The first thing that occurred between the king and the Muslims was as follows: The king ordered the translator to take his place between the king and the Muslims. Then he said: "Ask them what they call these garments." The translator asked al-Nuʿmān (b. Muqarrin), who was heading the delegation: "What is the name of your garment?" Al-

---

140. The purpose of bringing along additional horses seems to have been to increase the pomp of the delegation and to create the impression of power and abundance. See Dozy, *Supplément*, s.v. *j-n-b*.

141. Neighing of horses carries special significance in Islamic tradition. When God created the horse, He said: "I gave you my blessing. I shall frighten the polytheists by your neighing . . . " (*bāraktu fīka bi-ṣahīlika urhib al-mushrikīn*). See Ibn Juzayy, *Khayl*, 32. Satan is also said to be vexed by neighing of horses; see Ibn Juzayy, *Khayl*, 37. These traditions may well explain why the neighing of horses is mentioned in our context. The description of the Persians' reaction to the behavior of the horses (p. 2239, above) points in the same direction. See also Ṭabarī, I, 2435 l. 9; and Sarakhsī, *Sharḥ al-siyar*, I, 83.

142. See *EI²*, s.v. "Libās" (Y. K. Stillman and N. A. Stillmann); and Dozy, *Vêtements*, 59–64 (*burd*); 421–24 (*naʿl*); Suyūṭī, *Aḥādīth*, 6 (section 15).

143. Cf. Yaʿqūbī, *Taʾrīkh*, II, 163, who also stresses the impressive attire of the delegation (*dakhalū ʿalayhi fī aḥsani ziyyin wa ʿalayhim al-burūd wa-al-naʿl*).

Nuʿmān answered: "It is a cloak (*burd*)." The king saw an evil omen in this and said: "He has carried off the world (*burd jahān*)."[144] The Persians became pale and distressed. Then the king said: "Ask them about their footwear." The translator asked: "What is the name of these shoes?" Al-Nuʿmān said: "Sandals (*niʿāl*)." The king reacted as before and said: "Alas, alas (*nāla nāla*) for our country!" Then he asked al-Nuʿmān what he had in his hand. Al-Nuʿmān said: "A whip (*sawṭ*)." (*Sawṭ* means in Persian "burning.") The king said: "They have burned Persia. May God burn them!"[145] The king's augury[146] lay heavy upon the Persians, and they were full of sorrow because of his words.

Al-Sarī—Shuʿayb—Sayf—ʿAmr—al-Shaʿbī related the same tradition and then added: The king then said: "Ask them: 'Why did you come here? What induced you to attack us and covet our country? Did you muster courage against us because we left you alone and were busy with other matters?'" Al-Nuʿmān b. Muqarrin said to the members of his delegation: "If you wish, I shall answer on your behalf. If anybody else desires [to speak], I shall prefer him to do so." They said to him: "Speak," and they said to the king: "This man speaks on behalf of us all."

Al-Nuʿmān said:

> God has had mercy upon us and has sent to us a messenger who showed us what is good and ordered us to practice it; he made evil known to us and ordered us to abstain from it. If we should respond to him, he promised us the goodness of this world and of the next. All tribes whom he invited to join him became divided: One group drew near him, and an-

144. In Thaʿālibī, *Ghurar*, 739, the discussion is not with the king but with Rustam, who says: *bādshāhī burd* "he carried away the kingdom." See also Kūfī, *Futūḥ*, I, 197.

145. The king's play on words is made possible by the different meanings of words that sound similar in Arabic and Persian: *burd* "cloak" (Arabic), "carried" (Persian); *niʿāl* "sandals" (Arabic), *nālah* "lament" (Persian); *sawṭ* "whip" (Arabic), *sūkht* "burned" (Persian).

It is noteworthy that according to the account of Ibn Kathīr (*Bidāyah*, VII, 41), which is also attributed to Sayf b. ʿUmar, Yazdagird saw in the Arabs' replies to his questions a good omen, but God transformed it into a bad one (*tafāʾala fa-radda Al-lāh faʾlahu ʿalā raʾsihi*).

146. Reading *taṭayyuruhu* with Wellhausen, *Skizzen*, 152, and the Egyptian edition, rather than *naẓīruhu* of the Leiden edition.

other remained aloof. Only the elect embraced his religion.
[2240] He acted in this manner as long as God wanted him to act. Then he was ordered to dissociate himself from the Arabs who opposed him, and he began to act [against them]. Willingly or unwillingly, all of them joined him. Those who joined him unwillingly, [eventually] became content, while those who joined him willingly grew more and more satisfied. We all came to understand the superiority of his message over our former condition, which was replete with enmity and destitution. Then he ordered us to start with the nations adjacent to us and invite them to justice. We are therefore inviting you to embrace our religion. This is a religion which approves of all that is good and rejects all that is evil. If you refuse our invitation, you must pay the poll tax. This is a bad thing, but not as bad as the alternative; if you refuse [to pay], it will be war. If you respond and embrace our religion, we shall leave with you the Book of God and teach you its contents,[147] provided that you will govern according to the laws included in it. We shall leave your country and let you deal with its affairs as you please. If you protect yourself against us by paying the poll tax, we shall accept it from you and ensure your safety. Otherwise we shall fight you!

Then Yazdagird spoke, saying:

I know of no other nation on earth that was more miserable, smaller in numbers, and more rancorous than you. We used to entrust the outlying villages with our defense against you, and they were sufficient for the task. The Persians did not attack you, and you had no hope to hold your ground against them. If [your] numbers are now at par [with ours], let it not delude you [into attacking] us. If it is hardship that has caused you [to move against us], we shall allocate provisions for you in order to increase your prosperity. We shall honor your nobles, we shall provide you with clothing, and
[2241] we shall appoint for you a king who will treat you gently.

147. For *aqāma ʿalā* in this sense, see *Glossary* to Balādhurī, *Futūḥ*; and Dozy, *Supplément*, s.v. *q-w-m*.

The Arabs remained silent. Al-Mughīrah b. Zurārah b. al-Nabbāsh al-Usaydī stood up and said:

> O king, these are Arab chieftains of high rank. They are noblemen, diffident in their relationship with other noblemen. Only noblemen can honor other noblemen; only noblemen can enhance the rights of other noblemen, and only noblemen can treat other noblemen with respect. They therefore did not tell you all they had been sent with, and they did not reply to everything you had said. They did the right thing and did nothing except that which would befit people of their kind. Speak, therefore, with me; I shall give you the information, and they shall witness to it.[148] In your description of us, you said things of which you had no knowledge.[149] As for the destitution that you mentioned, there was nobody more destitute that we were. As for our hunger, it was not hunger in the usual sense. We used to eat beetles of various sorts (*khanāfis, ji'lān*),[150] scorpions, and snakes, and we considered this our food. Nothing but the bare earth was our dwelling. We wore only what we spun from the hair of camels and sheep. Our religion was to kill one another and to raid one another. And if there was among us such as would bury his daughter alive, recoiling from her eating from our food[151] — the our condition in the past had, indeed, been what I mentioned to you.
>
> But then God sent to us a well-known man. We knew his lineage, his face, and his birthplace. His land is the choice part of our land. His glory and the glory of his ancestors are

148. Al-Mughīrah implies that he will not be as reserved and inhibited in his speech as were the other members of the delegation.

149. Meaning that the conditions in which the Arabs lived in the pre-Islamic period were worse than would appear from the king's description.

150. The inferior food of the Arabs was one of the arguments frequently used by the Shu'ūbiyyah in order to deprecate them. Cf. Goldziher, *Muslim Studies*, I, 152 n. 1. Here it is used to describe the conditions in which the Arabs lived in the Jāhiliyyah and to demonstrate the fundamental transformation that they experienced as a result of the emergence of Islam.

151. The reference is to female infanticide (*wa'd al-banāt*), which was practiced in pre-Islamic Arabia. As in this passage, poverty is usually given as its cause. See, for instance, Iṣfahānī, *Aghānī*, XXX, 8519–20. For Qur'ānic criticism of the custom, see Qur'ān 6:137, 140, 151; 16:58, 59; 17:33. For a novel interpretation, see Lichtenstaedter, "*Gharānīq.*"

the most memorable among us. His family is the greatest of our families, and his tribe is the best of our tribes. He himself was the best among us and at the same time the most truthful and the most forbearing. He invited us to embrace his religion. Nobody responded to his call before [Abū Bakr], who was a person of his age[152] and became his successor af-
[2242] ter his death. He spoke, and we spoke; he spoke the truth, and we lied. He grew in stature, and we became deficient. Everything he said came to pass. God instilled in our hearts belief in him and [caused us] to follow him. He stood between us and the Lord of the Worlds. Whatever he said to us was the word of God, and whatever he commanded us to do was the commandment of God. He said: "Your Master says, I am God,[153] alone. I have no partner. I existed when there was nothing. Everything perishes except My face;[154] I created everything and to Me will everything return. My mercy has reached you, and I have sent to you this man in order to show you the way by means of which I shall save you from My punishment after death and cause you to dwell in My Abode, the Abode of Peace."[155]

We witnessed that he brought the truth from God. He[156] said: "Whoever follows you in this [religion] has the same rights and the same obligations as you have, but whoever refuses, offer him (payment of) the poll tax. If he agrees, protect him from everything that you protect yourself from, but whoever refuses [to pay], fight him, and I shall be the judge between you. I shall admit those who are killed to My garden, and to those who survive I shall give victory over their opponents." [Al-Mughīrah continued, addressing the king]:

152. According to a tradition, Abū Bakr was born three years after "the year of the elephant" and died at the same age as the Prophet: sixty-three years. He was thus three years younger than the Prophet. See Ṭabarī, I, 2128–9. The tradition according to which Abū Bakr was the first person to have embraced Islam is not the only one on this topic; see Ṭabarī, *Ta'rīkh*, I, 1165ff. for traditions according to which he had been preceded by others.

153. Qur'ān 28:30.

154. Qur'ān 28:88: "Everything perishes except His face."

155. Qur'ān 6:127.

156. The following paragraph is al-Mughīrah b. Zurārah's restatement of ideas from the Qur'ān and the *ḥadīth*. Although the pronoun refers to God, these are not exact quotations from the Qur'ān.

"If you wish, choose to pay the poll tax out of hand and in humilation.[157] If you wish (to reject this offer), it is the sword, unless you embrace Islam and save your soul."

[The king] said: "Do you [dare to] face me with such things?" [Al-Mughīrah b. Zurārah] said: "I faced only the one who spoke to me. Had somebody else spoken to me, I would not have faced you with this." The king said: "But for the custom not to kill envoys, I would have killed you. I have nothing for you."

Then the king said: "Bring me a load of soil,." And he said: "Load it on the most noble of them and drive him out of the gate of al-Madā'in." [And to the Arabs he said]: "Return to your chief and tell him that I am sending to you Rustam to finish you and your chief off in [2243]
the moat of al-Qādisiyyah. He will punish you severely as an example for others. Then I shall send him to your country and make you mind your own affairs in a manner more harsh than that which you suffered at the hands of Sābūr."[158] Then he asked: "Who is the most noble among you?" The Arabs remained silent. ʿĀṣim b. ʿAmr, who had decided to take the load without consulting anyone, said: "I am the most noble. I am their chief. Load it on me." The king asked: "Is it so?" The Arabs said: "Yes." The king loaded the soil on his neck and drove him out of the hall and out of the building. ʿĀṣim went to his camel, loaded it with the burden, and quickly rode away. All of them traveled to Saʿd. ʿĀṣim overtook them, and, passing near the gate of Qudays, he said: "Bring the tidings of victory to the amīr. God willing, we have won." He went to put the soil in a safe place, then returned, entered to Saʿd, and informed him about the matter. Saʿd said: "By God, rejoice, because God gave us the keys to their kingdom!" ʿĀṣim's companions returned. The strength of the Muslims began to increase day by day, and their enemy grew weaker day by day.

---

157. Paraphrasing Qur'ān 9:29. For an exhaustive discussion of the meaning attached in Qur'ānic exegesis to the expression "out of hand" (*ʿan yadin*), see Kister, "ʿAn yadin."

158. The king refers to Shāhpūr b. Hurmuz, who ruled the Sasanid kingdom between A.D. 310 and 379. He is known in the Arab tradition for his military exploits against the Arabs and for his cruel treatment of Arab prisoners of war, whose shoulders he is said to have dislocated. On the strength of this tradition he was dubbed "the man of the shoulders" (*dhū al-aktāf*). See Ṭabarī, I, 838–89, 843–44; Thaʿālibī, *Ghurar*, 517–21; and Ibn Qutaybah, *Maʿārif*, 656–67; for a discussion of this and other interpretations of *dhū al-aktāf*, see Christensen, *Sassanides*, 235 n. 2.

The action of the king and the acceptance of the soil by the Muslims lay heavily on the king's associates. Rustam came from Sābāṭ in order to see the king. He asked him what had come to pass between him and the Muslims and what was his opinion of them. The king said: "I did not think that there were among the Arabs men like those whom I saw in my presence. You are not wiser than they are, nor do you have a better presence of mind and ability to reply." He informed Rustam of what the Muslim spokesman had said and added:

> These people spoke to me truthfully. They promised a thing, and they will either achieve it or die for its sake. But I found that the most noble among them was also the biggest fool. When they mentioned the poll tax, I gave him [a load] of soil. He carried it on his head and went out. If he had wanted, he could have guarded himself against it by loading it on somebody else, and I would never have known [who is the most noble among them].

Rustam said: "O king, he is the wisest among them. He saw a good
[2244] omen in this[159] and perceived the matter, while his companions did not."

Rustam left the king's presence dejected and angry. Being an astrologer and a priest, he sent someone to follow the delegation and said to a confidant of his: "If the messenger catches up with them, we have put things right and saved our country. If they outstrip him, God will deprive you of your country and of your sons." The messenger returned from al-Ḥīrah, reporting that they had already gone. Rustam said: "These people have carried your country away without any doubt. Kingship is not an affair for the son of a woman cupper.[160] They have taken the keys to our kingdom."

This was one of the ways in which God infuriated the Persians.

After the delegation set out to meet Yazdagird, the Muslims sent out a raiding party. The party apprehended some fishermen with their catch. Sawād b. Mālik al-Tamīmī went to al-Nijāf.[161] Al-

---

159. *Taṭayyara bi-* usually means "he regarded something as a bad omen." Here we have *taṭayyara ilā* in the opposite sense, which does not seem to be listed in the classical dictionaries but was noted by de Goeje in *Glossary*, s.v. *ṭ-y-r*.

160. For the tradition about the birth of Yazdagird to Shahriyār and a cupper slave girl, see Ṭabarī, I, 1044.

161. I am not able to identify this place.

Firāḍ[162] was close to it. He led away three hundred animals, comprising mules, donkeys, and bulls. They loaded the fish upon them, drove them away, and reached the camp in the morning. Saʿd distributed the fish and the animals among the people, liberally distributing the fifth, except for what was given of it to the warriors, and dividing up the captives (*wa-ashama ʿalā al-saby*). This was "the Day of the Fish" (*yawm al-ḥītān*).

Āzādmard b. Āzādbih[163] went in pursuit [of Sawād's raiding party]. Sawād and the horsemen who were with him attacked him and fought him at the bridge of Ṣaylaḥūn.[164] When they were satisfied that the [animals taken as] booty were safe, they followed them and brought them to the Muslims.

The Muslims longed for meat; as for wheat, barley, dates, and other grains, they got hold of quantities sufficient even for a long stay. The objective of the forays was therefore to obtain meat, and the Muslims named their battles accordingly. Among the "meat battles" (*ayyām al-laḥm*) were "the Day of the Bulls" and "the Day of the Fish."

Mālik b. Rabīʿah b. Khālid al-Taymī (from Taym al-Ribāb) al- [2245]
Wāthilī[165] and Musāwir b. al-Nuʿmān al-Taymī al-Rubayyiʿī were sent with another raiding party. They attacked al-Fayyūm[166] and seized camels belonging to Banū Taghlib and Banū al-Namir. They drove the camels and the people of the village out and brought them in the morning to Saʿd. The camels were slaughtered, providing the Muslims with abundant food.

ʿAmr b. al-Ḥārith raided al-Nahrayn.[167] They found a great many cattle at Bāb Thawrāʾ;[168] took them across the area of Shīlā,[169] known today as Nahr Ziyād;[170] and brought them to the Muslim

162. Al-Firāḍ is described by Ṭabarī (I, 2073) as "the border area between Syria, Iraq, and the Jazīrah."

163. See note 84, above.

164. See p. 2232 n. 106, above.

165. See Ibn Ḥajar, *Iṣābah*, V, 724 no. 7635.

166. A village in the vicinity of Hīt on the Euphrates. See Yāqūt, *Muʿjam*, III, 933.

167. Probably a subdistrict of which the main city was Karbalāʾ, but not all the references in the sources point in this direction. See Ṣ. A. ʿAlī, "Minṭaqat al-Kūfah," 234–36; Morony, *Iraq*, 151 and index.

168. I am unable to identify this locality; cf. Ṣ. A. ʿAlī, "Minṭaqat al-Kūfah," 235.

169. According to Yāqūt (*Muʿjam*, III, 358), Shīlā was an area near al-Kūfah.

170. An ancient canal in the vicinity of al-Kūfah, named in the Islamic period after Ziyād b. Abīhi, who is said to have reopened it. See Yāqūt, *Muʿjam*, III, 358 and IV, 840–41.

camp. ʿAmr said: "At that time there were only two canals in the area."

More than two years passed between the coming of Khālid (b. al-Walīd) to Iraq and the camping of Saʿd in al-Qādisiyyah. Saʿd stayed there for more than two months, until he achieved victory.

According to the previous chain of transmission:[171] The following events took place between the Persians and the Arabs after the battle of Buwayb. Al-Anūshajān b. al-Hirbidh set out from the rural area of al-Baṣrah in the direction of the people of Ghuḍayy.[172] Four men who were leading various clans of Tamīm confronted him in front of the people of Ghuḍayy. These were al-Mustawrid and ʿAbdallāh b. Zayd, alternately commanding[173] al-Ribāb; Jazʾ b. Muʿāwiyah[174] and Ibn al-Nābighah, alternately commanding Saʿd; al-Ḥasan b. Niyār and al-Aʿwar b. Bashāmah, alternately commanding ʿAmr; and al-Ḥusayn b. Maʿbad and al-Shabah, alternately commanding Ḥanẓalah. They killed al-Anūshajān in defense of the people of Ghuḍayy. When Saʿd (b. Abī Waqqāṣ) came, they joined him together with the people of Ghuḍayy and all the clans mentioned above.

[2247][175] According to al-Sarī — Shuʿayb — Sayf — Muḥammad and Ṭalḥah and ʿAmr: The people of the *sawād* appealed to Yazdagird b. Shahriyār for help. They sent him a message, saying:

> The Arabs are camping at al-Qādisiyyah in a warlike manner. Nothing can endure their actions since they have camped at al-Qādisiyyah and remain intact. They have ruined everything that was between them and the Euphrates. Nobody remains in this area except in the forts. Animals and food that could not be contained in the forts have been destroyed. The thing that will come next is that they will demand that we come down from the forts. Should help be

---

171. See p. 2239, above.

172. See note 18, above.

173. For this meaning of *sānada*, see de Goeje's *Glossary* and Dozy, *Supplément*, s.v. The alternating pattern of command explains why Anūshajān was confronted by four commanders only, though eight names are mentioned in the text. See also Ṭabarī, I, 821 ll. 8–10: *fa-qātalāhu mutasānidayni yuqātiluhu hādha yawman wa-hādha yawman*. See now also M. Lecker, *The Banū Sulaym*, 152 n. 65.

174. Jazʾ (or Jazy) b. Muʿāwiyah b. al-Ḥusayn later became a governor of Ahwāz on behalf of ʿUmar. See (ʿI.) Ibn al-Athīr, *Usd*, I, 282–83; Ibn Ḥajar, *Iṣābah*, I, 474 no. 1151.

175. There is no p. 2246 in the Leiden edition.

> slow in coming, we shall surrender [everything] with our own hands.

The chieftains (*al-mulūk*) who had estates in the border area (*al-ṭaff*)[176] [also] wrote to Yazdagird about it and assisted the people of the *sawād* in this matter. They urged him to dispatch Rustam [against the Arabs].

When Yazdagird made up his mind to dispatch Rustam, he sent for him. Rustam entered into his presence, and Yazdagird said to him: "I wish to entrust you with this mission.[177] One must make preparations for an affair according to its magnitude. Today you are the [most prominent] man among the Persians. You see that the people of Persia have not faced a situation like this since the family of Ardashīr[178] assumed power."

It seems that Rustam agreed and praised the king. The king said: "I wish to consider [the information that] you have and to find out what you think. Describe to me the Arabs and their exploits since they have camped in al-Qādisiyyah and describe to me what the Persians have suffered at their hands." Rustam said: "I would describe them as a pack of wolves, falling upon unsuspecting shepherds and annihilating them."

Yazdagird said:

> It is not like that. I put the question to you in the expectation that you would describe them clearly and that then I would be able to reinforce you so that you might act according to the [real situation]. But you did not say the right thing. You must therefore understand what I have to say. The Arabs [2248] and the Persians are comparable to an eagle who looked upon a mountain where birds take shelter at night and stay in their nests at the foot of it. When morning came, the birds looked around and saw that he was watching them. Whenever a bird became separated from the rest, the eagle

---

176. *Al-ṭaff* was used for the part of the Arabian desert that was closest to the cultivated land of Iraq. From there the word acquired the meaning of border area in general; more specifically, al-Ṭaff is also used for the environs of al-Kūfah. See Yāqūt, *Muʿjam*, III, 539–40; cf. Morony, *Iraq*, 187 and index.

177. Literally: "I wish to send you in this direction."

178. Ardashīr (Artaxerxes) I was the founder of the Sasanian dynasty, which ruled Persia from A.D. the third century until the Muslim conquest. See *CHI*, III, index s.v.

> snatched him. When the birds saw him [doing this], they did not take off out of fear. Whenever a bird became separated from the rest, the eagle snatched him. If they had taken off all at once, they would have repelled him. The worst thing that could happen to them would be that all would escape save one. But if each group acts in turn and takes off separately, they all perish. This is the similarity between them and the Persians. Act according to this.[179]

Rustam said to him: "O king, let me [act in my own way]. The Arabs still dread the Persians, as long as you do not rouse them against me. It is to be hoped that my good fortune will last and that God will save us the trouble. We shall employ the right ruse and follow the right idea in war, because the right idea and ruse are more beneficial than some victories." The king refused and said: "What is it, them, that remains [for us to do]?" Rustam said: "In war, patience is superior to haste, and the order of the day is now patience. To fight one army after another is better than a single [and total] defeat and is also harder on our enemy." But the king was obdurate and refused [to accept Rustam's view]. Hence Rustam set out to establish his camp at Sābāṭ.

Envoys began coming to the king, one after the other, asking him to consider the dismissal of Rustam and the dispatch of somebody
[2249] else around whom the people would rally. Also, spies from al-Ḥīrah and from Banū Ṣalūbā[180] reported these matters to Saʿd, and he wrote about them to ʿUmar.

The cries for help brought to Yazdagird by al-Āzādmard b. al-Āzādbih on behalf of the *ahl al-sawād* grew in number. The king's soul became frightened, and he wanted to protect himself from the war by [dispatching] Rustam. He abandoned all prudence, became impatient and obstinate, and urged Rustam on. Rustam repeated what he had told him before and said:

> O king, abandonment of prudence has forced me to step out of bounds and to vindicate my soul. If I had an alternative, I would not speak these words. I implore you by God, for your

---

179. Cf. Thaʿālibī, *Ghurar*, 738–39.

180. Banū Ṣalūbā are identified as "people of al-Ḥīrah, Kalwādhā, and villages on the Euphrates." See Ṭabarī, I, 2061.

> sake, for the sake of your people, and for the sake of your kingdom, let me stay in my camp and send al-Jālnūs. If victory will be ours, then all is well; if not, I shall be alert and ready[181] to send someone else.[182] Then, when there is no alternative and we have made them weak and tired, we shall hold our ground against them while we are rested [and in full strength].

But the king insisted on Rustam's departure.

According to al-Sarī — Shuʿayb — Sayf — al-Naḍr b. al-Sarī al-Ḍabbī — Ibn al-Rufayl — his father: Having established camp at Sābāṭ and collected the military equipment, Rustam sent al-Jālnūs commanding the vanguard, with forty thousand men. He said: "Move forward, and do not rush [into battle] without my instructions." He appointed al-Hurmuzān to command his right wing, Mihrān b. Bahrām al-Rāzī his left wing, and al-Bayruzān his rear guard.

Rustam said, in order to raise the morale of the king: "If God gives us victory over them, we shall turn to their kingdom in their land, and we shall keep them busy in their place of origin until they agree to reconciliation or become again satisfied with their erstwhile condition." [2250]

When the delegation of Saʿd returned from their meeting with the king, Rustam had a dream that he disliked and perceived as a bad omen. He did not want to set out and to encounter the Arabs because of it. He lost his equanimity and became confused. He asked the king to send al-Jālnūs and to let him stay so that he might consider what [the Arabs] were doing. He said:

> The ability of al-Jālnūs is similar to mine, though they dread my name more than his. If he is victorious, this is what we want; if not, I shall send out someone like him, and we shall ward these people off for some time. The people of Persia still look up to me. As long as I am not defeated, they will act eagerly [on my command]. I am also all this time

---

181. For the expression *anā ʿalā rijlin* see Lane, *Lexicon*, s.v.; al-Azharī, *Tahdhīb*, XI, 30; Ibn Manẓūr, *Lisān al-ʿArab*, s.v. *rijl*.

182. Compare similar considerations in the Muslim camp, with regard to the question whether ʿUmar himself should lead the expedition against Persia. See Ṭabarī, I, 2213–15.

> dreaded by the Arabs; they dread to move forward as long as I do not confront them. But once I do confront them, they will, at last, take heart, and the people of Persia will, in the end, be defeated.

Rustam sent out his vanguard with forty thousand men and himself set out with sixty thousand. His rear guard set out with twenty thousand.

According to al-Sarī—Shuʿayb—Sayf—Muḥammad, Ṭalḥah, Ziyād, and ʿAmr: Rustam set out with one hundred and twenty thousand men, all of them accompanied by dependents. Together with the dependents they numbered more than two hundred thousand. He set out from al-Madāʾin with sixty thousand men, accompanied by dependents.

According to al-Sarī — Shuʿayb — Sayf — Hishām b. ʿUrwah — ʿĀʾishah: Rustam moved against Saʿd in al-Qādisiyyah with sixty thousand men, accompanied by dependents.

[2251] According to al-Sarī—Shuʿayb—Sayf—Muḥammad, Ṭalḥah, Ziyād, and ʿAmr: When the king insisted on [Rustam's] going [into battle], Rustam wrote to his brother and to the chiefs of the people of his country:

> From Rustam to al-Binduwān, the Marzubān of al-Bāb[183] and the arrow of the people of Persia, who is equal to every event, by means of whom God will break up every powerful army and conquer every impregnable fort, and (from Rustam) to those who follow him. Strengthen your forts, prepare [for war], and be ready, as if the Arabs have already arrived in your country to fight for your land and for your sons. I suggested that we should ward them off and thus gain time until their auspicious stars become unlucky, but the king refused.

According to al-Sarī—Shuʿayb—Sayf—al-Ṣalt b. Bahrām—a certain man: When Yazdagird ordered Rustam to set out from Sābāṭ,

183. Al-Bāb (or Bāb al-Abwāb) is the old name for the city of Darband, on the western shore of the Caspian Sea. It served as a fortification against invasions from the north and as a point of entry for visitors from that direction into the Persian empire. See Yāqūt, *Muʿjam*, I, 437–42; Christensen, *Sassanides*, 369, 415; *EI²*, s.vv. "Bāb al-Abwāb" (D. M. Dunlop); "al-Ḳabḳ" (C. E. Bosworth).

Rustam wrote to his brother a letter similar to the previous one and added:

> Pisces rendered the water turbid; Pegasus (*al-Naʿāʾim*) is in beautiful form, and so is Venus; Libra is balanced, and Mars has disappeared.[184] I think that these people are going to overcome us and to take possession of what belongs to us. The gravest matter that I have seen is that the king has said: "Either you go to [fight] them, or I am going myself." Therefore I am going.

According to al-Sarī — Shuʿayb — Sayf — al-Naḍr b. al-Sarī — Ibn al-Rufayl — his father: The person who encouraged Yazdagird to [2252] send Rustam was the servant of Jābān, the king's astrologer, who was from the people of Furāt Bādaqlā.[185] Yazdagird sent to him [a message], saying: "What is your view of Rustam's departure and of the war against the Arabs today?" The servant was, however, afraid to speak the truth and lied to the king.

Rustam knew astrology and was unwilling to go forth because of what he knew. For the king it was an easy matter, because [the astrologer] deceived him. The king said to Jābān's servant: "I want you to tell me something that will reassure me with regard to your view." The servant said to Zurnā the Indian: "Tell him." Zurnā said to the king: "Ask me." The king asked him, and Zurnā said: "O king, a bird will draw near and will alight at your palace, and something will drop from his beak on this spot," and he drew a circle. The servant said: "He spoke the truth. The bird is a crow (*ghurāb*), and the thing in his beak is a dirham."

Jābān[186] was informed that the king had been looking for him, so he came and entered into the king's presence. The king asked him about what the servant had said. After some reflection, Jābān said: "He spoke the truth, but he was not accurate. The bird is a magpie (*ʿaqʿaq*), and the thing in his beak is a dirham. It will fall on this

---

184. Rustam is described as an astrologer (Ṭabarī, I, 2167). See also Yaʿqūbī, *Taʾrīkh*, II, 164, where another letter of astrological content, also addressed to Rustam's brother, is quoted.

185. Furāt Bādaqlā was a subdistrict (*ṭassūj*) in the vicinity of al-Ḥīrah. See Morony, *Iraq*, 150; Oppenheimer *et al.*, *Babylonia*, 32–33 n. 15, 336 n. 4.

186. In addition to his position at the court, Jābān was the ruler of Ullays. For Ullays, see Donner, *Conquests*, 329 and index.

spot, but Zurnā has lied. The dirham will bounce and come to rest on that spot," and he drew another circle. Before they could get up, a magpie landed on the battlements; a dirham fell from its beak on the first line, bounced, and came to rest on the second line.

The Indian became hostile to Jābān for having exposed his error. A pregnant cow was brought to them. The Indian said: "Its lamb will be black, with a white spot on its forehead (*gharrāʾ*)." Jābān said: "You are lying. It will rather be black with a white spot on its
[2253] tail (*ṣabghāʾ*)." The cow was slaughtered and the lamb extracted. Its tail was between its eyes. Jābān said: "By this Zurnā was deluded."[187] Both[188] encouraged the king to dispatch Rustam, and the king ordered him to go forth.[189]

Jābān wrote to Jushnasmāh[190] saying: "The affair of the Persians is over, and their enemy has prevailed over them. The Zoroastrian kingdom has passed away, the kingdom of the Arabs has emerged victorious, and their religion has gained the ascendancy. Make a contract of protection with them, and do not allow yourself to be deceived. Hurry, hurry before you are taken captive." When he received the letter, Jushnasmāh went out to the Arabs and came to al-Muʿannā. Al-Muʿannā was at al-ʿAtīq with his horsemen. He sent him to Saʿd. Jushnasmāh made a contract [of protection] for himself, for his family, and for those who followed him.[191] Saʿd instructed

---

187. For this meaning of the passive form *utiya*, see Ibn Manẓūr, *Lisān al-ʿArab*, s.v. *a-t-y* (XIV, 16); and Lane, *Lexicon*, s.v. *a-t-y*.

188. Jābān and Zurnā, or Jābān and his servant, who increased their credibility by winning the magicians' contest with Zurnā.

189. Fearful of disclosing what the stars had in store for the Persians, the astrologers encouraged the king to send Rustam into battle and presumably made favorable predictions about its outcome. It seems, however, that the choice of the birds in the story by the Muslim traditionist is intended as a hint that their predictions were false and that the Persian empire was doomed. In Arab ornithomancy the crow is considered the worst of all omens. One of the reasons is that the crow did not return to Noah's ark after he had been sent out to report on the situation of the flood. See Jāḥiẓ, *Ḥayawān*, II, 316; III, 443, 457 (an evil omen if he cries once and a good omen if he cries twice). See also Damīrī, *Ḥayawān*, II, 172–81 (especially 173 last line–174 l. 1). Cf. Fahd. *Divination*, 506–10; Fahd, "Présages." The magpie (*ʿaqʿaq*) was considered evil because popular etymology derived its name from *ʿuqūq* "filial disobedience." The intensity of popular feelings about the magpie can be gauged from the legal controversy over whether a person who set out on a journey, heard the sound of the magpie, and therefore returned should be considered an infidel for believing in ornithomancy or not. See Damīrī, *Ḥayawān*, II, 148–49.

190. Jushnasmāh was one of Jābān's military commanders. See Ṭabarī, I, 2168.

191. Apparently those who surrendered to the Arabs with him.

Jushnasmāh to return [to his place], and he became a spy for the Muslims.

Jushnasmāh presented al-Muʿannā with some *fālūdhaq*.[192] Al-Muʿannā said to his wife: "What is this?" She said: "I think that his miserable wife tried to prepare *ʿaṣīdah*[193] but failed." Al-Muʿannā said: "May misery befall her!"

According to al-Sarī—Shuʿayb—Sayf—Muḥammad, Ṭalḥah, Ziyād, and ʿAmr: When Rustam left Sābāṭ, Jābān met him on the bridge and said to him in complaint: "Do you not see what I see?" Rustam said: "I am being led by the nose and can see no alternative except submission."[194] Rustam ordered al-Jālnūs to proceed to al-Ḥīrah. He set out and established his camp in al-Najaf. Rustam set out for Kūthā and wrote to al-Jālnūs and al-Āzādmard: "Capture for me an Arab from the army of Saʿd." Each rode forward by himself, [2254] captured a prisoner, and sent him to Rustam in Kūthā; Rustam interrogated him and then killed him.

According to al-Sarī—Shuʿayb—Sayf—al-Naḍr b. al-Sarī—Ibn al-Rufayl—his father: When Rustam went forth and ordered al-Jālnūs to move in the direction of al-Ḥīrah, he also ordered him to capture an Arab for him. He and al-Āzādmard went out with a raiding party of one hundred men, reached al-Qādisiyyah, captured a man before the Qādisiyyah bridge, and took him away. The Muslims rallied to his rescue but were not able to catch up with the Persians. They managed only to hit some of those who lagged behind. When the Persians reached al-Najaf, they sent the man to Rustam, who was in Kūthā. Rustam said to him: "What brought you here? What

---

192. Originally a Persian dessert, *falūdhaq* (or *falūdhaj*) was made of crushed almonds and sugar; cf. modern Persian *palūda*; Jawālīqī, *Muʿarrab*, 295; Ibn Manẓūr, *Lisān al-ʿArab*, s.v. *f-l-dh*. Arab tradition speaks of ʿAbdallāh b. Judʿān as the first person who introduced the Arabs to this dish after his visit to the Persian king. Our anecdote seems to indicate that it was still not very well known among the Arabs in the first decades of Islam. In later periods it is said to have been considered one of the most exquisite dishes (*min ashraf mā ʿarafūhu min ṭaʿām*). See Jāḥiẓ, *Bukhalāʾ*, 253. Muslim tradition considers the adoption of *falūdhaq* as a sign of the great prosperity that the Arabs came to enjoy as a result of the conquests (see Ibn Mājah, *Sunan*, II, 1108–9, *Kitāb al-aṭʿimah, bāb* 46). For the recipe, see Baghdādī, *Ṭabīkh*, quoted in Rodinson, "Recherches," 149 (with ample bibliography and discussion); *EI*², s.v. "Ghidhāʾ" (M. Rodinson), II, 1067a.

193. *ʿAṣīdah* is porridge made with flour and oil. See Ibn Manẓūr, *Lisān al-ʿArab*, s.v. *ʿa-ṣ-d*; Rodinson, "Recherches," 141 (with ample bibliography).

194. Both Rustam and Jābān are astrologers and know in advance what the outcome of the conflict will be.

is it that you want?" The man said: "We came to seek what God promised to us." Rustam said: "And what is that?" The man said: "Your land, your sons, and your blood, if you refuse to embrace Islam." Rustam said: "And if you are killed before you accomplish this?" The man said: "God has promised us that He will give those of us who are killed before then a place in Paradise. For those who survive, He will fulfill [the promise] that I mentioned. We are confident and assured." Rustam said: "Have we then been placed at your mercy?" The man said: "Poor Rustam! It is your deeds that have put you [in this situation]. Because of them God has delivered you to us. And let not what you see delude you; you are not fighting human beings but, rather, irrevocable fate." Rustam exploded in anger and ordered the man to be killed.

Rustam left Kūthā and camped at Burs.[195] His men robbed the people of their possessions, raped the women, and drank wine. The Persians[196] cried out to him and complained about the damage to their property and the suffering brought upon their sons. Rustam rose to address his men and said:

[2255] O people of Persia, the Arab spoke the truth. By God, nothing save our deeds has delivered us to them. By God, though we are at war with them, the Arabs treat our people better than you do. God would have given you victory over the enemy and strengthened your position in the land if your behavior had been upright, if you had refrained from injustice, if you had lived up to your commitments and had performed good deeds. But, if you go astray and engage in these [evil] actions, I believe that God will change your circumstances [for the worse], and I am not confident that He will not take His dominion away from you.

Rustam sent his men out to arrest some people against whom complaints were lodged. They were brought to him, and he struck their heads off. Then he rode out and called upon the people to march. He set out and camped opposite Dayr al-Aʿwar.[197] Then he

---

195. Yāqūt identifies Burs as "a place in Babylon (*Bābil*), in which there are some remnants from [the time of] Nebuchadnezzar. It is on a very high hill." See Yāqūt, *Muʿjam*, I, 565 l. 24.

196. The text has *ʿulūj*, sg. *ʿilj*, which is a pejorative term.

197. A place on the outskirts of al-Kūfah (*ẓāhir al-Kūfah*; cf. glossary to *BGA*, IV, 294). See Yāqūt, *Muʿjam*, II, 644; Oppenheimer et al., *Babylonia*, 384 n. 5.

moved down to al-Milṭāṭ[198] and camped on the bank of the Euphrates, opposite the people of al-Najaf, opposite al-Khawarnaq,[199] and near al-Ghariyyān.[200] He summoned the people of al-Ḥīrah, threatened them, and made up his mind to act against them. Ibn Buqaylah[201] said to him: "You cannot have it both ways, [i.e.,] to be unable to help us and at the same time to blame us for defending ourselves and our land." Rustam was reduced to silence.

According to al-Sarī—Shuʿayb—Sayf—ʿAmr—al-Shaʿbī and al-Miqdām al-Ḥārithī—other transmitters mentioned: Rustam summoned the people of al-Ḥīrah (his tent was at that time near the monastery)[202] and said: "O enemies of God! You are pleased that the Arabs have forced their way into our country. You have been spying for them against us. You have reinforced them with money."

The people of al-Ḥīrah wanted Ibn Buqaylah to protect them [2256] against Saʿd and said to him: "You will be the one to speak to him." Ibn Buqaylah stepped forward and said:

> You have said that we were pleased with the Arabs' coming into the country. What then have they done [to please us]? By which of their actions should we be pleased? Should it be so because they say that we are their slaves? They do not belong to our religion, and they attest that we are destined for Hell. You said that we were spying for them. But why should they be in need of our spying? Your people have fled from them, abandoned the villages to them, and nobody prevents them from moving in whatever direction they please. If they wish, they can go to the right or, if they wish, to the left. You said that we have strengthened them with money. [The truth of the matter is that] we have bribed them with money for fear that we should be taken as prisoners, that we should be plundered, and that our fighting men would be killed. All

---

198. Al-Milṭāṭ was the name for the area along the Euphrates in the vicinity of al-Kūfah. See Yāqūt, *Muʿjam*, IV, 633.

199. See note 97, above.

200. The Ghariyyān were two high buildings on the outskirts of al-Kūfah. They were built by al-Mundhir b. Imriʾ al-Qays, king of al-Ḥīrah. For the traditions surrounding them, see Yāqūt, *Muʿjam*, III, 790–95.

201. Ibn Buqaylah was one of the leaders (*nuqabāʾ*) of al-Ḥīrah and the first man to sue for peace. He cooperated with the Muslims in various ways. See Ṭabarī, index, s.v. ʿAmr b. ʿAbd al-Masīḥ.

202. Probably Dayr al-Aʿwar; see note 197, above.

> this has happened because you did not protect us. None of you who confronted the Arabs was able to hold his ground against them. Now we are weaker than you are. I swear that you are preferable to us and have more valor in our eyes. Protect us from the Arabs, and we shall help you. We are like the scum of the *sawād*, slaves of those who prevail!

Rustam said: "The man has spoken the truth on your behalf!"

According to al-Sarī—Shuʿayb—Sayf—al-Naḍr—Ibn al-Rufayl—his father: Rustam dreamed in the monastery that an angel came, entered the Persian camp, and put a seal on all the weapons.

According to al-Sarī—Shuʿayb—Sayf—Muḥammad and his companions and al-Naḍr: When Rustam regained his peace of mind, he ordered al-Jālnūs to march from al-Najaf. He set out with the vanguard and camped between al-Najaf and al-Saylaḥūn. Rustam departed also and camped in al-Najaf. Between the departure of Rus-
[2257] tam from al-Madāʾin, his camping in Sābāṭ, his departure from there, and his confrontation with Saʿd four months elapsed. During this time he did not move forward and did not fight. He was hoping that the Arabs would become disgusted with the place, would become exhausted, and would leave. He disliked the idea of fighting them because he was afraid that he would fare no better than those who [had fought the Arabs] before him. He temporized, but the king rushed him, incited him, and urged him forward; finally, he forced his hand [to engage in battle].

When Rustam camped in al-Najaf, he had the dream again and saw the same angel. With him were the Prophet and ʿUmar. The angel seized the Persian weapons, put a seal on them, and handed them to the Prophet.[203] The Prophet handed them to ʿUmar. When Rustam woke up, his gloom increased. Al-Rufayl noticed it and developed a desire to embrace Islam, and this was the reason for his conversion.

ʿUmar knew that the Persians would temporize with the Muslims. He therefore instructed Saʿd and the Muslims to camp on the border of Persia and to temporize with the Persians indefinitely, in order to throw them off balance. The Muslims camped in al-Qādisiyyah. They made up their minds to be patient and to temporize. God willed to make His light perfect. The Muslims remained [in

203. Cf. Thaʿālibī, *Ghurar*, 741.

their places] with calm and assurance. They raided the *sawād*, plundered the area around them, and gathered the spoils. They prepared for some protracted maneuvering, and accordingly came prepared to endure until God should grant them victory. ʿUmar supplied them with provisions to supplement what they gained by plunder.

When the Persian king and Rustam saw this, became aware of their situation, and received information about the deeds of the Arabs, the king understood that the Arabs were not going to desist and that, if he were to remain [in his place without doing anything], the Arabs would not leave him alone. He saw fit to send Rustam forth. Rustam saw fit to camp between al-ʿAtīq and al-Najaf, to temporize, and at the same time to engage [the Muslims] in combat.[204] He thought that this was the best thing they (i.e., the Persians) could do until they should achieve the aim of their restraint or until fortune should turn in their favor.

According to al-Sarī—Shuʿayb—Sayf—Muḥammad, Ṭalḥah, and [2258]
Ziyād: The raiding parties roamed [the land]. Rustam was in al-Najaf, al-Jālnūs between al-Najaf and al-Saylaḥūn, Dhū al-Ḥājib between Rustam and al-Jālnūs. Al-Hurmuzān and Mihrān were in charge of the two wings, and al-Bayruzān commanded the rear guard. Zād b. Buhaysh, the ruler of Furāt Siryā,[205] commanded the infantrymen, and Kanārā the light cavalry. The army of Rustam consisted of one hundred and twenty thousand men. Sixty thousand were accompanied by servants (*shākirī*); from the [other] sixty thousand, fifteen thousand were noblemen accompanied [by dependents]; and they had chained themselves together in order to bear the brunt of the fiercest battle.[206]

204. It seems that the intended combat was on a small scale, perhaps only occasional duels between two warriors. For *munāzalah* (also *nizāl* and the special imperative form *nazāli*), see Ibn Manẓūr, *Lisān al-ʿArab*, s.v. *n-z-l*; and Abū Tammām, *Ḥamāsah*, I, 29.

205. See Morony, *Iraq*, 149–50; Yāqūt, *Muʿjam*, III, 87–88.

206. Ṭabarī and other Muslims writers report that both the Byzantines and the Persians used to tie some of their soldiers together with chains, so that they could not run away from the battlefield. See Balādhurī, *Futūḥ*, 135, 303; Ibn Kathīr, *Bidāyah*, VII, 44; Ṭabarī, I, 2089, 2294, 2337, 2356, 2598, 2632; Abū Yūsuf, *Kharāj*, 83; Yāqūt, *Muʿjam*, IV, 9. Cf. de Goeje, *Mémoire*, 121; Christensen, *Sassanides*, 207; Noth, *Studien*, 122–23.

In a forthcoming article Dr. L. Conrad maintains that the term *silsilah*, which is used in some of these texts, originally referred to a Byzantine military formation. Only later was it taken to mean a chain and a device to prevent soldiers from fleeing

According to al-Sarī — Shuʿayb — Sayf — Muḥammad b. Qays — Mūsā b. Ṭarīf: The people said to Saʿd: "We are fed up with this place. Move forward." Saʿd scolded the speaker and said: "As your opinion is not needed, do not take the trouble [of offering it]. We shall move forward only on the advice of the people of judgment. Be quiet as long as we do not speak to you." Saʿd sent out Ṭulayḥah[207] and ʿAmr (b. Maʿdīkarib) on a scouting mission without horses. Sawād (b. Mālik al-Tamīmī) and Ḥumayḍah (b. al-Nuʿmān) set out with one hundred men each and raided al-Nahrayn.[208] Saʿd had forbidden them to venture so far. When Rustam received information about the raid, he sent his horsemen against them. When Saʿd heard that Rustam's cavalry had gone in pursuit, he summoned ʿĀṣim b. ʿAmr
[2259] and Jābir al-Asadī[209] and sent them after Sawād and Ḥumayḍah, to follow in their trail and to take the same way. He said to ʿĀṣim: "If you join battle with the Persians, you will be the commander." ʿĀṣim encountered them between al-Nahrayn and Iṣṭīmiyā.[210] The Persian horsemen were encircling the Arab raiding party, trying to extract the spoils from their hands. Sawād said to Ḥumayḍah: "Make your choice: either stand up to the Persians and I shall carry away the spoils, or I shall stand up to them and you shall carry away the spoils."[211] Ḥumayḍah replied: "Stand up to them, hold them back, and I shall deliver the spoils for you."

Sawād held out against the Persians, and Ḥumayḍah hastened to leave. ʿĀṣim b. ʿAmr encountered him. Ḥumayḍah thought that it was another group of Persian horsemen, so he made a turn to avoid them. When they recognized each other, Ḥumayḍah went on with the spoils. ʿĀṣim marched to [the aid of] Sawād. The Persians managed to recover some of the spoils. When they saw ʿĀṣim, they fled. Sawād took possession of what they had recovered and brought the spoils to Saʿd, returning safe and victorious.

---

the battlefield. Historically speaking, there were therefore no soldiers who fought fettered (private communication, November 8, 1989).

I thank my former student David Marmer for drawing my attention to Dr. Conrad's work.

207. Ṭulayḥah b. Khuwaylid al-Asadī was an important leader of the *riddah*. See *EI*[1], s.v. "Ṭulaiḥa b. Khuwailid" (V. Vacca); Ṭabarī, I, 1797, 1798, 1871, and index.

208. See note 167, above.

209. See Ibn Ḥajar, *Iṣābah*, I, 441 no. 1041.

210. I am unable to identify this locality.

211. The verb *istāqa*, which is used here, indicates that the spoils consisted of cattle and horses.

Ṭulayḥah and ʿAmr had gone forth [from the camp]. Saʿd ordered Ṭulayḥah to confront the camp of Rustam, whereas ʿAmr was ordered to confront the camp of al-Jālnūs. Ṭulayḥah went alone, while ʿAmr went with a group of men. Saʿd sent Qays b. al-Hubayrah[212] after them and said to him: "If a battle takes place, you will be commander over them." Saʿd wanted to humiliate Ṭulayḥah because of his rebelliousness. ʿAmr, on the other hand, was obedient to him. Qays b. Hubayrah set out, met ʿAmr, and asked him about Ṭulayḥah. ʿAmr said: "I know nothing of him." When they reached al-Najaf from the direction of the valley, Qays said: "What do you intend to do?" ʿAmr said: "I want to raid the nearest part of their camp." Qays said: "With these men?" ʿAmr said: "Yes." Qays said: "By God, I shall not allow you to do this. Are you going to expose [the Muslims] to an intolerable [danger]?" ʿAmr said: "And what say do you have in this?" Qays said: "I have been made commander over you. But [even] if I were not [your] commander, I would not have allowed you to do it." Al-Aswad b. Yazīd attested in the presence of a [2260]
number of people: "Saʿd made him commander over you and over Ṭulayḥah, if both of you should happen to be in the same place." ʿAmr said: "By God, O Qays! A time in which you are commander over me will be a time of evil. I prefer to renounce this religion of yours, revert to my former faith, and fight for it until death, rather than suffer you to be my commander another time." He added: "If your master should send you with such a matter again, we shall most certainly dissolve any connection with him." Qays said: "It is up to you the next time."

Qays took ʿAmr back [to camp]. They returned with information [about the enemy], some Persian [captives], and some horses. Each of them complained against the other; Qays complained of ʿAmr's insubordination, and ʿAmr complained of the rude behavior of Qays. Saʿd said: "O ʿAmr! The information that you have brought and your safe return are more pleasing to me than to sustain one hundred ca-

212. Qays b. Hubayrah (or b. Makshūḥ) belonged to the tribe of Murād. The question whether he embraced Islam during the lifetime of the Prophet or later is disputed in the *rijāl* literature. In addition to al-Qādisiyyah, he fought in the battle of Nihāwand and was killed in the battle of Ṣiffīn. In the Jāhiliyyah there was a rivalry between him and ʿAmr b. Maʿdīkarib; this explains ʿAmr's unwillingness to serve under the command of Qays; see p. 2260, below. See Ibn Saʿd, *Ṭabaqāt*, V, 390; (ʿI.) Ibn al-Athīr, *Usd*, IV, 227–8; Ibn Ḥajar, *Iṣābah*, V, 538–41 no. 7318; Caskell and Strenziok, *Ǧamharat an-nasab*, II, 549.

sualties for the price of killing a thousand enemies. Do you intend to go to the Persian battlefield and make an attack against them with one hundred men? I thought that you knew about war more than you do." ʿAmr said: "It is as you say."

Ṭulayḥah went forth and entered the Persian camp on a moonlit night and examined the situation within it. He cut the ropes of a man's tent and led his horse away. Having come out of this camp, he passed near the camp of Dhū al-Ḥājib,[213] wrecked a man's tent, and untied his horse. Then he slipped into the camp of al-Jālnūs, wrecked another man's tent, and untied his horse. Then he left the place and went to al-Kharrārah.[214] The three men—one from al-Najaf, the other from the camp of Dhū al-Ḥājib, and the third from the camp of al-Jālnūs—pursued him. The first man to catch up with him was the Jālnūsī, the second the Ḥājibī, and the third the Najafī. Ṭulayḥah killed the first two and took the last one prisoner. He brought him to Saʿd and informed Saʿd of what had happened. The prisoner embraced Islam, and Saʿd named him "Muslim." He attached himself to Ṭulayḥah and was with him during all the [sub-
[2261] sequent] wars of conquest.

According to al-Sarī—Shuʿayb—Sayf—Abū ʿAmr—Abū ʿUthmān al-Nahdī: When ʿUmar sent Saʿd to Persia he instructed him to take with him any man of strength, valor, and leadership whom he should meet in an oasis on his way. If anyone were to refuse to join, he was to take him by force. ʿUmar issued the orders, and Saʿd reached al-Qādisiyyah with twelve thousand men. They consisted of those who participated in [earlier] battles (*ahl al-ayyām*),[215] as well as non-Arabs (*al-ḥamrā'*)[216] who had responded to the Muslims and assisted them. Some of them embraced Islam before the fight-

---

213. A commander of the Persian army, also known as Bahman Jādhawayhi, who defeated the Muslims in the battle of the Bridge. See Ṭabarī, I, 2174–75, and index, s.v. "Bahman Jādhawayhi."

214. A place near al-Saylaḥūn. See Yāqūt, *Muʿjam*, II, 409.

215. These are the Muslims who fought with al-Khālid b. al-Walīd in the earlier campaigns in Iraq and Syria. See Donner, *Conquests*, 207, and index.

216. For this meaning of *al-ḥamrā'* see Ibn Manẓūr, *Lisān al-ʿArab*, s.v. *ḥ-m-r*: "The Arabs used [the word] *al-ḥamrā'* for the non-Arabs whose complexion is mostly fair, such as the Byzantines, the Persians, and others who lived in their proximity" (*kānat al-ʿArab taqūlu li-'l-ʿajam alladhīna yakūnu al-bayāḍ aghlaba alwānihim mithl al-Rūm wa-al-Furs wa-man ṣāqabahum innahum al-ḥamrā'*). See Goldziher, *Muslim Studies*, I, 243–44; Morony, *Iraq*, 197–98.

ing, and some did it afterward. They were allowed to take part in [the distribution of] the spoils and received shares identical with those of the [other] participants in the battle of al-Qādisiyyah, i.e., two thousand [dirhams] each. They asked about the most powerful Arab tribe, and accordingly associated themselves with the tribe of Tamīm.[217]

When Rustam drew near and camped in al-Najaf, Saʿd sent out scouts and ordered them to capture a man whom he could interrogate about the situation of the Persians. The scouts went out, after some disagreement. After all the Muslims had agreed that a scouting party might consist of from one to ten men, they gave their permission, and Saʿd sent out Ṭulayḥah with five men and ʿAmr b. Maʿdīkarib with the same number. That was on the morning when Rustam had ordered al-Jālnūs and Dhū al-Ḥājib to march forward. The Muslims did not have knowledge of their departure from al-Najaf. When the scouts had marched only slightly more than a *farsakh*,[218] they saw the Persian armed men[219] and their mounts filling the outposts of the Ṭaff region.[220]

Some of them said: "Return to your amīr because he has sent you out on the assumption that the Persians are [still] in al-Najaf, and bring the information to him. Return, lest your emeny be forewarned."[221] ʿAmr then said to his companions: "You are right," but Ṭulayḥah said to his companions: "You are wrong. You were not sent to bring information about their mounts (*sarḥ*) but simply to [2262]
bring back secret information (*khubr*)." They said: "What do you want to do?" Ṭulayḥah said: "I wish to brave the Persians or else to perish." They said: "You are a man with treachery in your soul, but you will not succeed[222] after the killing of ʿUkkāshah b. Miḥṣan.[223]

---

217. Literally "they counted themselves among the Tamīm." In other words, they became the *mawālī* of this tribe.

218. A *farsakh* equals approximately 6 kilometers. See Hinz, *Masse*, 62.

219. For *masāliḥ* in this sense, see de Goeje's *Glossary* to Balādhurī, *Futūḥ*; and to Ṭabarī.

220. This seems to be the meaning of *ṭufūf* in this context. For al-Ṭaff, see note 176, above.

221. The text uses the plural form of the imperative, and the translation is literal. The meaning is "we should return . . . ," etc.

222. The Muslims doubt that Ṭulayḥah will succeed in becoming a faithful Muslim after his exploits during the *riddah* rebellion. See note 223, below.

223. For another description of this episode, see Dīnawarī, *Akhbār*, 119–20. In this version Ṭulayḥah's companions explicitly accuse him of the desire to join the Per-

Take us back!" However, Ṭulayḥah refused. Saʿd heard about the departure [of Ṭulayḥah's unit], sent out Qays b. Hubayrah, placed one hundred men under his command, and also appointed him to command the scouting parties if he should meet them. Qays reached them only after they had split up. ʿAmr saw him and said [to his companions]: "Show him your determination." They showed him their desire to embark on a raid, but Qays refused permission. He found that Ṭulayḥah had already left; hence he returned to Saʿd with ʿAmr's scouting party and informed Saʿd about the proximity of the Persians.

Ṭulayḥah went forth on the riverbank, opposite the watering places in the Ṭaff region (*wa ʿāraḍa al-miyāha ʿalā al-ṭufūf*).[224] He slipped into Rustam's camp and remained there during the night, spying, looking, and trying to learn from what he saw. When the night was almost over, Ṭulayḥah passed on his way out by [the tent of] the Persian who he thought was the most noble, on the edge of the camp. None of the Persians had a horse like the one he had, and his white tent was unique. Ṭulayḥah drew his sword, cut the reins of the horse, and tied them to the reins of his own horse. Then he stirred his horse and left the camp in a gallop. When the owner of the horse and the Persian infantrymen became aware of what happened, they summoned each other and rode after him on every available mount.[225] Some of them rushed in his pursuit without saddling their horses. A Persian horseman caught up with Ṭulayḥah at dawn. When he fell upon him and pointed his spear to stab him, Ṭulayḥah made his horse swerve, and the Persian fell on the ground in front of him; Ṭulayḥah then attacked him and broke his back with the spear. Then another Persian caught up with him, and Ṭulayḥah did the same. Then a third Persian came. Having seen the death of his two companions, who were his cousins, he flew into a rage. When he

---

sians. They doubt that God will guide Ṭulayḥah back to Islam after he has killed ʿUkkāshah. For the killing of ʿUkkāshah b. Miḥsan by Ṭulayḥah during the *riddah* wars, see Ṭabarī, I, 1888.

224. The text of this passage is dubious and the translation tentative.

225. The text reads *rakibū al-ṣaʿbata wa-al-dhalūla* "they rode both the refractory and the tractable she-camels." This is an example of merismus, a fairly common literary device in Arabic. Cf. such expressions as *al-aswad wa-al-aḥmar,* "the Arabs and the non-Arabs = all humanity"; *al-ins wa-al-jinn,* "people and jinns = all creatures"; *al-layl wa-al-nahār,* "night and day = all the time." See Lane, *Lexicon,* s.v. *ṣaʿb;* and Goldziher, *Muslim Studies,* I, 243–44.

caught up with Ṭulayḥah and pointed his spear at him, Ṭulayḥah made his horse swerve, and the Persian fell in front of him. Ṭulayḥah [2263]
attacked him and urged him to accept captivity. The Persian understood that Ṭulayḥah would [otherwise] kill him and submitted himself as a captive; Ṭulayḥah ordered him to run in front of him, and this is what the Persian did. Now the [other] Persians arrived and saw that the two horsemen had been killed and the third had been taken prisioner. Meanwhile, Ṭulayḥah was now near[226] their (i.e., the Muslim) camp. They left him alone and withdrew.

Ṭulayḥah went forward and reached the Muslim camp, the army being in battle array. The soldiers were alerted and escorted him to Saʿd. When Ṭulayḥah came to him, Saʿd said: "Poor you! What is behind you?"[227] Ṭulayḥah said: "I entered their camp and have spied on them since last night. I captured a man who appears to be the most noble of them, but I do not know whether I am right or wrong.[228] Here he is; question him."

A translator was brought in and stood between Saʿd and the Persian captive. The Persian said: "Will you spare my life if I tell you the truth?" Saʿd said: "Yes. We prefer truthfulness in war to falsehood." The Persian said:

> I shall tell you about this companion of yours before I inform you about those who are with me. I have participated in wars, I have heard about heroes, and I have encountered them from the time when I was a boy until I reached the situation in which you see me now. But I have not seen a man similar to this one, nor have I heard of one like him. This man has crossed two camps [so strong] that heroes had not been courageous enough to take them on. He reached a [third] camp, which consists of seventy thousand men. Each of them is attended by five or ten people, or fewer. He was not content to get out in the same way as he got in; rather, he robbed a prominent horseman of the army, cut the ropes of his tent, and thereby alerted him. All of us were also alerted and went in his pursuit. The first man to catch up with him

---

226. For *shārafa* in this sense, see de Goeje's *Glossary* to Balādhurī, *Futūḥ*, s.v.
227. *Mā warāʾaka* is a question frequently addressed to someone who has been sent out to bring some information. See Maydānī, *Amthāl*, III, 188, 240.
228. Regarding the man's standing among the Persians.

> was a prominent horseman[229] who equals a thousand, but he killed him. Then another horseman, similar [in prowess] to the first one, caught up with him and was killed as well. Then I myself came. I do not think that I left behind some-one who is equal to me, for I was trying to take revenge for
> [2264] the two slain men, who were my cousins. I saw that death was imminent, so I submitted myself as a captive.

The prisoner then told Saʿd about the Persians, saying that the army consisted of one hundred and twenty thousand men, with an equal number of men serving them. The man embraced Islam, and Saʿd named him "Muslim."[230] He then returned to Ṭulayḥah and said: "By God, you will not be defeated as long as you are as faithful, truthful, benign, and charitable as I see you now. I do not need [any-more] to be associated with Persia." On that day, he acquitted him-self well.[231]

According to al-Sarī — Shuʿayb — Sayf — Muḥammad b. Qays — Mūsā b. Ṭarīf: Saʿd said to Qays b. Hubayrah al-Asadī: "You heed-less man![232] Go forth and care for nothing of this world until you bring me information about the Persians." Qays set out. Saʿd also sent ʿAmr (b. Maʿdīkarib) and Ṭulayḥah. Qays reached the area op-posite to the bridge, marched a little, and came upon a large group of the Persian horsemen, who were emerging from their camp. Rustam had left al-Najaf and halted where Dhū al-Ḥājib had been before. Al-Jālnūs also moved, and Dhū al-Ḥājib camped in his place. Al-Jālnūs went in the direction of Ṭayzanābād,[233] halted there, and ordered the horsemen to move forward.

Saʿd sent Ṭulayḥah and ʿAmr with Qays because of an utterance by ʿAmr that came to his knowledge and because of what ʿAmr had

229. Literally "the horseman of the people."

230. It was normal practice for converts to abandon their pre-Islamic names and adopt new, Islamic ones.

231. Probably meaning that he displayed valor in battle on the side of the Muslims.

232. The Leiden edition has *ʿāqil* "wise." I am translating *ghāfil* "heedless," using the version preferred by Kosegarten. It seems to give a better sense in the context: Qays is instructed to stop caring for this world, which is, in the Muslim tradition, a characteristic of those who are heedless of their fate in the hereafter.

233. Ṭayzanābād was situated 1 mile from al-Qādisiyyah, on the way to the Ḥijāz. Yāqūt (*Muʿjam*, III, 569–70) describes it as a resort, surrounded by vineyards, wine-presses, trees, and inns. It was a place "of amusement and idleness."

previously said to Qays b. Hubayrah.[234] ʿAmr said: "O Muslims, fight your enemy!" He then started the battle and fought the Persians for a while. Then Qays attacked them, and they suffered a defeat. He killed twelve men and took three prisoners. He took booty, brought it to Saʿd, and provided him with information. Saʿd said: [2265] "These are good tidings. God willing, when you confront the main body of their army and their valiant men, the result will be the same." Then he summoned ʿAmr and Ṭulayḥah and said to them: "What is your view of Qays?" Ṭulayḥah said: "We think that he was the bravest among us," and ʿAmr said: "The amīr has more understanding of men than we have." Saʿd said:

> By means of Islam God has revived us, brought life to hearts that had been dead, and death to hearts that had been alive. I warn you not to prefer the affair of the Jāhiliyyah, lest your hearts die while you are still alive. Stick to obedience and recognize the [people's] rights. Nobody has ever seen people like those whom God has made strong by means of Islam.[235]

According to al-Sarī—Shuʿayb—Sayf—Muḥammad, Ṭalḥah, and ʿAmr; also Ziyād, Mujālid, and Saʿīd b. al-Marzubān: On the morning that followed his camping in al-Saylaḥūn Rustam ordered al-Jālnūs and Dhū al-Ḥājib to move forward. Al-Jālnūs marched out and halted before the bridge, opposite Zuhrah (b. al-Ḥawiyyah) and next to the commander of the vanguard. Dhū al-Ḥājib camped in his stead in Ṭayzanābād; Rustam camped instead of Dhū al-Ḥājib in al-Kharrārah. He ordered Dhū al-Ḥājib to march forward. When he reached al-ʿAtīq, he turned left. Then, when he was opposite Qudays, he dug a moat. Al-Jālnūs set off and joined him. Saʿd had Zuhrah b. al-Ḥawiyyah commanding the vanguard, and ʿAbdallāh b. al-Muʿtamm and Shuraḥbīl b. al-Simṭ al-Kindī commanding the [2266] two wings. ʿĀṣim b. ʿAmr commanded the light cavalry, another man the archers, another man the footmen, and Sawād b. Mālik the scouts. Rustam's vanguard was commanded by al-Jālnūs; his two

234. Saʿd's anxiety is probably the result of ʿAmr b. al-Maʿdīkarib's unwillingness to accept Qays b. Hubayrah as his commander and his threat to renounce Islam; cf. pp. 2259–60, above.

235. Saʿd demands that past rivalries not be allowed to interfere with the unity of the Muslims.

wings by al-Hurmuzān and Mihrān, his light cavalry by Dhū al-Ḥājib, and his scouts by al-Bayruzān, with Zād b. Buhaysh commanding the footmen.

When Rustam reached al-ʿAtīq, he stopped on its banks, opposite the camp of Saʿd. He assigned to his men their positions, and they occupied them one after the other, until their entire multitude assembled.[236] He remained there during the night, with the Muslims' refraining from attacking them.

According to Saʿīd b. al-Marzubān: When the Persians woke up after spending the night on the bank of al-ʿAtīq, Rustam's astrologer advised Rustam of the vision that he had been shown during the night. He said: "I saw Aquarius in the sky in the form of a bucket emptied of water. I saw Pisces in the form of fish in shallow water and in a state of commotion; and I saw Pegasus (*al-Naʿāʾim*) and Venus shining." Rustam said: "Woe to you! Did you tell anyone about it?" The astrologer said: "No." Rustam said: "Keep it secret!"

According to al-Sarī—Shuʿayb—Sayf—Mujālid—al-Shaʿbī: Rustam was an astrologer and was weeping because of what he saw in his dreams and because of [the visions?] coming to him. When he was in the outskirts[237] of al-Kūfah, he dreamed that ʿUmar entered the Persian camp accompanied by an angel. The angel put a seal on the weapons of the Persians, tied them into a bundle, and handed them to ʿUmar.

According to al-Sarī — Shuʿayb — Sayf — Ismāʿīl b. Abī Khālid — Qays b. Abī Ḥāzim (who participated in the battle of al-Qādisiyyah): Rustam had with him eighteen elephants, and al-Jālnūs had fifteen elephants.

According to al-Sarī — Shuʿayb — Sayf — al-Mujālid — al-Shaʿbī:
[2267] Rustam has with him in the battle of al-Qādisiyyah thirty elephants.

According to al-Sarī — Shuʿayb — Sayf — Saʿīd b. al-Marzubān — another man: Rustam had with him thirty-three elephants, including the white elephant of Sābūr, to whom the (other) elephants kept close; he was the biggest and oldest among them.

According to al-Sarī — Shuʿayb — Sayf — al-Naḍr — Ibn al-Rufayl — his father: Rustam had thirty-three elephants, eighteen of whom

---

236. I have not translated *yunziluhum fa-yanzilūn*; the meaning seems to be the same as *wa-nazzala al-nāsa wa-mā zālū yatalāḥaqūn*.

237. For *ẓahr* in this sense, see *Glossary* to *BGA*, IV, 294.

were in the central part of the army and fifteen in the two wings.

According to al-Sarī — Shuʿayb — Sayf — Mujālid, Saʿīd, Ṭalḥah, ʿAmr, and Ziyād: When Rustam woke up after the night which he spent near al-ʿAtīq, he went riding with his horsemen. He observed the Muslims and then went up in the direction of the bridge. Having estimated the number of the Muslims, he stood facing them on the near side of the bridge, and sent them a messenger, saying: "Rustam says to you: Send to us a man who will speak to us, and we shall speak to him." The messenger returned. Zuhrah then sent someone to inform Saʿd of this, and Saʿd sent al-Mughīrah b. al-Shuʿbah to Rustam. Zuhrah accompanied al-Mughīrah to al-Jālnūs, and al-Jālnūs escorted him to Rustam.

According to al-Sarī — Shuʿayb — Sayf — al-Naḍr — Ibn al-Rufayl — his father: Rustam camped near al-ʿAtīq and spent the night there. On the next morning, he went to examine the situation and to estimate the number of the Muslims. He went along al-ʿAtīq in the direction of al-Khaffān[238] until he reached the end of the Muslim camp, and then he went up until he reached the bridge. He observed the Muslims and then came to a place from which he could look at them from above. When he stood on the bridge, he sent a message to Zuhrah, who went toward him until Rustam asked him to stop; he wanted to make peace with the Muslims and give Zuhrah a stipend on the condition that they should depart. He said, among other things:

> You are our neighbors, and some of you have been under our rule. We have given them protection, we have kept all harm away from them, and we have given them many useful things. We have kept them safe among the people living in their desert, we have allowed them to graze their flocks on our pastures and have provided them with supplies from our country. We did not prevent them from trading in any part of our land, since their livelihood was based on this. [2268]

[He was alluding to peace but spoke about the good deeds of the Persians. His purpose was peace, but he did not say so explicitly].

Zuhrah said:

---

238. A place in the vicinity of al-Kūfah, on the way to Mecca. See Yāqūt, *Muʿjam*, II, 456.

> You have spoken the truth. In the past the situation was as you described it. But our concern is not what the concern of our forbears was, and our desire is different from theirs. We did not come to you looking for things of this world; our desire and aspiration is the hereafter. In the past we were as you said; those of us who came to your country were obedient to you, humbled themselves before you, and sought what was in your hands. Then God sent to us a Prophet, who called us to his Lord, and we responded. God said to His Prophet: "I have given to this community dominion over those who did not embrace my religion. By means of this community I shall take revenge upon those, and I shall make this community prevail as long as they affirm this religion. This is the religion of truth; none will shun it without suffering humiliation, and none will embrace it without gaining honor and strength."

Rustam said: "And of what does it consist?" Zuhrah said: "Its essential pillar[239] is to testify that there is no god except Allāh and that Muḥammad is His messenger, and to affirm what he has brought from God." Rustam said: "Excellent! And what else?" Zuhrah said: "To extricate people from servitude to [other] people and to make them servants of God." Rustam said: "Good. And what else?" Zuhrah said: "Men are sons of Adam and Eve, brothers born of the
[2269] same father and mother." Rustam said: "How excellent is this!" And he added: "If I agree to this matter and respond to you, together with my people, what will you do? Will you return (to your country)?" Zuhrah said: "By God, indeed we will, and we shall never draw near your land except for [purposes of] trade or some necessity." Rustam said: "You have spoken to me truthfully. But, by God, since Ardashīr[240] ascended the throne, the Persians did not allow any lowly person to leave his work. They used to say: 'If they leave their work, they overstep their bounds and become hostile to their nobles.'" But Zuhrah said to him: "We are the best people for the sake of others. We cannot be as you say. We obey God with regard to the lowly, and we are not harmed if someone disobeys God with regard to us."

---

239. Literally "Its pillar, without which none of its parts is sound. . . ."
240. See note 178, above.

Rustam went away. He summoned the Persians and spoke to them about this, but they went into a rage and scornfully rejected (Zuhrah's proposals). Rustam said: "May God curse you and afflict you! May God disgrace the greatest weaklings and cowards among us!" When Rustam left, I [sc. Ibn al-Rufayl] felt sympathy for Zuhrah. I embraced Islam and associated myself with him, and he allotted to me shares in the spoils equally with the participants in the battle of al-Qādisiyyah.

The same tradition was transmitted also by al-Sarī—Shuʿayb—Sayf—Muḥammad, Ṭalḥah, and Ziyād: They [also] said: Saʿd sent for al-Mughīrah b. al-Shuʿbah, Busr b. Abī Ruhm, and ʿArfajah b. Harthamah,[241] Ḥudhayfah b. Miḥṣan,[242] Ribʿī b. ʿĀmir,[243] Qirfah b. Zāhir al-Taymī al-Wāthilī, Madhʿūr b. ʿAdī al- ʿIjlī,[244] Muḍārib b. Yazīd al-ʿIjlī,[245] and Maʿbad b. Murrah al-ʿIjlī, who was one of the [2270] shrewdest of the Arabs. Saʿd said to them: "I am sending you to the Persians. What do you think of it?" All of them said: "We shall follow your orders to the utmost. Should something which you did not mention come up, we shall consider what is the most appropriate and the most beneficial thing for the people, and we shall tell them." Saʿd said: "This is what prudent people do. Go and prepare yourselves!" Ribʿī b. ʿĀmir said: "The Persians have their own views and their customs. If we all come to them, they will think that we have gone out of our way to honor them, so do not send more than one man." All of them agreed. Ribʿī then said: "Send me," so Saʿd sent him [alone].

Ribʿī set out in order to enter into Rustam's camp. The Persians on the bridge arrested him, and he was sent to Rustam immediately upon his arrival. Rustam consulted the Persian dignitaries and asked them: "What do you think? Should we enter into a contest

241. See Ibn Saʿd, *Ṭabaqāt*, IV/ii, 78; (ʿI.) Ibn al-Athīr, *Usd*, III, 401; Ibn Ḥajar, *Iṣābah*, V, 271.

242. Ḥudhayfah b. Miḥṣan al-Qalfānī (or al-Ghalfānī) later became governor of ʿUmān on behalf of Abū Bakr and governor of Yamāmah on behalf of ʿUmar. See (ʿI.) Ibn al-Athīr, *Usd*, I, 390; Ibn Ḥajar, *Tahdhīb*, II, 44 no. 1648.

243. Ribʿī b. ʿĀmir also participated in the battle of Nihāwand and later became governor of Ṭukhāristān. See Ibn Ḥajar, *Iṣābah*, II, 454–55 no. 2574; Crone, *Slaves*, 118–19.

244. See Ibn Ḥajar, *Iṣābah*, VI, 63–64 no. 7867; (ʿI.) Ibn al-Athīr, *Usd*, IV, 342.

245. See Ibn Ḥajar, *Iṣābah*, VI, 125 no. 8011. For a discussion of the historicity or otherwise of this list, see Noth, *Studien*, 95–96.

with him (*a-nubāhī*) or should we treat him with disdain?"[246] All of them decided to treat him with disdain. They displayed ornaments, spread carpets (*busuṭ*) and pillows (*namāriq*), and did not leave any ornament without using it. A gold-plated seat[247] was set up for Rustam, decorated with rugs (*anmāṭ*), and cushions (*wasāʾid*) laced with gold. Ribʿī came in on a hairy, short-legged mare, having with him a polished sword whose scabbard was made of shabby cloth. His spear was bound with a strap of sinew,[248] and he had a shield made of cowhide, whose exterior was of bright color (*aḥmar*), like a thick, round loaf of bread. He also had with him a bow and arrows.

When he entered upon the king,[249] reached him, and reached the edge of the carpets, the Persians said to him: "Dismount!" but Ribʿī drove the horse onto the carpet. [Only] when the horse stood on the carpet did he dismount. He tied the horse to two cushions, tore them up, and put the rope inside them; they could not stop him from doing this but could only treat him with disdain. He knew what their in-
[2271] tention was and wanted to cause them distress. He had a shield shining like a pond,[250] and his coat was the cover of his camel, in which he made a hole, used it as a shield, and tied it to his waist with a bark of reeds. He was the hairiest of the Arabs, and he tied to his head a piece of cloth which was the girth of his camel. On his head he had four locks of hair which protruded like horns of a goat. The Persians

---

246. The Persians seem to be considering two alternatives: to enter into a verbal contest with Ribʿī by expatiating on their superiority vis-à-vis the Arabs or to show their contempt for him by an ostentatious display of their finery, which would put his shabby appearance into sharp relief.

247. The text reads *sarīr al-dhahab*, "golden seat," but see Sadan, *Le mobilier*, 51. See this work, *passim*, for materials on *bisāṭ*, *numruq*, and *wisādah*.

248. *Rumḥ maʿlūb* is a spear bound with sinews (*ʿilbāʾ*) taken from a camel's neck. The Arabs used to bind a cracked spear with a fresh and moist sinew, which would then dry out and make the weapon strong and usable again. Cf. Schwarzlose, *Waffen*, 233–34. This carries in our context a special significance: It reflects the rugged ways of the Arabs—which are considered praiseworthy—in contradistinction to the luxury of the Persians. See Bukhārī, *Ṣaḥīḥ*, II, 226 (*Kitāb al-jihād*, *bāb* 83): "The conquests were accomplished by people whose swords were not embellished by gold and silver but by sinews, lead, and iron" (*la-qad fataḥa al-futūḥa qawmun mā kānat ḥilyatu suyūfihim al-dhahab wa-lā al-fiḍḍah wa-innamā kānat ḥilyatuhā al-ʿalābī wa-al-ānuk wa-al-ḥadīd*).

249. Ribʿī is about to meet Rustam, not Yazdagird, but high officials of the Persian empire were frequently called "kings." See Morony, *Iraq*, 186–87.

250. For this meaning of *aḍāt*, see Ibn Manẓūr, *Lisān al-ʿArab*, s.v. ʾ-ḍ-w; *Glossary*, s.v. ʾ-ḍ-w. For the comparison of the shield with a pond, see Schwarzlose, *Waffen*, 348.

said to him: "Lay down your arms," but Ribʿī said: "I have not come to you [on my own initiative] so that I should have to lay down my arms on your orders. You invited me here; and if you do not want me to come as I please, I shall return."

The Persians notified Rustam of this. He said: "Let him come in; he is only one man." Ribʿī came in, leaning on his spear. Its lower end[251] was (as sharp as) the blade. He walked with short steps and pierced their carpets and cushions, so that he did not leave even one cushion or carpet without destroying it and left them torn to shreds. When he came close to Rustam, the guards seized him. He sat on the floor, plunging his spear into the carpets. They said: "Why are you doing this?" Ribʿī said: "We do not like to sit on this finery of yours." Then Rustam spoke to him and asked him: "What has brought you here?" Ribʿī said:

> God has sent us and has brought us here so that we may extricate those who so desire from servitude to the people [here on earth] and make them servants of God; that we may transform their poverty in this world into affluence; and that we may free them from the inequity of the religions and bestow upon them the justice of Islam. He has sent us to bring His religion to His creatures and to call them to Islam. Whoever accepts it from us, we shall be content. We shall leave him on his land to rule it without us; but whoever refuses, we shall fight him, until we fulfill the promise of God.

Rustam said: "And what is the promise of God?" Ribʿī said: "Paradise for him who dies while fighting those who have refused [to embrace Islam] and victory for him who survives."

Rustam said: "I have heard your speech. Are you willing to delay this matter until both parties consider it?" Ribʿī said: "How long a [2272]

251. It may be worthwhile to speculate on the symbolic content of this description. The lower end (*zujj*) of the spear was not normally used to stab the enemy but rather to stick the weapon into the ground. It was therefore a symbol of peaceful intentions. In our context the *zujj* is, indeed, stuck into the ground, but in a way that destroys the objectionable finery of the Persians. That the lower end of the spear is described as being as sharp as the blade may be taken as a hint that peaceful resolution of the conflict is not envisaged. See Ibn Manẓūr, *Lisān al-ʿArab*, s.v. *z-j-j*; Schwarzlose, *Waffen*, 232, and index; Anbārī, *Sharḥ al-qaṣāʾid*, 280–81 (on the *Muʿallaqah* of Zuhayr b. Abī Sulmā, v. 47).

delay would you like? One day or two days?" Rustam said: "No [I wish a longer delay], until we exchange letters with our men of judgment and with the leaders of our people." (He wanted to attract him and to put him off [at the same time].) Ribʿī said:

> The custom that has been established for us by the Messenger of God and put into effect by our leaders is that we should not listen to the enemy nor delay the fight with them for more than three days. We shall therefore go back and leave you alone for three days. Look into your affair and into the affair of your people and choose—within this period—one of three options. Choose Islam, and we shall leave you alone on your land; or choose [to pay] the poll tax, and we shall be content and refrain from fighting you. If you do not need our help, we shall leave you alone; and if you need it, we shall protect you. Otherwise it will be war on the fourth day. We shall not attack you between now and the fourth day unless you attack us. You have my guarantee on behalf of my companions and on behalf of all those [Muslims] whom you see.

Rustam said: "Are you their chief?" Ribʿī said: "No, I am not, but the Muslims are like one body. They are all parts of a whole (*baʿḍuhum min baʿḍin*). The most humble among them can promise protection on behalf of the most noble."[252]

Rustam went into private consultation with the Persian chieftains and said: "What is your opinion? Have you ever heard a statement more lucid and more honorable that the statement of this man?" They said: "May God save you from inclining toward something like that and abandoning your religion to this dog! Did you not see his clothing?" Rustam said: "Woe to you! Do not look at his

252. This is a reference to the idea that an assurance of safety or protection given by any Muslim is binding on the entire community. See Bukhārī, *Ṣaḥīḥ*, II, 296 (*Kitāb al-jizyah, bāb* 10): "The assurance of safety or protection of the Muslims is one; the most humble of them is entitled to take it upon himself" (*dhimmat al-muslimīn wa-jiwāruhum wāḥidah yasʿā bihā adnāhum*). Explaining this tradition, Qasṭallānī (*Irshād*, V, 238) says: "Whoever gives an assurance of safety to someone from the People of War, his assurance is binding on all the Muslims. It is immaterial whether he is lowly or noble, slave or free, man or woman" (*inna kulla man ʿaqada amānan li-aḥadin min ahl al-ḥarb jāza amānuhu ʿalā jamīʿal-muslimīn daniyyan kāna aw sharīfan ʿabdan aw ḥurran rajulan aw imraʾatan*). See also Bukhārī, II, 298; Qasṭallānī, *Irshād*, V, 243; and Ṭabarī, *Jihād*, 25ff.

clothing! Look rather at his judgment, his speech, and his conduct. The Arabs attach no importance to clothing and food. They protect their ancestral glory (*aḥsāb*) instead. They are not like you in regard to clothing and they do not see in it what you do." They approached [2273] Ribʿī, took his weapons in their hands, and belittled their worth. He said: "Do you want to show me [your ability] and I shall show you [mine]?" He drew his sword from its rags like a flame of fire. The Persians said: "Sheathe it." Ribʿī complied. Then he shot at a shield (of theirs), and they shot at his leathern shield; their shield was pierced, while his remained intact. Ribʿī said: "O people of Persia, you attach great importance to food, clothing, and drink, whereas we belittle all these." Then he returned, so that they might consider the matter within the allotted time.

On the next morning, the Persians sent a message, saying: "Send this man to us again," but Saʿd sent to them Ḥudhayfah b. Miḥṣan. He came dressed in a similar attire. When he came to the nearest carpet, the Persians said: "Dismount!" He said:

> You would have the right to speak in this fashion if I were to come asking for something. Ask your king whether he wants to ask for something or whether I do. If he says that I came here to ask for something, he is lying and I shall return and leave you. If he says that he wants to ask for something, then I am not coming except as I please.

Rustam said: "Let him come in." Ḥudhayfah came in and stood near Rustam, who was sitting on his seat. Rustam said: "Dismount!" Ḥudhayfah said: "I shall not." When Ḥudhayfah refused, Rustam asked him: "Why have you come rather than the man who was here yesterday?" Ḥudhayfah said: "Our amīr treats us justly in distress as well as in comfort; it is now my turn." Rustam said: "What has brought you here?" Ḥudhayfah said:

> God the Exalted has favored us with His religion and showed us His signs. We have come to know Him after we had denied Him. Then He ordered us to summon the people to one of three options. Whichever you accept will be accepted by us. (If you embrace) Islam, we shall leave you alone. If [you agree to pay] the poll tax, we shall protect you if you need our protection. Otherwise, it is war.

Rustam said: "Or truce till a certain day?" Ḥudhayfah said: "Yes—for three days, beginning yesterday."

When Rustam could not get from Ḥudhayfah anything except that, he sent him away. Then he came to his companions and said:

> Woe to you! Do you not see what I do? The first one came to us yesterday, forced his way into our land, debased what we
> [2274] honor, made his horse stand on our finery, and tied him to it. He came on an auspicious day [for him] and bore away our land and all that is in it to them.[253] He had superior intelligence. The second one came today. He stopped here on an auspicious day, standing on our land before us.

This continued until Rustam and his companions enraged each other. On the next morning, Rustam sent a message, saying: "Send another man to us," so the Muslims sent al-Mughīrah b. Shuʿbah.

According to al-Sarī—Shuʿayb—Sayf—Abū ʿUthmān al-Nahdī: When al-Mughīrah reached the bridge and crossed over to the Persians, they detained him and asked Rustam for permission to let him pass. They did not change anything in the setting in order to intensify their disdain. When al-Mughīrah b. Shuʿbah arrived, the Persians were in their attire, wearing crowns and clothing laced with gold. Their carpets were a bow shot long. Nobody could reach their chief without walking on them all this distance. Al-Mughīrah came in, having four locks of hair on his head. He walked through and sat down with Rustam on his seat and cushion.[254] The Persians fell upon him, seized him violently, dragged him down, and gave him a light beating. Al-Mughīrah said:

> We have heard about your moderation and self-restraint, but I think that there is no nation more excitable and stupid than you are. We, the Arabs, are (all) equal (to each other). We do not enslave each other, except if someone fights against the other [and is taken prisoner]. I thought you treated your people as equals as we do. Instead of what you
> [2275] did, it would have been better if you had informed me that

---

253. See p. 2244, above.

254. This tradition can be found in Abū Yūsuf, *Kharāj*, 83. According to Abū Yūsuf's version, al-Mughīrah seated himself on Rustam's throne on purpose, in order to provoke his anger.

> some of you are masters over others, that behavior [such as mine] is unacceptable among you, and that we should not engage in it. I have not come [on my own initiative]; you have invited me. Today I have come to know that your affair will come to nought and that you will be defeated. A kingdom cannot be based on such conduct, nor on such minds [as yours].

The lowly people said: "By God, the Arab is speaking the truth." The landowners (*dahāqīn*) said: "By God, he has said things to which our slaves have always been inclined. May God curse[255] our forbears! How foolish they were when they disparaged this nation!"

Rustam made a joke in order to blot out [the impression of] what had been done. He said: "O Arab, the king's attendants sometimes do things with which the king does not agree, but he is soft on them for fear that he would destroy their willingness to do the right thing [in the future]. We are faithful and truthful, the way you want us to be. And what are the spindles that you have with you?"[256] Al-Mughīrah said: "A burning coal does not deteriorate because it is not long." He then competed with them in shooting arrows. Rustam said: "Why is your sword old?" and al-Mughīrah replied: "Its covering is shabby, but its blade is sharp," and he fought a mock fight with them. Rustam said: "Speak, or shall I myself speak?" Al-Mughīrah said: "You are the one who sent for us, so speak!"

Rustam ordered the translator to take his place between them. Rustam began to speak. He praised his people and glorified them, saying:

> We are firmly established in the land, victorious over our enemies, and noble among the nations. None of the kings has our power, honor, and dominion. We triumph over others, and they do not triumph over us, except for a day or two, or a month or two, and this is [only] because of our transgressions. When God takes His revenge to His satisfac- [2276]
> tion, He will restore our honor and we shall assemble for our enemy [an army which will fight him on] the worst day that

---

255. For this meaning of *qātalahu Allāh*, see Ibn Manẓūr, *Lisān al-ʿArab*, s.v. *q-t-l*.

256. Cf. p. 2236, above.

ever came upon him. Furthermore, there was never among the people a nation which we considered more contemptuous than you. You were people who lived in misery and privation. We thought nothing of you and held you of no account. When your land was famine-striken and you were afflicted with drought, you sought help in the border area of our country, and we would provide you with dates and barley and send you back. I know that the only cause of what you are doing is the distress which you face in your land. I shall supply your chief with a garment, a mule, and one thousand dirhams. I shall provide every one of you with a load of dates and two garments, and you will then leave our country, for I have no desire to kill you or to take you in captivity.

Al-Mughīrah b. Shuʿbah began to speak. He praised God, extolled Him, and then said:

God is the creator of everything![257] When somebody makes something, it is [really] He who makes it and it belongs to Him.[258] As for your victories and your firm position in the land and your powerful dominion in the world which you have mentioned with regard to yourself and with regard to the people of your country, we know this and do not deny it. But it is God who has done this to you and entrusted you with it; all this is His, not yours. As for our destitution, privation, and dissension which you mentioned, we know it [also] and do not deny it. It is God who has put us to the test by it and reduced us to this condition. Fortune in this world is transitory; people afflicted with calamities hope for prosperity until they achieve it, and people of prosperity expect that calamities will afflict them.[259] And even if you were grateful to God for what He has bestowed upon you, your gratitude would fall short of what you were given. The inadequacy of [your] gratitude would cause a change of [your]
[2277] condition for the worse. And if we were ungrateful with regard to our tribulations, then the greatest afflictions which

257. Qurʾān 13:18, 39:62.

258. I am translating according to de Goeje's suggested emendation: *wa-huwa lahu*, instead of *wa-alladhī lahu* of the text.

259. I have not translated *wa yaṣīru ilayhā*.

> kept coming at us time and again from God would seem like acts of mercy through which He has alleviated our suffering.[260] But the matter is different from what you think, and we are not the people whom you knew in the past. God has sent to us a messenger. . . .

Then al-Mughīrah mentioned things identical with those which had been related before.[261] When he reached the sentence: "And if you need our protection, then be our slave, and pay the poll tax out of hand, while being humiliated;[262] otherwise, it is the sword," Rustam snorted, flew into a rage, and swore by the sun: "Dawn will not break upon you tomorrow before I kill you all."

Al-Mughīrah went away. Seeking conciliation, Rustam met in private with the Persian [dignitaries] and said:

> How different are these people from you! What is going to happen after this? The first two men came, annoyed you, and caused you distress. Then this one came. There were no differences between them; they followed the same way and held fast to the same matter. By God, these are [veritable] men, whether they speak the truth or lie. By God, if they speak the truth and if their intelligence and secretiveness are such that no difference between them can be discerned, then they are more effective than anybody else in expressing their purpose. Nothing can stand against them.

The Persians wrangled with each other and feigned boldness. Rustam said: "I know that you incline to my words, and all this is dissimulation on your part," but their wrangling intensified.

According to al-Sarī—Shuʿayb—Sayf—al-Naḍr—Ibn al-Rufayl—his father: Rustam sent a man to accompany al-Mughīrah. He said to him: "When he crosses the bridge and reaches his companions, cry out to him: 'The king[263] is an astrologer. He made calculations with regard to you, looked into your affair, and said that one of [2278] your eyes would be put out tomorrow.'"[264] The messenger did as he

260. This is to say that, if the Arabs had been ungrateful to God, He would have brought upon them suffering of such magnitude that their former tribulations would appear merely as acts of His mercy when compared with it.

261. By the Muslims who had met Rustam before al-Mughīrah.

262. Paraphrasing Qur'ān 9:29.

263. The title evidently refers to Rustam.

264. Al-Mughīrah did, indeed, lose an eye in the wars of conquest. According to one

was told to do. Al-Mughīrah said: "You have given me good tidings about my reward. If I did not have to fight polytheists like you in the future, I would have wished that my other eye had gone as well."[265] The messenger saw that the Arabs laughed at what al-Mughīrah said and admired his determination.[266] He returned to the king with his report. Rustam said: "O people of Persia, obey me. I see that God is about to inflict punishment on you. You will not be able to ward it off."

The horses of the Persians and of the Muslims clashed on the bridge and nowhere else. The Persians were incessantly engaging the Muslims in battle, while the Muslims nevertheless left them alone for three days and did not attack them. When the Persians started up the fighting, the Muslims repelled and turned them back.

According to al-Sarī — Shuʿayb — Sayf — Muḥammad — ʿUbaydallāh — Nāfiʿ — Ibn ʿUmar: The translator of Rustam was a man from al-Ḥīrah. His name was ʿAbbūd.

According to al-Sarī — Shuʿayb — Sayf — Mujālid — al-Shaʿbī and Saʿīd b. al-Marzubān: Rustam asked al-Mughīrah to come, and the latter came in and sat down on Rustam's seat. Rustam then summoned his translator, who was an Arab from the people of al-Ḥīrah named ʿAbbūd. Al-Mughīrah said to him: "O wretched ʿAbbūd! You are one of the Arabs. Inform him of what I say in the same way as you inform me of what he says." Rustam said to al-Mughīrah the same things [that had been related before], as did al-Mughīrah. [He said:] "... [you have] one of three options: Islam, in which case you will have the same rights and the same obligations as we have. There will be no difference between us. Or [to pay] the poll tax out of hand, while being humiliated." Rustam asked: "What does 'while being
[2279] humiliated' mean?" Al-Mughīrah said: "It means that a Persian will stand on his feet in order to pay the poll tax to one of us and will

---

tradition, this happened in al-Ḥudaybiyyah; according to another, in al-Qādisiyyah. See Ibn Ḥabīb, *Muḥabbar*, 261, 302.

265. Classical Islamic literature, and especially the chapters on *jihād*, frequently contains utterances in which the warriors express their desire to be wounded or even killed while fighting the infidels. See, e.g., Bukhārī, *Ṣaḥīḥ*, II, 206 (*Kitāb al-jihād, bāb* 21), and IV, 408 (*Kitāb al-tamannī, bāb* 1), for prophetic traditions on this topic. See also Noth, *Studien*, 129–30.

266. For this meaning of *baṣīrah* see de Goeje's *Glossary*, s.v., and Blachère *et al.*, *Dictionnaire*, I, 646.

267. Muslim jurisprudents and commentators on the Qurʾān are concerned with

praise the Muslim for agreeing to accept it from him."[267] Al-Mughīrah completed his statement and said: "Islam is the option we prefer [you to choose]."

According to al-Sarī—Shuʿayb—Sayf—ʿUbaydah—Shaqīq: I participated in the battle of al-Qādisiyyah as a young man, after attaining puberty. Saʿd came to al-Qādisiyyah with twelve thousand men, among whom were participants in previous battles (*ahl al-ayyām*). The vanguard of Rustam moved toward us, and then he marched forward with sixty thousand men. When he saw our camp, he said: "O Arabs, send to us a man who will speak to us and we shall speak to him." Saʿd sent to him al-Mughīrah b. Shuʿbah with a group of people. When they came to Rustam, al-Mughīrah sat down on [Rustam's] seat. Rustam's brother snorted. Al-Mughīrah said: "Do not snort, for this will not increase my honor, nor will it detract from your brother's." Rustam said: "You were people of misery . . . " and continued until he reached the words: "If there is something besides this, let me know."[268] Then Rustam took an arrow from al-Mughīrah's quiver and said: "Do not think that these spindles will be of any avail to you." Responding, al-Mughīrah mentioned the Prophet and said: "Among the things with which God has provided us through the Prophet was a seed which grows in this country of yours. When we gave it to our families to taste, they said: 'We cannot endure without it.' We therefore came in order to let them eat it or else to die." Rustam said: "Die you indeed will, or be killed." Al-Mughīrah said: "In that case, those of us who will be killed will enter Paradise, and those of you whom we shall kill will enter the Fire. Those of us who survive will be victorious over those of you who survive. We give you the choice of three options . . . ," and he com-

---

the ways in which the Qur'ānic requirement to humiliate the payer of the poll tax is to be implemented. One of the frequently mentioned devices for achieving this is to have the payer stand while the payee is comfortably seated. This seems to be the background of al-Mughīrah's response to Rustam's question. See Ṭabarī, *Tafsīr*, X, 77 last line–78: "The commentators were divided concerning the meaning of humiliation that God intended in this verse (9:29). Some said: 'He (i.e., the *dhimmī*) should pay it standing while the [Muslim] who takes it is sitting (. . . an yuʿṭiyaka wa-huwa qā'im wa-al-ākhidh jālis).'" See also Fattal, *Le statut*, 286–88, and Kūfī, *Futūḥ*, I, 200. Al-Mughīrah also expresses the idea that the acceptance of the poll tax is a favor that the Muslims do for their non-Muslim subjects, one for which the latter should be grateful.

268. See pp. 2275–76 for Rustam's speech.

pleted his speech. Rustam said: "There will be no peace between us."

According to al-Sarī—Shuʿayb—Sayf—Muḥammad, Ṭalḥah, and
[2280] Ziyād: Saʿd sent to the Persians the best people of judgment, who numbered three.[269] They went forth and came to Rustam in order to reproach him severely, and said to him:

> Our chief says to you that good neighborliness (*jiwār*) keeps rulers safe. I call upon you to accept what is good for us and what entails well-being for you. If you accept the call of God, we shall return to our country and you shall return to yours. We shall be closely associated with one another, but your land will be yours and your affairs will be in your hands. Whatever you seize beyond your borders will be yours and we shall have no part in it. Should anyone intend [to attack] you or overpower you, we shall come to your help. O Rustam, fear God and do not let your people perish at your hands! Nothing except embracing Islam and expelling Satan from your self by means of it stands between you and the attainment of happiness and prosperity.

Rustam replied:

> I have spoken to a few people from among you. If they had only understood what I said, I would have hoped that you would also understand. Parables are clearer than many a speech, so I shall therefore apply a parable to you. You must understand that you were people whose livelihood was meager and whose appearance was shabby, and the places where you lived were neither fortified nor difficult of access; nor did you insist on getting what was due to you. We did not treat you badly, nor did we stop sharing our wealth with you. Time and again you were forced out of your country [and into ours] by the drought, and we used to provide you with
> [2281] supplies and then send you back home. You used to come to us as hirelings and merchants, and we treated you well. After you partook of our food, drank of our drink, and rested in

269. I am translating according to the version found in (ʿI.) Ibn al-Athīr, *Kāmil,* II, 361: *wa-kānū thalāthatan.*

> our shade, you described this in favorable terms to your people, invited them to come, and brought them to us. Your relationship with us regarding this is similar to that of a man who had a vineyard and saw a fox in it. [He did nothing] and said: "What is one fox?" The fox went away and called the foxes to this vineyard. When they gathered together, the owner closed behind them the hole through which they had come and killed them. I know that only greed, covetousness, and privation caused you to do this. Go back this year, supply yourselves with provisions, and you can return whenever you are in need, for I have no desire to kill you.

According to al-Sarī—Shuʿayb—Sayf—ʿUmārah b. al-Qaʿqāʿ al-Ḍabbī—a man from Yarbūʿ who was present [at the meeting with Rustam]: Rustam said:

> Many of your people took whatever they wanted from our land; then they were killed or had to run away. He who established this custom among you was better and stronger than you are. You have seen the situation: Whenever they took something, some of them were hurt and some of them escaped and had to abandon whatever they took. With regard to the deeds that you perpetrate, you are like rats who used to come regularly to a jar full of grain. In the jar there was an opening. The first rat went in and stayed there. The other rats began to carry the grain away and to come back [for more]. They spoke to the rat inside about returning but he refused. He became extremely fat, longed for his family, [2282] and wanted to show them his excellent condition. The opening was now too narrow for him. He became worried, complained to his companions, and asked them to help him out, but they said: "You cannot get out before you return to the size that you had been before you went in." He starved himself and was full of fear, but, when he finally returned to his former size, the owner of the jar came along and killed him. Get out, therefore, and let not this parable be applicable to you.

According to al-Sarī—Shuʿayb—Sayf—al-Naḍr—Ibn al-Rufayl—his father: Rustam said:

God never created creatures more covetous and more harmful than flies. O Arabs, do you not see the destruction into which your greed leads you? I shall apply a parable to you. When flies see honey, they fly toward it and say: "He who enables us to reach it will have two dirhams." When they get to it, they refuse to listen to anyone who tries to drive them away. When they plunge into the honey, they drown and become stuck in it, and then they say: "He who extricates us will have four dirhams."

He also said:

You are like a fox, emaciated and weak, who entered a vineyard through a hole, and used to eat whatever God wanted him to eat. The owner of the vineyard saw his condition and took pity on him. After he stayed in the vineyard for a long time, he became fat, his condition improved, and his leanness disappeared. He began to behave with pride and self-conceit, to fool around in the vineyard, and to destroy more than he could eat. This became unbearable for the vineyard owner, and he said: "I shall not endure this from him." He took a piece of wood, asked his servants to help him, and they went after the fox. The fox began to play tricks with them in the vineyard. When he saw that they did not desist,
[2283] he tried to get out by means of the hole through which he had entered, but he got stuck in it; the hole was big enough for him when he was lean but too small when he became fat. The vineyard owner caught up with him in this condition and did not cease beating him until he killed him. You came here lean; now you have become somewhat fat. Consider the way in which you will get out.[270]

Rustam also said:

A man took a basket and put his food in it. The rats came along, pierced a hole in his basket, and got into it. The man

270. Al-Thaʿālibī (*Ghurar*, 739–40) records, in addition to a shorter version of Rustam's parable, the following response of al-Mughīrah b. Shuʿbah: "'His (i.e., the fox's) being killed after attaining his aim and fulfilling his desire is better than death by hunger and emaciation.' Rustam admired al-Mughīrah's forceful reply and understood that the Arabs were firmly resolved to overcome the Persians." (The word *s-r-y* in this sentence is not clear.)

wanted to block the hole, but was told: "Do not do it, because they will pierce it again. Rather, make a hole opposite it and put in a hollow tube. When the rats come, they will enter it and come out through it, and whenever a rat appears, you can kill it." I have blocked your way and I warn you not to force your way into the tube, for none will emerge from it without being killed. What has caused you to do this? I see neither numbers nor weapons.[271]

According to al-Sarī—Shuʿayb—Sayf—Muḥammad, Ṭalḥah, and Ziyād: The Muslims spoke, saying:

As for what you have said about our miserable and unsettled situation in the past, you have not grasped its essence.[272] Those of us who died went into the Fire. Those of us who survived lived in distress. While we were in this extremely bad situation, God sent to us a messenger who was one of our own.[273] He sent him to all creatures[274] as a mercy to those whom He wanted to treat with mercy and as a punishment to those who rejected His generosity. The messenger approached us tribe after tribe. Nobody treated him more harshly, nobody denied his message more completely, and [2284]
nobody made a greater effort to kill him and to refute what he had brought than his own tribe and, after them, the people who were close to them. All of us eventually agreed to help in this and treated him with hostility. He was a lonely man, who stood alone, and no one except God was with him. Nevertheless, he was given victory over us. Some of us embraced Islam willingly, others as a result of coercion. Then all of us recognized his truth and veracity in view of the miraculous signs that he brought to us. One of the ideas that he brought from our Lord was to wage war against those who were closest to us first. We acted upon it among ourselves and saw that there was no turning away from what he

271. This is to say that neither the numbers of the Muslims nor the weapons at their disposal are sufficient to give them a chance of victory.

272. Meaning that the situation of the Arabs in the pre-Islamic period was even worse than would appear from Rustam's description. Cf. note 149, above.

273. Echoing Qur'ān 3:164: "Truly God was gracious to the believers when He raised up among them a Messenger from themselves . . . " (Arberry's translation).

274. *Al-ins wa-al-jinn;* cf. note 225, above.

had promised us or any revoking of it. The Arabs agreed on this, though their dissension had been such that in the past no one could bring about a reconciliation between them. Now we came to you by order of our Lord, fighting for His sake. We act upon His orders and seek the fulfillment of His promise. We call upon you to embrace Islam and to accept its authority. If you agree, we shall let you alone; we shall return [to our country] and leave with you the Book of God. If you refuse, the only permissible thing for us to do is to engage you in battle unless you ransom yourselves by paying the poll tax. If you pay this, well and good; if not, then God has already bequeathed to us your country, your sons, and your property. Heed, therefore, our advice. By God, we prefer your conversion to Islam to taking your spoils, but we would rather fight you than make peace with you.[275] As for what you mentioned concerning our shabby appearance and our small numbers, [you must understand that] our weapon is obedience to God and our fighting is [based on] endurance. As for the parables that you applied to us, you were using ridicule with regard to [honorable] men, weighty matters, and
[2285] a serious affair. But we shall [also] apply a parable to you. You are like a man who cultivated a tract of land, chose for it the trees and the seeds, and made canals flow through it. He embellished the land with castles and settled peasants on it, intending them to live in the castles and to tend the gardens. The peasants behaved in the castles in a way of which he did not approve and did the same with the gardens. He was patient with them for a long time, but, when they themselves did not feel shame because of what they had done, he asked them to mend their ways. They behaved toward him with haughtiness and conceit, so he expelled them from his land and invited others in their stead. If they should leave the land, they were to be seized and carried away by force. If they should remain, they were to become servants of these [who would come to replace them]. They were ruled by them, not

275. The idea is that, if the Persians do not embrace Islam and do not agree to pay the poll tax, then the Muslims will fight them, rather than make peace with them without securing the payment.

made kings over them, and were humiliated forever. By God, if what we are telling you were not true, and if it were not connected only with this world, we would not have been so patient with your luxurious life and the finery that we have become accustomed to see on you; we would have fought you and taken it away from you by force.[276]

Rustam said: "Will you cross [the canal] to our side, or shall we cross to yours?" The Muslims replied: "Cross to our side." The Muslims left Rustam in the evening. Saʿd ordered them to take up their positions and sent a message to the Persians: "Cross [the canal] as you please." They wanted to cross on the bridge, but he sent a message to them, saying: "By no means! We shall not restore to you something that we took from you by force. Take pains to prepare for yourselves a crossing other than a bridge." Hence the Persians spent the night filling the al-ʿAtīq canal with their chattels.

The Day of Armāth[277]

According to al-Sarī—Shuʿayb—Sayf—Muḥammad—ʿUbaydallāh—Nāfiʿ—al-Ḥakam: When Rustam decided to cross over, he ordered the damming up of al-ʿAtīq opposite Qādis,[278] which then was [2286]
farther downstream than it is today, near ʿAyn al-Shams.[279] They spent the night, until the morning, filling al-ʿAtīq with soil, reeds, and saddles and preparing a crossing through it. It was ready on the next day, after dawn.

According to al-Sarī—Shuʿayb—Sayf—Muḥammad, Ṭalḥah, and Ziyād: At night Rustam had a dream in which he saw an angel who descended from heaven, took the bows of his companions, put a seal

276. The last passage of the Muslims' speech reflects the ascetic idea of the absolute worthlessness of this world. Had the world not been worthless, God—or the Muslims—would not have allowed the infidels to enjoy anything of it. Only because of the worthlessness of the world did God and the Muslims allow the Persians to enjoy it until now. For this idea in Ṣūfī literature, see Sarrāj, *Lumaʿ*, 47.

277. The meaning of Armāth in this context is not clear. *Rimth* is a kind of shrub; *ramath* means a raft, a worn-out rope, or the remains of milk in the udder after milking. Yāqūt (*Muʿjam*, I, 211) does not know why the first day of the battle of al-Qādisiyyah was so called.

278. According to Ṭabarī (I, 2351) Qādis was a village near ʿUdhayb (see note 92, above).

279. ʿAyn al-Shams is a spring between al-ʿUdhayb and al-Qādisiyyah. See Yāqūt, *Muʿjam*, III, 793.

on them, and ascended back to heaven with them. Rustam woke up full of anxiety and grief. He called in his close associates and related the dream to them. He said: "God is exhorting us! I wish the Persians would let me take heed! Do you not see that victory has been taken away from us? You see that the enemy is going to gain the ascendancy, and we cannot stand up to them in deed or word. But the Persians, in their insolence, still want to have a fight!" They crossed [the canal] with their baggage and camped on the [other] bank of al-ʿAtīq.

According to al-Sarī—Shuʿayb—Sayf—al-Aʿmash: On "the day of the damming up" [of al-ʿAtīq], Rustam put on two pieces of armor and a helmet. He took his weapons and ordered his horse to be saddled. The horse was brought to him. He mounted the horse without touching [his sides] and without putting his feet into the stirrup. He said: "Tomorrow we shall crush them to pieces." A certain man added, "God willing," but Rustam said: "Even if He is not willing!"

According to al-Sarī b. Yaḥyā — Shuʿayb — Sayf — Muḥammad, Ṭalḥah, and Ziyād: Rustam said: "The fox makes speeches when the lion is dead." He reminded his companions of the death of
[2287] Kisrā[280] and told them: "I am afraid that this will be the year of the apes."

When the Persians crossed the canal, they arrayed themselves in battle lines. Rustam sat on his throne,[281] and a sunshade[282] was placed on it. He placed eighteen elephants with palanquins (*ṣanādīq*) and men in the center of the army; in the two wings he placed [respectively] eight and seven elephants with palanquins and men. He placed al-Jālnūs between himself and the right wing, and al-Bayruzān between himself and the left wing. Thus the bridge was between two units of horsemen, Muslims and polytheists.

When Yazdagird sent Rustam out, he placed a man at the door of his hall and ordered him to stay near him and to pass any information back to him. Another man was placed where he could be heard

280. After the murder of Khusraw II in 628 several Persian monarchs were murdered, and it is not clear which one is meant here. See *CHI*, III/i, 170–71.

281. For the Sasanian custom of bringing the royal throne to the battlefield, even when the battle is not directed by the king but by one of his generals, see Christensen, *Sassanides*, 211.

282. For *ṭayyārah* in this sense, see Dozy, *Supplément*, s.v., and de Goeje's *Glossary*, s.v.

from the palace, and another one outside the palace. At each "hearing distance,"[283] Yazdagird placed a man. When Rustam encamped [at Sābāṭ], the man in Sābāṭ said: "He has encamped." The man next to him said the same. [The information was transmitted in this way] until the man standing at the door of the king's hall said it. Yazdagird placed a man at each "hearing distance."[284] When Rustam camped, moved out, or something happened, the man [on the scene] described it; then the man next to him said it until it was said by the man standing at the door of the king's hall. Yazdagird placed men in this manner between al-ʿAtīq and al-Madāʾin. He dispensed with the messenger service,[285] which was the regular way [of gathering information].

The Muslims stood in battle lines. Zuhrah (b. Ḥawiyyah) and ʿĀṣim (b. ʿAmr) were placed between ʿAbdallāh (b. al-Muʿtamm) and Shuraḥbīl (b. al-Simṭ). The commander of the scouts was charged with the attack. Saʿd mixed the warriors from the center with those of the two wings. His herald (*munādī*) proclaimed: "Envy is permissible only in *jihād* for the sake of God. O men, be envious and jealous of each other in matters of *jihād*!"

At that time, Saʿd was not able to ride or sit since he was suffering from boils. He had to lie face down, leaning on a pillow under his chest. From the castle he watched the Muslims and sent written or- [2288]
ders to Khālid b. ʿUrfuṭah, who was in a place lower than his. The Muslim lines were adjacent to the castle. Khālid was somewhat like Saʿd's deputy, except that Saʿd was present and watching.

According to al-Sarī—Shuʿayb—Sayf—al-Qāsim b. al-Walīd al-Hamdānī—his father—Abū Nimrān: When Rustam crossed [al-ʿAtīq], Zuhrah and al-Jālnūs changed places. Saʿd ordered Zuhrah to move to [Shuraḥbīl] Ibn al-Simṭ's place, and Rustam ordered al-Jālnūs to move to al-Hurmuzān's place. Saʿd was suffering from ischial pain (*ʿirq al-nasā*) and from boils and had to lie face down. He appointed Khālid b. ʿUrfuṭah as his deputy, but the people turned against him. Saʿd said: "Carry me to an elevated place and let me observe the army from there." They took him [to such a place] and

283. For this meaning of *daʿwah*, see de Goeje, *Glossary*; several additional examples of this usage are also noted in the *Glossary* to *BGA*, IV, 234.

284. It is not clear to me what is meant by the expression *ʿalā kulli marḥalatayni* in this context.

285. See *EI*², s.v. "Barīd" (D. Sourdel).

he lay down watching the army. The battle line [of the Muslims] was at the foot of the wall of Qudays.[286] Saʿd issued orders to Khālid, and Khālid transmitted them to the troops.

Some of the leading men conspired against Saʿd. He cursed them and said: "By God, if you were not facing the enemy, I would have punished you as an example for others." He imprisoned them and chained them up in the castle; [the poet] Abū Miḥjan al-Thaqafī[287] was among them. Jarīr (b. ʿAbdallāh al-Bajalī) said: "In my oath of allegiance to the Prophet, I pledged to obey any man whom God should appoint to lead us, even if he be an Abyssinian slave." Saʿd said: "From now on nobody will hold the Muslims back from [fighting] their enemy or keep them busy while facing him. [Should this happen again], it would turn into a custom for which my successors would be chastised."

According to al-Sarī—Shuʿayb—Sayf—Muḥammad, Ṭalḥah, and
[2289] Ziyād: On that day Saʿd addressed those who were under his command. It was on a Monday in the month of Muḥarram in the year 14, after Saʿd vented his rage on those who had opposed Khālid b. al-ʿUrfuṭah. Having praised God and extolled Him, he said:

> God is the Truth. He has no partner in His dominion and His words will never go unfulfilled. God has said: "For We have written in the Psalms, after the Remembrance, 'The earth shall be the inheritance of My righteous servants.'"[288] This land is your inheritance and the promise of your Lord. God permitted you to take possession of it three years ago. You have been tasting it and eating from it, and you have been killing its people, collecting taxes from them, and taking them into captivity. All this is by virtue of [the defeats] that the participants in the previous battles[289] had inflicted upon the Persians. Now this army of theirs has come against you. You are Arab chiefs and notables, the elect of every tribe, and the pride of those who are behind you. If you renounce this world and aspire for the hereafter, God will give you both this world and the hereafter. This will not bring the death of anyone closer. But, if you should be flagging, weak,

286. A place in the neighborhood of al-Qādisiyyah; see Yāqūt, *Muʿjam*, IV, 42–43.
287. See note 360, below.
288. Qurʾān 21:105 (Arberry's translation).
289. See note 215, above.

and feeble, then you will lose your predominance and ruin your share in the hereafter.

ʿĀṣim b. ʿAmr stood up to address the light cavalry and said:

God has made it permissible for you to fight the people of this land. In the last three years you have been inflicting harm upon them and they have not been inflicting harm upon you. You have the upper hand[290] and God is with you. If you stand firm and fight them with courage, their property, their women, their sons, and their country will be yours; but should you become flagging and weak—and God is your protector from this—this [Persian] army will not spare even a remnant of you for fear that you would bring perdition upon them again. By God! Remember the [previous] days [of battle] and remember what God has bestowed upon you. Do you not see that the land behind you is a desolate desert without a place of hiding or refuge in which one can take shelter and which is inaccessible [to the enemy]? Place your aspirations on the hereafter!"

Saʿd wrote to the [army commanders entrusted with the] flags in the following terms: [2290]

I have appointed Khālid b. ʿUrfuṭah as my deputy. Nothing except the pain that afflicts me recurrently and the boils from which I suffer prevents me from being in his place. I am lying face down, but you can see my body. Listen to Khālid and obey him because he commands you only according to my orders and acts according to my judgment.

The message was read to the troops, and it improved their morale. They finally accepted Saʿd's opinion and urged each other to obey him, agreeing that Saʿd had an excuse [for not leading the army in battle] and becoming content with what he did.

According to al-Sarī—Shuʿayb—Sayf—Ḥallām—Masʿūd: The commander of each group addressed his companions and made [Saʿd's speech] known to them.[291] They urged each other to obey and

290. See Qurʾān 3:139, 47:35.

291. This translation of *sayyara fīhim* is tentative. Cf. *sāʾir* in the sense of "current, commonly known."

to stand firm and admonished each other [to do good]. Each commander returned to his position with the companions who were with him in the [previous] battles. Saʿd's herald called for the noon prayer and Rustam called out: "*Pādishahān-i marandar*. ʿUmar consumed my liver; may God burn his! He taught the Arabs until they gained knowledge!"[292]

According to al-Sarī—Shuʿayb—Sayf—al-Naḍr—Ibn al-Rufayl:
[2291] When Rustam halted at al-Najaf, he sent a spy to the Muslim camp. He merged with the Arabs in al-Qādisiyyah, as if he were someone who had strayed from them, and he saw them cleaning their teeth with toothpicks before each prayer.[293] Then they prayed and dispersed to their positions. The spy returned to Rustam and informed him about the Muslim way of life. Rustam asked him: "What is their food?" The spy said: "I stayed among them for one night. By God, I did not see any one of them eating anything. They merely suck twigs when they go to sleep in the evening and before they rise in the morning." When Rustam halted between the fort and al-ʿAtīq, he encountered the Muslims after the *muʾadhdhin* of Saʿd had called for the morning prayers. He saw them move and called upon the Persians to mount their horses. He was asked the reason for this, and he said to them: "Do you not see that your enemy has been given the summons and is moving against us?" His spy said: "They are moving in order to pray." He then spoke in Persian, and what follows is its Arabic translation: "In the morning I heard a voice. It was ʿUmar speaking to the dogs and teaching them reason." When they crossed [the canal], they faced the Muslims. The *muʾadhdhin* of Saʿd called for prayer, and Saʿd prayed. Rustam said: "ʿUmar has consumed my liver."

According to al-Sarī—Shuʿayb—Sayf—Muḥammad, Ṭalḥah, and Ziyād: Saʿd sent men of the best judgment, of the greatest valor, and of manifold virtues. Among the men of judgment was the group who
[2292] came to Rustam: al-Mughīrah (b. Shuʿbah), Ḥudhayfah (b. Miḥṣan), ʿĀṣim b. ʿAmr, and their companions. Among the people of valor were Ṭulayḥah (b. Khuwaylid), Qays (b. Hubayrah) al-Asadī, Ghālib

---

292. It is not clear what the meaning of *pādishahān-i marandar* is. De Goeje maintains that the text is corrupt. See his discussion of the matter in *Glossary*, s.v. *marandar*, and Houtsma's suggested emendation in *Addenda et Emendanda*, DCXVII.

293. This is a well-known *sunnah* of the Prophet. See, e.g., Ibn Ḥanbal, *Musnad*, I, 237: "I have been commanded to use the toothpick . . ." (*umirtu bi-ʾl-siwāk* . . .), and numerous other references in Wensinck *et al.*, *Concordance*, s.v. *siwāk*.

b. ʿAbdallāh al-Asadī, ʿAmr b. Maʿdīkarib, and their like. Among the poets were al-Shammākh,[294] al-Ḥuṭay'ah,[295] Aws b. al-Maghrā',[296] and ʿAbdah b. al-Ṭabīb,[297] and he also sent people like them from other groups. Saʿd addressed them before sending them out and said: "Go forth and speak to the people about your obligations and their obligations on the battlefield. You are people of great importance among the Arabs. You are their poets and orators, their men of judgment and valor, and their chieftains. Go therefore to the people, admonish them, and exhort them to fight."

They went out among the people. Qays b. Hubayrah al-Asadī said: "O people, praise God for the guidance that He has given you and for the favor that He has bestowed upon you, so that He may give you more. Remember God's favors and pray to Him at the customary times. Either Paradise or spoils wait in front of you. Beyond this castle there is nothing except desert, wasteland, rough stones, and open country that [even] guides do not cross."

Ghālib said:

> O people! Praise God for the favor that He has bestowed upon you. Ask Him and He will give you more; pray to Him and He will respond. O men of Maʿadd,[298] what excuse do you have today? You are in your fortresses (meaning the horses), and you are in possession of those that do not dis- [2293]
> obey you (meaning the swords). Remember what the people will say in the future; tomorrow you will be the first about whom people will speak, and [only] then they will speak about those who will follow you.

Ibn al-Hudhayl al-Asadī said:

> O men of Maʿadd, make your swords your fortresses. Handle your enemies like lions of the forest, be stern like tigers, and

294. On al-Shammākh, see note 105, above.

295. Jarwal b. Aws al-Ḥuṭay'ah was a famous *mukhaḍram* poet from the tribe of ʿAbs, best known for his satirical poems. See *EI*², s.v. "al-Ḥuṭay'a" (I. Goldziher [Ch. Pellat]); *GAS*, II, 236–38.

296. Aws b. Maghrā' was a *mukhaḍram* poet from the tribe of Tamīm. See Jumaḥī, *Ṭabaqāt*, 129, and index; Ibn Qutaybah, *Shiʿr*, 432; *GAS*, II, 381–82.

297. ʿAbdah b. al-Ṭabīb was a *mukhaḍram* poet from the tribe of Tamīm. See Ibn Qutaybah, *Shiʿr*, 456–57; *GAS*, II, 198–99.

298. Maʿadd is considered an ancestor of the northern Arabs; see Caskell and Strenziok, *Ǧamharat an-nasab*, index.

let dust be your armor.[299] Trust in God and lower your eyes.[300] If your swords become blunt—and this happens to them as a result of the [divine] command—throw stones at your enemies, because it is permitted to do with stones what is not permitted to do with iron.

Busr b. Abī Ruhm al-Juhanī said:

Praise God and make your words credible by means of your deeds! You have praised God for the guidance that He has given to you and have declared His oneness. There is no god except Him. You have proclaimed His greatness and believed in His Prophet and in His messengers. Do not die except as Muslims.[301] Let nothing be more worthless in your eyes than this world, because this world makes itself available to those who despise it. Do not incline toward it, lest it run away from you in order to deflect you [from the straight path]. Help God, and He will help you.

ʿĀṣim b. ʿAmr said:

O Arabs, you are Arab notables and you stood up to Persian notables. You risk Paradise, while they risk [only] this world. Let them not protect this world more assiduously than you protect the next. Do not do things today that will make you the disgrace of the Arabs tomorrow.

Rabīʿ b. al-Balād al-Saʿdī said:

O Arabs, fight for the religion and for this world. Hasten to forgiveness from your Lord and to a garden whose breadth is as the heavens and the earth, prepared for the God-fearing
[2294] ones.[302] And if the devil depicts the affair [of this war] as formidable [in order to discourage you], remember the stories that will be related about you during the fairs and festivals forever and ever.[303]

---

299. Galloping horses raise clouds of dust that are described here as protecting the Muslim warriors.

300. Lowering of the eyes is a sign of modesty; cf. Qur'ān 24:30.

301. See Qur'ān 2:132.

302. Qur'ān 3:133 (Arberry's translation, slightly modified).

303. Literally "as long as there are people who relate stories." Cf. Noth, *Studien*, 87, for a German translation of this and some of the preceding passages.

Rib'ī b. ʿĀmir said:

> God has guided you to embrace Islam, has united you by means of it, and has caused you to experience prosperity. In endurance there is repose; train yourself to endure, so that endurance becomes your habit. Do not fall into the habit of showing unrestrained grief lest this become your habit.

All of them spoke in this vein. The people entered into mutual agreements, made pledges to each other, and roused one another to do their duty. The Persians did the same among themselves: They entered into mutual agreements, enjoined each other to do good, and bound themselves with chains. The number of those who bound themselves was thirty thousand.[304]

According to al-Sarī—Shuʿayb—Sayf—Mujālid—al-Shaʿbī: The Persians numbered one hundred and twenty thousand men. They had thirty elephants. With each elephant were four thousand men.

According to al-Sarī b. Yaḥyā—Shuʿayb—Sayf—Ḥallām—Masʿūd b. Khirāsh: The battle line of the polytheists was on the bank of al-ʿAtīq, and the battle line of the Muslims was at the wall of Qudays, with the moat behind them. The Muslims and the polytheists were between the moat and al-ʿAtīq. The polytheists had thirty thousand men bound with chains and thirty fighting elephants. There were also elephants on which the leaders were standing and which did not fight. Saʿd ordered Sūrat al-Jihād[305] to be read to the troops and they were learning it.

According to al-Sarī—Shuʿayb—Sayf—Muḥammad, Ṭalḥah, and Ziyād: Saʿd said:

> Stay in your positions and do not move anything before you perform the noon prayer. When you complete the noon prayer, I shall proclaim "God is most great!" Proclaim the same and prepare yourselves. Know that none before you [2295]
> was given [the right to proclaim] "God is most great," and know that it was given to you as a sign of support for you. Then when you hear me proclaiming "God is most great"

---

304. See note 206, above.

305. There is no sūrah bearing this name in the canonical version of the Qur'ān. As de Goeje noted, (ʿI.) Ibn al-Athīr (*Kāmil*, II, 364) maintains that the intended sūrah was Qur'ān 8, "The Spoils" (*Sūrat al-anfāl*).

for the second time, proclaim the same and let your equipment be ready. When I proclaim "God is most great" for the third time, proclaim the same, and let your horsemen encourage the people to step forward and charge their adversaries. When I proclaim "God is most great" for the fourth time, all of you must move forward, mingle with the enemy, and say: "There is no power or strength except in God!"

Al-Sarī — Shuʿayb — Sayf — ʿAmr b. al-Rayyān — Muṣʿab b. Saʿd transmitted the same tradition.

According to al-Sarī—Shuʿayb—Sayf—Zakariyyāʾ—Abū Isḥāq: On the day of al-Qādisiyyah, Saʿd sent to the army a message, saying: "When you hear the cry 'God is most great,' tie the straps of your sandals. When I proclaim 'God is most great' for the second time, get ready. When I proclaim it for the third time, stick doggedly to your purpose[306] and attack."

According to al-Sarī b. Yaḥyā — Shuʿayb — Sayf — Muḥammad, Ṭalḥah, and Ziyād: When Saʿd performed the noon prayer, he ordered the young man whom ʿUmar ordered to stay with him, and who was a Qurʾān reader, to read Sūrat al-Jihād, and all the Muslims were learning it. He read Sūrat al-Jihād to the military unit that was near him. It was [then] read in every unit. The hearts and eyes of the people became cheerful, and in reading this sūrah they experienced repose (*sakīnah*).[307]

According to al-Sarī—Shuʿayb—Sayf—Muḥammad, Ṭalḥah, and Ziyād: When the Qurʾān readers finished [their reading], Saʿd proclaimed "God is most great." Those who were close to him did likewise. One after the other, the Muslims proclaimed "God is most great," and they began to move. Then Saʿd proclaimed "God is most great" for the second time, and the Muslims completed their preparations. Then he proclaimed it for the third time, and men of valor
[2296] went forth and started the battle. Men of similar qualities from among the Persians went forth and exchanged blows with the Muslims. Ghālib b. ʿAbdallāh al-Asadī went forth, reciting:

The courageous woman, coming to the garrisons,[308]

---

306. The text has *shuddū al-nawājidh ʿalā al-aḍrās*.

307. For the changes that the meaning of the Hebrew word *shekhinah* underwent in Arabic, see Goldziher, "*Sakîna.*"

308. Translating *wāridat al-masāliḥ* with Masʿūdī, *Murūj*, IV, 208 (= ed. Pellat, II, 55), instead of *wāridat al-masāʾiḥ* of our text.

with white breast and fingers, knows
That I am venom to the fighting warrior
and I bring relief to the grievous and oppressive affair.

Hurmuz, who was one of the kings of al-Bāb[309] and had a crown, went to encounter him. Ghālib took him captive and brought him into Saʿd's presence. Then he returned to the fighting. ʿĀṣim b. ʿAmr went forth, reciting:

The woman of white complexion and silvery breast,
like silver covered with gold, knows
That I am not a man helped by connections;[310]
any defect will provoke a man like me against a man like you.[311]

ʿĀṣim fought with a Persian man, who ran away from him with ʿĀṣim in pursuit. When he mingled in their battle line, he encountered a horseman with a mule. The horseman abandoned the animal and sought refuge with his companions, who gave him protection. ʿĀṣim carried off the mule with the saddle and the load. When he reached the Muslim lines, it became clear that the man was the king's baker and had with him delicacies for the king: a variety of sweet dishes (*akhbiṣah*)[312] and crystallized (*maʿqūd*) honey. ʿĀṣim brought all this to Saʿd and returned to his position. When Saʿd [2297] looked at it, he said: "Take it to the people of his position," and he said: "The amīr gave this to you, so eat it," and he gave it to them.

When the Muslims were expecting Saʿd to proclaim "God is most great" for the fourth time, Qays b. Ḥidhyam b. Jurthumah, the commander of the footmen of Banū Nahd, stood up and said: "O Banū Nahd, attack (*inhadū*), because you were called Nahd only in order that you should do it."[313] Khālid b. ʿUrfuṭah sent to him a message, saying: "Stop it, or I shall appoint someone else in your place," so Qays stopped.

---

309. See note 183, above.

310. Masʿūdī, *Murūj*, IV, 209 (= ed. Pellat, III, 55), has *nasab* "lineage," instead of *sabab*.

311. *Mithlī ʿalā mithlika yughrīhi al-ʿatab* is not well connected to the preceding material; the text is dubious and the meaning not clear. Some manuscripts of Masʿūdī, *Murūj*, ed. Pellat, III, 55, have *mithlī ʿalā mithlika yughrīhi al-katab*; both editors of Masʿūdī have preferred not to include this line in their text.

312. See Baghdādī, *Ṭabīkh*, 71–74; Rodinson, "Recherches," 148, 150.

313. The name Nahd is derived from the same triliteral root as the verb *nahada* "he attacked."

When the horses and the horsemen fought each other, a man went forth shouting: "Man to man!" (*mard o mard*).[314] ʿAmr b. Maʿdīkarib, who was opposite him, took up the challenge; he fought him, seized him by the neck, threw him down, and slew him. Then he turned to the people and said: "When a Persian loses his bow, he becomes [stupid like] a goat." Then both sides formed into fighting units.

According to al-Sarī—Shuʿayb—Sayf—Ismāʿīl b. Abī Khālid—Qays b. Abī Ḥāzim: ʿAmr b. Maʿdīkarib passed by us between the lines and roused the people, saying: "When a Persian drops his spear, he becomes [stupid like] a goat."

While he was rousing us in this manner, a Persian went forth, stood between the lines, and shot an arrow. He hit the curved part of the bow that ʿAmr was carrying on his shoulders. ʿAmr turned toward the Persian, attacked him, and seized him by the neck. Then he grabbed his belt, lifted him, and threw him down in front of him. Then he carried him farther, and when he drew near us he broke his neck. Then he put his sword on his throat and slew him, hurled his
[2298] corpse down, and said: "This is what you should do to them!" We said: "O Abū Thawr,[315] who is able to do what you are doing?" According to some transmitters [of the last tradition], except Ismāʿīl: ʿAmr b. Maʿdīkarib took from the Persian his two bracelets, his belt, and a brocaded coat[316] that he wore.

According to al-Sarī—Shuʿayb—Sayf—Ismāʿīl b. Abī Khālid—Qays b. Abī Ḥāzim: The Persians sent in the direction of the tribe of Bajīlah thirteen elephants.

According to al-Sarī—Shuʿayb—Sayf—Ismāʿīl b. Abī Khālid: The battle of al-Qādisiyyah took place at the beginning of Muḥarram of the year 14. A [Muslim] man went out to the Persians. They said to him: "Direct us!" He directed them toward Bajīlah, and they sent in the direction of Bajīlah sixteen elephants.

According to al-Sarī—Shuʿayb—Sayf—Muḥammad, Ṭalḥah, and Ziyād: When the fighting units came into formation after the [ini-

---

314. For the Sasanian custom of starting a battle by challenging the enemy to engage in individual combat, see Christensen, *Sassanides*, 216.

315. Abū Thawr was the *kunyah* of ʿAmr b. Maʿdīkarib. See *EI²*, s.v. "ʿAmr b. Maʿdīkarib" (Ch. Pellat).

316. For *dībāj* "brocade," see Dozy, *Vêtements*, 113 n. 9; Mayer, *Mamluk Costume*, 40, and index, s.v. "Brocade."

tial] attack, the elephant drivers attacked the Muslims and drove a wedge between their units. The horses panicked. Bajīlah was on the verge of being annihilated. Their horses and the horses of those who were with them in their positions fled in terror, and only the infantrymen stationed there remained. Saʿd sent a message to the tribe of Asad, saying: "Defend Bajīlah and the men who are attached to them." So Ṭulayḥah b. Khuwaylid, Ḥammāl b. Mālik, Ghālib b. ʿAbdallāh, and al-Ribbīl b. ʿAmr set out with their fighting units. They confronted the elephants so that the drivers turned them [in another direction]. Every elephant was ridden by twenty men.

According to al-Sarī — Shuʿayb — Sayf — Muḥammad b. Qays — [2299]
Mūsā b. Ṭarīf: When Saʿd called [upon the tribe of Asad] to come to the rescue [of Bajīlah], Ṭulayḥah stood up to address his people and said:

> O my tribe, the one whose name is mentioned is the trusted one! If Saʿd knew that some other tribe was more suitable than you to help Bajīlah, he would have asked for their help. Attack them first and forcefully! Attack them like ferocious lions! You were called Asad ("lion") only in order that you should act like one. Charge and do not turn back! Attack and do not run away! How excellent is [the tribe of] Rabīʿah! What a feat are they going to accomplish! And of what an adversary are they going to take care! Are their positions going to be accessible? Take care of your positions! May God help you! Attack them in the name of God.

Al-Maʿrūr b. Suwayd and Shaqīq said: By God, they fell upon the Persians, stabbed them, and hit them until we were able to keep the elephants back from Bajīlah. The elephants retreated. A Persian chieftain came out against Ṭulayḥah, but the latter fought him and killed him in no time.

According to al-Sarī—Shuʿayb—Sayf—Muḥammad, Ṭalḥah, and Ziyād: Al-Ashʿath b. Qays stood up and said: "O people of Kindah! How excellent is [the tribe of] Asad! What a feat are they going to accomplish! How quickly do they use today the sword in defense of their positions! Every tribe takes care of [defending] the area next to them, but you await someone who will save you the trouble. I bear
witness that today you have not followed well the example of your [2300]

people, the Arabs. They are being killed and are fighting, while you look on, squatting on your knees!"

But at that, ten of them jumped to him and said: "May God vitiate your fortune! You are trying hard to humiliate us, yet we are the most firm in holding our ground. And where have we let down our people, the Arabs? Where have we not lived up to their example? Here we are with you!" Al-Ashʿath b. Qays made a dash at the enemy. The men of Kindah dashed with him and drove away the Persians who were opposite them.

When the Persians saw what the elephants were suffering at the hands of the Asadī unit, they struck the Muslims with their weapons. Commanded by Dhū al-Ḥājib and al-Jālnūs, they attacked the Muslims,[317] who were expecting Saʿd to proclaim "God is most great" for the fourth time. The Persian cavalry, accompanied by the elephants, gathered against Asad. The Asadīs stood their ground. Saʿd proclaimed "God is most great" for the fourth time. The Muslims then moved [to assist] the Asadīs, around whom the fiercest battle was being fought. The elephants attacked the horses on the two wings [of the Muslim army], and the horses were recoiling and swerving aside. The Muslim horsemen insistently asked the infantrymen to urge the horses on.[318] Saʿd sent a message to ʿĀṣim b. ʿAmr, saying: "O people of Tamīm, you are owners of camels and horses: Do you not have in store a trick against these elephants?" They said: "We certainly have, by God." ʿĀṣim then summoned some archers from his tribe, as well as men skilled in the use of the sword, and said to them: "O archers, drive the elephant riders away from the Muslim horsemen with arrows!" and he went on to say, "O
[2301] swordsmen, get near the elephants from behind, and cut their girths!"[319] He himself set out to defend the Asadīs, around whom the fiercest battle was being fought. The right and left wings wheeled around not far away. ʿĀṣim's men drew near the elephants, seized

317. The Cairo edition reads *badara* (instead of *badarū*) *al-muslimīna al-shaddata ʿalayhim Dhū al-Ḥājib wa-al-Jālnūs;* in this version Dhū al-Ḥājib and al-Jālnūs would be the subjects of the sentence. The editor does not indicate the basis of this version, and it does not seem to be in any way superior to that of the Leiden edition.

318. Translating *yashmuṣūna* instead of *yashmusūna* of the text. The two roots are interchangeable. See de Goeje's *Glossary,* s.v.; and Ibn Manẓūr, *Lisān al-ʿArab,* s.v. *sh-m-s.*

319. With which the palanquin is fastened to the elephant's back.

their tails and the ornaments hanging from their litters, and cut their girths. The elephants' trumpeting was intense. On that day, no Persian elephant remained without [his back] being exposed; the elephant drivers were killed, the Muslims faced each other,[320] and the Asad were relieved. The Muslims repelled the Persians to their positions. They fought until sunset, and during a part of the night, and then both sides withdrew. Five hundred Asadīs were killed on that evening, having been the mainstay of the Muslims and ʿĀṣim having been their leader in war and their protector. This was the first day of the battle of al-Qādisiyyah, and it is called the Day of Armāth.

According to al-Sarī—Shuʿayb—Sayf—Ghusn b. al-Qāsim[321]—a man from Kinānah: The wings [of the Muslim army] wheeled around on the Day of Armāth and the tribe of Asad was engaged in the fiercest fight, so that five hundred of them were killed on that evening. ʿAmr b. Shās al-Asadī[322] recited:

We brought to Kisrā horsemen from the sides of a high mountain, [2302]
    and he confronted them with horsemen [of his own].
The horses left them in distress in al-Aqsām [2303]
    and in al-Haqwān, for days on end.
We left in Persia many a woman praying
    and weeping whenever she sees the new moon.
We killed Rustam and his sons violently,
    and the horses raised sand over them.
At the place of our encounter we left
    [dead] men[323] who have no intention of moving again.
Al-Bayruzān fled without protecting [his men];
    he brought calamity upon his troops.
Al-Hurmuzān was saved by the prudence of his soul
    and by the swift running of the horses.

---

320. *Taqābala al-nās* probably means that the tribe of Asad, which had been surrounded by the Persians, again came in contact with the other Muslims.

321. For the reading Ghuṣn b. al-Qāsim (instead of Ghuṣn *ʿan* al-Qāsim), see *Addenda et Emendanda*, DCXVII.

322. ʿAmr b. Shās is described as a prolific poet of the pre-Islamic period, who was well respected in his tribe and embraced Islam together with them. Except for his participation in the battle of al-Qādisiyyah little is known of his life. Most material included in the classical sources is of an anecdotal nature. See, e.g., al-Iṣfahānī, *Aghānī*, XI, 3982–89. The poetry of ʿAmr b. Shās, as well as the scanty biographical material included in the classical sources, has been collected in Jabūrī, *Shiʿr*. See also *GAS*, II, 228.

323. Reading *fiʾāman*, with Jabūrī, *Shiʿr*, 87, instead of *qiyāman*.

The Day of Aghwāth

According to al-Sarī — Shuʿayb — Sayf — Muḥammad and Ṭalḥah: Saʿd married in Sharāf Salmā bint Khaṣafah, who had been the wife
[2304] of al-Muthannā b. Ḥārithah. He brought her to al-Qādisiyyah. When the Muslim soldiers were wheeling around on the Day of Armāth, he could sit only in an upright, uncomfortable posture or [had to lie] on his belly. Saʿd became restless and began to wander[324] impatiently on the roof of the castle. When Salmā saw what the Persians were doing, she said: "Alas for Muthannā! The horsemen have no [one like] Muthannā today."[325] She said it in the presence of a man (i.e. Saʿd) who was distressed by the actions of his companions and by his own condition. He slapped her face and said: "How far is al-Muthannā from the unit around which the fiercest fight is going on!"[326] He meant the Asad and ʿĀṣim with his horsemen. She said: "Are you both jealous and cowardly?"[327] Saʿd said: "By God, nobody will today accept my excuse if you do not accept it while seeing my condition! The troops have a better reason [than you have] not to accept my excuse." The Muslims remembered it, and when they became victorious there was no poet who did not hold it against Saʿd. Yet he was not a coward, nor was he worthy of blame.

On the next morning, the troops were arranged in battle order. Saʿd put a group of men in charge of carrying the [corpses of the] martyrs and the wounded to al-ʿUdhayb. The wounded were turned over to the women, to be cared for until God should decide their fate. As for the martyrs, they buried them on both sides of the Musharriq valley: the one that was near al-ʿUdhayb and the one that was distant from it. (Musharriq is a valley between al-ʿUdhayb and ʿAyn Shams. Its near side extends to al-ʿUdhayb and its far side beyond it.)[328] The Muslims put off the [resumption of] fighting until the wounded and the dead were carried away.

---

324. Translating *yajūlu*, which is a variant reading mentioned by de Goeje, rather than *yaḥūlu* of the text.

325. This is taken as implied criticism of Saʿd's leadership, as compared to that of al-Muthannā, Salmā's late husband.

326. Meaning that al-Muthannā had never been in a military situation so difficult as the one in which this unit finds itself.

327. As noted by de Goeje, *a-ghayratan wa-jubnan!* became a proverb and was included in al-Maydānī, *Amthāl*, II, 415–16. It is used to describe a person flawed by two vices.

328. This geographical note by Ṭabarī appears in almost identical form in Yāqūt, *Muʿjam*, IV, 539.

When the camels rose to carry them in the direction of al-ʿUdhayb, the manes of the horses from Syria appeared. Damascus had been conquered one month before the battle of al-Qādisiyyah. When Abū ʿUbaydah received ʿUmar's letter ordering him to divert the Iraqis under Khālid (b. al-Walīd)'s command [to Iraq] without mentioning Khālid himself, he kept Khālid with him and did not let him go.[329] He then dispatched the army, which consisted of six thousand men: Five thousand were from Rabīʿah and Muḍar and one thousand from various southern tribes of Ḥijāz. Abū ʿUbaydah appointed Hāshim b. ʿUtbah b. Abī Waqqāṣ to be their commander. He placed the vanguard in charge of al-Qaʿqāʿ b. ʿAmr[330] and ordered him to hasten ahead of Hāshim, and he appointed Qays b. Hubayrah b. ʿAbd Yaghūth al-Murādī, who had not participated in the previous battles, to command one of the wings. He joined the army in Yarmūk when the Iraqis were being diverted [to Iraq] and went with them. Abū ʿUbaydah appointed al-Hazmāz b. ʿAmr al-ʿIjlī[331] to command the other wing, and Anas b. al-ʿAbbās[332] to command the rear guard. Al-Qaʿqāʿ traveled quickly, without stopping, and reached the Muslims [of al-Qādisiyyah] on the morning of the Day of Aghwāth. He had instructed his men, whose number was one thousand, to divide into groups of ten; whenever one such unit moved out of sight, they sent another in its wake. Al-Qaʿqāʿ reached the Muslims fighting at al-Qādisiyyah with a group of ten before the rest of his troops. He greeted them, announced the coming of his soldiers, and said: "O Muslims, I have come to you with men [of valor]! If they were in your place and then noticed you, they would envy you the good fortune [of martyrdom] and would attempt to take it all for themselves, leaving nothing for you.[333] So do as I do."

[2305] [2306]

329. See Donner, *Conquests*, 137. For another version of ʿUmar's letter, see Kūfī, *Futūḥ*, I, 158.

330. Al-Qaʿqāʿ b. ʿAmr belonged to the tribe of Tamīm and was a Companion of the Prophet. He participated in the battle of Yarmūk, as well as in the conquests of Damascus and al-Madāʾin. He had a reputation for extraordinary bravery and was also known for poems in which he described his military exploits. He was the brother of ʿĀṣim b. ʿAmr, another participant in the battle of al-Qādisiyyah. See (ʿI.) Ibn al-Athīr, *Usd*, IV, 207; Ibn Ḥajar, *Iṣābah*, V, 450–52 no. 7132.

331. Ibn Ḥajar, *Iṣābah*, VI, 537.

332. Anas b. al-ʿAbbās belonged to the tribe of Sulaym and embraced Islam after the conquest of Mecca. He participated in the battle of Yarmūk and in the conquest of Damascus. See Ibn Saʿd, *Ṭabaqāt*, I/ii, 49; Ibn Ḥajar, *Iṣābah*, I, 125 no. 271.

333. This should be understood in light of the extremely high value placed on martyrdom in the Islamic tradition. Al-Qaʿqāʿ says, in effect, that, if his men had been

He then stepped forward and called out: "Who is going to fight me?" [The Muslims applied to him the saying of Abū Bakr: "An army that has a man like this will not be defeated." They trusted him.] Dhū al-Ḥājib came out to fight him. Al-Qaʿqāʿ asked: "Who are you?" He said: "I am Bahman Jādhawayhi." Al-Qaʿqāʿ cried out: "Vengeance for Abū ʿUbayd,[334] Salīṭ,[335] and the warriors of the battle of the Bridge!" They fought each other, and al-Qaʿqāʿ killed his opponent. Al-Qaʿqāʿ's horsemen began to arrive group after group, and their arrival lasted until nightfall. The Muslims took heart from the arrival of [al-Qaʿqāʿ's] units, as if no calamity had befallen them on the day before, and as if their battle had started with the killing of the Ḥājibī.[336] For the same reason, the Persians became dejected. Al-Qaʿqāʿ called out again: "Who is going to fight me?" Two men came out to fight him: One of them was al-Bayruzān, and the other al-Binduwān. Al-Qaʿqāʿ was joined by al-Ḥārith b. Ẓabyān b. al-Ḥārith of the Banū Taym al-Lāt. Al-Qaʿqāʿ fought al-Bayruzān, struck him, and cut off his head, and Ibn Ẓabyān fought al-Binduwān, struck him, and cut off his head. The Muslim horsemen gradually became entangled with the Persians. Al-Qaʿqāʿ exclaimed: "O Muslims, strike them with the swords, because men are killed by the swords!"[337] The Muslims roused each other, and all of them rushed toward the Persians, fighting with their swords until the evening. On this day the Persians did not experience anything which they liked, and the Muslims slew a great number of them. On this day also, the Persians did not fight on elephants: Their palanquins had been broken on the previous day. They started repairing them in the morning, but they were not in place until the following day.

[2307] According to al-Sarī—Shuʿayb—Sayf—Mujālid—al-Shaʿbī: A woman from the tribe of al-Nakhaʿ had four sons who participated in the battle of al-Qādisiyyah. She said to her sons: "You have embraced Islam and have not exchanged it for anything else; you have

---

in the difficult military situation facing the Muslims at al-Qādisiyyah, they would have refused help from anyone, in order not to share the distinction of martyrdom; they would have preferred to keep this distinction jealously and exclusively for themselves.

334. Abū ʿUbayd b. Masʿūd was killed in the battle of the Bridge; see Ṭabarī, I, 2174 ff.; Donner, *Conquests*, 192.

335. Like Abū ʿUbayd, Salīṭ b. Qays was killed in the battle of the Bridge. See Ṭabarī, I, 2179.

336. This name refers to Dhū al-Ḥājib, who was mentioned above.

337. Meaning that the killing of men is what the swords are for.

emigrated [with the Prophet from Mecca to Medina] and no blame has been attached to you; you were not unable to stay in [your] land or forced out of it by drought. Nevertheless, you brought your aged, old mother and placed her in front of the Persians. By God, you are verily the sons of one man and one woman! I have not betrayed your father, nor have I brought disgrace upon your maternal uncle. Go forth and fight the battle from the beginning till the end!" They advanced quickly. When they moved out of her sight, she raised her hands to the sky and said: "O God, protect my sons!" Having acquitted themselves well in battle, they returned to her, with none of them injured. I saw them afterward receiving their pay, two thousand [dirhams] each. Then they came to their mother and gave her their pay;[338] she returned it to them and divided it between them in a just and satisfactory way.

According to al-Sarī—Shuʿayb—Sayf—Muḥammad, Ṭalḥah, and Ziyād: Al-Qaʿqāʿ was assisted on that day by three men from the tribe of Yarbūʿ, the clan of Riyāḥ.[339] Whenever a unit [of his horsemen] appeared, al-Qaʿqāʿ proclaimed "God is most great!" and the Muslims did the same; then he attacked and the Muslims followed suit. The Yarbūʿīs were Nuʿaym b. ʿAmr b. ʿAttāb, ʿAttāb b. Nuʿaym b. ʿAttāb b. al-Ḥārith b. ʿAmr b. Hammām, and ʿAmr b. [2308]
Shabīb b. Zinbāʿ b. al-Ḥārith b. Rabīʿah, one of the Banū Zayd.

On that day a messenger of ʿUmar arrived and brought with him four swords and four horses for distribution among those whose valor in war was the greatest. The messenger called upon Ḥammāl b. Mālik, al-Ribbīl b. ʿAmr b. Rabīʿah (both Wālibīs), Ṭulayḥah b. Khuwaylid al-Faqʿasī[340] (these three belonged to the tribe of Asad), and upon ʿĀṣim b. ʿAmr al-Tamīmī and gave them the swords; then he called upon al-Qaʿqāʿ b. ʿAmr and the Yarbūʿīs and let them ride the horses. Thus the three Yarbūʿīs received three-quarters of the horses, and the three Asadīs received three-quarters of the swords. Al-Ribbīl b. ʿAmr said concerning this:

---

338. Literally "they placed their pay in her bosom." A similar tradition is included in Kūfī, *Futūḥ*, I, 206–7, where the mother is the poetess al-Khansāʾ (for whom see *EI*², s.v. "al-Khansāʾ" [F. Gabrieli]) and her four sons are martyred in the battle. This tradition has *wa-lā faḍaḥtu ḥālatakum*, instead of Ṭabarī's *wa-lā faḍaḥtu khālakum*. See also Nuwayrī, *Nihāyah*, XIX, 215–18.

339. See Caskel and Strenziok, *Ğamharat an-nasab*, I, 68; II, 9.

340. Both Wālibah and Faqʿas were tribal subdivisions of Asad. See Caskel and Strenziok, *Ğamharat, an-nasab*, I, 50.

The people knew that we were the most deserving of them,
 when they seized the sharp, cutting swords.
On the night of Armāth, my horsemen did not cease
 defending, group after group, the multitude of tribes;
During the morning hours,[341] till nightfall—
 and they became successful till the end of days.[342]

Al-Qaʿqāʿ recited concerning the horsemen:

The pure Arab horses did not know anyone equal to us
 on the night of Aghwāth, near al-Qawādis,[343]
[2309] On the night when we went with the lances,
 which looked on the troops like a variety of birds ready to take off.

According to al-Sarī—Shuʿayb—Sayf—al-Qāsim b. Sulaym b. ʿAbd al-Raḥmān al-Saʿdī—his father: The battle began each day with individual combat.[344] When al-Qaʿqāʿ arrived, he said: "O men, follow my example!" and called out: "Who is going to fight me?" Dhū al-Ḥājib came forth against him, and al-Qaʿqāʿ killed him. Then came al-Bayruzān, and al-Qaʿqāʿ killed him as well. Then the troops came from every direction and the battle began. Al-Qaʿqāʿ's kinsmen attacked on that day in groups of ten footmen, on camels that were covered and veiled and with their horses surrounding and protecting the camels. Al-Qaʿqāʿ ordered them to attack the Persian horses between the two battle lines, simulating elephants. The Muslims did to the Persians on the Day of Aghwāth what the Persians had done to them on the Day of Armāth. These camels were not able to withstand anything, yet the Persian horses took fright and fled. The horses of the Muslims pursued them, and when the other Muslim troops saw this they followed their example. On the Day of Aghwāth, the Persians suffered from the camels more than the Muslims had suffered on the Day of Armāth from the elephants.

---

341. For grammatical considerations with regard to the expression *ladun ghudwatan*, see Ibn Manẓūr, *Lisān al-ʿArab*, s.v. *l-d-n*.

342. For *ukhrā al-layālī al-qhawābiri* in this sense, see Arazi, *Poésie arabe*, 76.

343. Cf. note 278, above.

344. The text has *muṭāradah*. The more usual term for individual combat is *mubārazah* (see Fries, *Heereswesen*, 80), but the description that follows indicates that *muṭāradah* is used here in a similar sense.

A member of the tribe of Tamīm, whose name was Sawād and who was defending his kinsmen,[345] launched an attack, courting martyrdom. He was mortally wounded[346] after he launched the attack, but martyrdom was slow in coming. He stood up against Rustam, determined to kill him, but was himself killed before he could reach him.

According to al-Sarī — Shuʿayb — Sayf — al-Ghuṣn — al-ʿAlāʾ b. Ziyād and al-Qāsim b. Sulaym—his father: A Persian warrior came forth, calling out: "Who is going to fight me?" ʿIlbāʾ b. Jaḥsh al-ʿIjlī went forth against him. ʿIlbāʾ struck the Persian with his sword and pierced his chest, but the Persian struck ʿIlbāʾ with his sword and disemboweled him. Both fell to the ground, the Persian dying immediately. As for ʿIlbāʾ, his bowels spilled out and he could not get up; he attempted to put his bowels back but was unable to do it. Then a Muslim passed by, and ʿIlbāʾ said: "O so-and-so, help me with my belly!" The Muslim put his bowels back, and ʿIlbāʾ held the slit skin of his belly together and rushed toward the Persian lines, without turning his face to the Muslims. Death befell him thirty cubits from the place where he had been struck, in the direction of the Persian lines. He recited: [2310]

I hope I shall receive reward for this from our Lord;
I was one of those who fought well.

According to al-Sarī — Shuʿayb — Sayf — al-Ghuṣn — al-ʿAlāʾ and al-Qāsim — his father: A Persian warrior went forth, calling out: "Who is going to fight me?" Al-Aʿraf b. al-Aʿlam al-ʿUqaylī went forth against him and killed him. Then another Persian came forth and al-Aʿraf killed him as well. Then Persian horsemen surrounded him and threw him down; his weapon dropped to the ground and the

345. Translating *al-ʿashīrah*, according to the Cairo edition, instead of *al-ʿasharah* of the Leiden text.

346. The text has *qutila* "he was killed," but this does not make sense in the context. The suggested translation is not supported in the classical dictionaries. It is based on an inference from the meaning of *maqtal* "a place in the body where a wound causes death."

This is another instance of an early Muslim warrior's actively seeking martyrdom. Descriptions of such attitudes abound in classical Islamic literature; the Prophet himself is reported to have expressed his desire to experience martyrdom and then to be revived in order to experience it again and again. See Bukhārī, *Ṣaḥīḥ*, II, 201 (*Kitāb al-jihād, bāb tamannī al-shahādah*).

Persians seized it. He threw dust into their faces and returned to his companions, reciting [the following verses] concerning this event:

If they take my sword—I am an experienced man,
victoriously emerging from the calamity.
Verily, I am a defender of my kinsmen,
riding after my passion, managing the affair.

[2311] According to al-Sarī—Shuʿayb—Sayf—al-Ghuṣn—al-ʿAlāʾ and al-Qāsim — his father: Al-Qaʿqāʿ launched on that day thirty attacks. Whenever one of his units appeared, he launched an attack and hit someone. He began to recite verses in the *rajaz* meter[347] and said:

I throw them into disorder by beating;
I stab, hitting the target and causing [blood] to flow.
I hope [to be rewarded] for it by a multitude of people [entering] Paradise.[348]

According to al-Sarī—Shuʿayb—Sayf—Muḥammad, Ṭalḥah, and Ziyād: Al-Qaʿqāʿ killed on the Day of Aghwāth thirty people in thirty attacks. Whenever he launched an attack, he killed a man, the last of these being Buzurjmihr al-Hamadhānī. Al-Qaʿqāʿ recited concerning this:

I dealt him a blow that made his blood spurt
and froth, like a sun ray.[349]
On the Day of Aghwāth and the night of the Persians,
I drove the Persians[350] away violently,
So that my soul and my people find abundance.[351]

---

347. For a general survey of the classical Arabic poetic meters, see EI^2, s.v. "ʿArūḍ" (G. Weil).

348. The poet entertains the hope that a great number of people from his tribe will be admitted to Paradise as a reward for his valor.

349. For *jayyāshah* in this sense, see Bevan, *Naqāʾiḍ*, 987 ll. 9–14; and *Glossary*, 322; for a description of blood spurting out of the wound and frothing, see Abū Tammām, *Ḥamāsah*, I, 329, above. See also de Goeje's *Glossary*, s.vv. *j-y-sh*, *h-d-r*.

350. For *qawm* in this sense see note 112, above.

351. The poem can be found in a different (and to my mind unsatisfactory) version in Masʿūdī, *Murūj*, IV, 212 (= ed. Pellat, III, 57). The French translation in the first edition of *Murūj* is also unacceptable.

Al-Aʿwar b. Quṭbah fought Shahrbarāz Sijistān, and they killed each other. Al-Aʿwar's brother recited concerning this:

I have not seen a day more sweet and more bitter, worse[352] and better
than the Day of Aghwāth[353], when the frontier was opened
Without a smile.[354]

According to al-Sarī—Shuʿayb—Sayf—Muḥammad, Ṭalḥah, and Ziyād—and[355] Ibn Mikhrāq—a man from Ṭayyiʾ: The horsemen fought on the Day of the Military Units (*yawm al-katāʾib*)[356] from sunrise till midday. Toward the end of the day the [rest of] the troops marched toward each other and fought tumultuously till midnight. The Night of Armāth was called "tranquillity" (*al-hadʾah*), and the Night of Aghwāth was called "blackness" (*sawād*). The first part [of the night] was also called "blackness." [2312]

On the Day of Aghwāth the Muslims were witnessing victory in al-Qādisiyyah, and they killed the Persian notables. The central part of the Persian horsemen wheeled around, but their infantrymen stood firm. If their horsemen had not launched an attack, Rustam would have been taken prisoner. When the first part of the night passed, the Muslims spent the [rest of the] night in the same way as the Persians spent the Night of Armāth.[357] The Muslims kept on proclaiming their tribal affiliations[358] throughout the evening, until they retired. When Saʿd heard this in the evening, he went to sleep. He said to one of his companions: "If the Muslims persist in proclaiming their tribal affiliations, do not wake me up, because [this

---

352. Translating *aswaʾa* according to de Goeje's conjecture.

353. The Day of Aghwāth aroused mixed feelings in the heart of the poet; it ended victoriously, but many Muslims, including his brother, had been killed in the fighting.

354. This is a pun on *thaghr*, which means both the mouth (or the front teeth) and the Muslim frontier.

355. Here begins an additional, though partial, chain of transmission.

356. This is apparently another name for the Day of Aghwāth.

357. This sentence is not very clear. It may mean that the Muslims, who were victorious on the Day of Aghwāth, spent the following night celebrating and dividing the spoils, in the same way that the Persians had spent the Night of Armāth, after they had inflicted heavy casualties on the Muslims (five hundred Asadīs had been killed then; see p. 2301, above).

358. The text is *yantamūna*. In a similar description Masʿūdī (*Murūj*, IV, 213; ed. Pellat, III, 58) has *intimāʾ al-nās ilā ābāʾihim wa-ʿashāʾirihim*. See also note 404, below.

means that] they are stronger than their enemy. If they are quiet and the Persians do not proclaim their affiliations, do not wake me, because [this means that] they are equal. If you hear the Persians proclaiming their affiliations, wake me up, because their proclamation portends evil."

They related: The battle intensified during that night.[359] Abū Miḥjan[360] was imprisoned and fettered in the palace. In the evening he went up to Saʿd and asked his forgiveness, but Saʿd repelled him and sent him back. Abū Miḥjan came to Salmā bint Khaṣafah[361] and
[2313] said: "O Salmā, O daughter of the clan of Khaṣafah! Will you do me a favor?" She said: "And what is that?" He said: "Set me free and lend me al-Balqā'.[362] By God, if He keeps me safe, I shall come back to you and put my feet back in the fetters." She said: "What have I to do with this?" Abū Miḥjan started again to drag his feet in the fetters, and recited:

It is grievous enough that the horsemen gallop with the spears,
while I am left tied up, with my fetters on.
When I stand up, the iron hurts and the doors
are closed behind me, making the voice of the caller inaudible.
In the past I was a man of much wealth, and I had brothers;
now they have left me alone, having no brother.
By God, I took an oath, which I shall not break:
If [the door] is opened, I shall not visit the wine sellers' shops.[363]

Salmā said: "I have asked God for guidance, and I am satisfied with your oath." So she set him free and said: "As for the horse however, I shall not lend it," and she returned to her house. [Nevertheless,] Abū Miḥjan led the horse out through the palace gate, which was ad-

359. The text has *sawād*, which is a name of the Night of Aghwāth; see p. 2312, above.

360. Abū Miḥjan was a *mukhaḍram* poet of the tribe of Thaqīf, best known for his addiction to wine and his wine poems. See *EI²*, s.v. "Abū Miḥdjan" (N. Rhodokanakis–Ch. Pellat); *GAL*, I, 40; S. I, 70–71; *GAS*, II, 300–2. There is an extensive account of this episode in Iṣfahānī, *Aghānī*, XXI, 7225–33. The editor of the *Aghānī* has also provided a list of additional sources in which information about Abū Miḥjan may be found. See also Kūfī, *Futūḥ*, I, 207–9.

361. See Ibn Ḥajar, *Iṣābah*, VII, 705–6 no. 11311.

362. A horse belonging to Saʿd b. Abī Waqqāṣ. See Ibn Juzayy, *Khayl*, 137–40, where the whole episode is related.

363. See Ibn Qutaybah, *Shiʿr*, 252, for a slightly different version of this poem, with full textual apparatus. See also Masʿūdī, *Murūj*, IV, 212 (= ed. Pellat, III, 58).

jacent to the moat, mounted it, and moved slowly [toward the enemy]. When he was opposite the right wing [of the Muslims], he proclaimed "God is most great!" and attacked the left wing of the Persians, swinging his lance and weapon between the two battle lines. [The transmitters of this tradition] have said that he rode the horse saddled. Saʿīd and al-Qāsim said that he rode it without a saddle. [2314]

Abū Miḥjan then returned behind the Muslim lines, moved to the left wing, proclaimed "God is most great!" and attacked the right wing of the Persians, swinging his lance and weapon between the battle lines. Then he [again] returned behind the Muslim lines, moved to the center, came out in front of the Muslims, and attacked the Persians, swinging his lance and weapon between the two lines. On that night, the Muslim felt deep anguish.[364] They admired Abū Miḥjan, although they did not recognize him and had not seen him during daytime. Some of them said: "These are the [first] companions of Hāshim (b. ʿUtbah) or Hāshim himself."[365] Observing the Muslim troops while lying on the roof of the castle, Saʿd said: "By God, if Abū Miḥjan were not in prison, I would say that this is Abū Miḥjan and the horse is al-Balqāʾ!" Some people said: "If al-Khaḍir[366] were participating in the wars, we would think that the rider of al-Balqāʾ is al-Khaḍir!" Others said: "Had it not been that angels do not participate in fighting,[367] we would think an angel was supporting us." The Muslims did not remember Abū Miḥjan, nor did they take notice of him, because he was in prison.

At midnight the Persians and the Muslims disengaged from each other and retreated. Abū Miḥjan approached [the castle], entered it at the same place where he had gone out, put down [his weapon] and [the saddle] of the horse, placed his feet in the fetters, and recited:

The tribe of Thaqīf know—and this is not boasting— [2315]
that we have the most noble swords among them.

---

364. The text here is difficult and de Goeje's vocalization *al-nāsa* does not seem to be the best one possible. I follow Nöldeke's translation, published in his review of Abel, *Abû Miḥjan*, in *WZKM*, II (1888), 81: "... die Leute hatten ... arge Beklemmung gefühlt."

365. See p. 2305 and note 137, above, Hāshim b. ʿUtbah was appointed to command the reinforcements sent to al-Qādisiyyah by Abū ʿUbaydah.

366. For the legendary figure of al-Khaḍir in the Islamic tradition, see EI^2, s.v. "al-Khaḍir" (A. J. Wensinck).

367. But see the traditions about the participation of angels in the battle of Badr in Ṭabarī, *Tafsīr*, IV, 50ff. (on Qurʾān 3:124–25).

We have the fullest armor,
and we hold our own firmly when they are not willing to stand up.
Every day we act on their behalf;
if they are [too] blind to [see it], ask a man knowledgeable about them.
On the night of Qādis they were not aware of me,
and I did not let the troops notice my departure.
If I am imprisoned, it is my affliction;
if I am released, I shall make [the enemy] taste death.

Salmā said to him: "O Abū Miḥjan, for what reason did this man imprison you?" He said: "By God, he did not imprison me because of a forbidden thing that I ate or drank. But I was drinking in the Jāhiliyyah. Because I am a poet, poetry creeps to my tongue, which sometimes sends it to my lips, and my reputation is damaged because of this; this is why he has put me in prison. I recited:

[2316] When I die, bury me at the foot of a grapevine,
so that its roots will moisten my bones after death.
And do not bury me in the desert,
for I fear that I shall not taste [the juice of] the grapevine after I die.
It will moisten my grave with the wine of al-Ḥuṣṣ,[368] because
I became its captive, after I tried to drive it away.

Salmā was angry with Saʿd on the Night of Armāth, on the Night of Tranquillity, and on the Night of Blackness. When she woke up, she came to him, made up with him, and informed him of what had passed between herself and Abū Miḥjan. Saʿd summoned him, released him, and said: "You are free to go; I shall not punish you for anything you say unless you actually do it." Abū Miḥjan said: "By God, I must never respond to my tongue's desire to describe abominable things."

The Day of ʿImās

According to al-Sarī b. Yaḥyā—Shuʿayb—Sayf—Muḥammad, Ṭalḥah, and Ziyād; and Ibn Mikhrāq—a man from Ṭayyiʾ: On the

368. Al-Ḥuṣṣ is identified as a place near Ḥimṣ. Yāqūt (*Muʿjam* II, 274) mentions that it was famous for its wine, but the only reference adduced by him is this verse of Abū Miḥjan.

morning of the third day, the Muslims and the Persians were in their positions. The area between the two armies — meaning the stony tract (*ḥarrah*) — was like a reddish watercourse (*rijlah ḥamrāʾ*).[369] The area between the two battle lines was one mile in width. Muslim casualties were two thousand wounded and dead, and the casualties of the polytheists were ten thousand wounded and dead. Saʿd said: "He who wishes will wash the martyrs, and he who wishes will bury them in their blood."[370] [2317]

The Muslims approached the fallen, took care of them, and placed them in the rear. Those who collected the bodies carried them to the graveyards and delivered the wounded to the women. Ḥājib b. Zayd was responsible for the care of the martyrs. For two days, on the Day of Aghwāth and the Day of Armāth, the women and the children were digging graves on both sides of the Musharriq valley.[371] Two thousand and five hundred of those who fought at al-Qādisiyyah and in the previous battles were buried. Ḥājib, some of the martyrs,[372] and the martyrs' kinsmen passed near the trunk of a palm tree between al-Qādisiyyah and al-ʿUdhayb, there being at that time no other palm tree between these two places. When the wounded were being carried away, they reached this tree. One of them, who was in the state of consciousness, asked to be allowed to stop under it and rest in its shade. Another wounded man, whose name was Bujayr, sheltered in its shade and recited:

O solitary palm tree between Qādis
and al-ʿUdhayb, be safe and well!

---

369. Probably because of the blood spilled in the fighting.

370. Saʿd's statement reflects the different views expressed in Islamic tradition on whether martyrs (*shuhadāʾ*) have to be ritually washed before burial. According to a tradition reported in the canonical collections, the Prophet ordered the burial of the martyrs of the battle of Uḥud "in their blood" (*idfinūhum fī dimāʾihim*); see Bukhārī, *Ṣaḥīḥ*, I, 337 last line–338, and Wensinck *et al.*, *Concordance*, s.v. *d-f-n*, for further references. The commentators explain this ruling in several ways. Some say that the martyrs' blood will diffuse scent (*yafūḥu miskan*) on the Day of Judgment (and therefore must be left unwashed). Others maintain that the angels perform the ritual washing for the martyrs (Qasṭallānī, *Irshād*, II, 441). The fact that the martyrs are not washed as are the other dead is also said to be an indication of their being alive, according to Qurʾān 3:169 (ʿAynī, *ʿUmdat al-qārī*, VIII, 154). See also ʿAbd al-Razzāq, *Muṣannaf*, III, 540–48; Sarakhsī, *Sharḥ al-siyar*, I, 232–37.

The opposite view, which favors the performance of ritual washing for the martyrs, is attributed to al-Ḥasan al-Baṣrī and Saʿīd b. al-Musayyab (Qasṭallānī, *Irshād*, II, 441, and ʿAynī, *ʿUmdat al-qārī*, VIII, 154.

371. Cf. note 328, above.

372. The wounded are also considered martyrs.

Another man, whose name was Ghaylān and who belonged to Banū Ḍabbah or to Banū Thawr, recited:

O palm tree on a sand hill, be safe and well!
You are surrounded by plants of *jummān* and *rughl*.[373]

[2318] A man from Banū Taym Allāh, called Ribʿī, recited:

O palm tree on a sand hill, oh hill of gravestones!
May the morning clouds and abundant rain provide you with water!

Al-Aʿwar b. Quṭbah recited:

O riders' palm tree, may you always be fresh and green!
May palm trees always grow around your hill!

ʿAwf b. Mālik al-Tamīmī (or al-Taymī, of Taym al-Ribāb), recited:

O palm tree on a hill near al-ʿUdhayb,
may morning clouds and rainy days provide you with ample water!

According to al-Sarī—Shuʿayb—Sayf—Muḥammad, Ṭalḥah, and Ziyād: Al-Qaʿqāʿ spent the whole night dispatching his companions to the place from where he parted from them on the previous evening. Then he said: "When the sun rises, come in groups of one hundred each. When one group of one hundred moves out of sight, let another group follow it. Should Hāshim come, then all is well; if not, you will revive the hope and determination of the Muslims."
[2319] They acted accordingly and nobody noticed it. In the morning the Muslims were in their positions, having taken care of their dead and delivered them to al-Ḥājib b. Zayd. The dead of the polytheists lay between the lines, having been neglected, since the Persians had not been attending to their dead. The place where the Persians were was determined by God as a ruse for the sake of the Muslims in order thereby to strengthen them. When the sun rose, al-Qaʿqāʿ was looking out for the horsemen. When their manes appeared, he proclaimed "God is most great!" and the Muslims followed suit and said: "Reinforcements have arrived!" ʿĀṣim b. ʿAmr was ordered to

373. See Aṣmaʿī, *Nabāt*, 63; Ibn Manẓūr, *Lisān al-ʿArab*, s.v. *r-qh-l*. I have not found references to *jummān*.

do the same [and to proclaim "God is most great!"]. Al-Qaʿqāʿ's men came from the direction of Khaffān.[374] The horsemen advanced; the fighting units went into formation and engaged in battle. The reinforcements were coming one after the other. The last of al-Qaʿqāʿ's men were closely followed by Hāshim (b. ʿUtbah) with seven hundred men. The Muslims informed him of al-Qaʿqāʿ's tactics[375] and described to him what al-Qaʿqāʿ had done in the past two days. Hāshim therefore arranged his men in groups of seventy, and as soon as the last of al-Qaʿqāʿ's men had arrived he went forth with seventy men, among whom was Qays b. Hubayrah b. ʿAbd Yaghūth, who had not participated in previous battles. He came to al-Yarmūk from the Yemen, responded to Hāshim's call [and joined his troops]. Hāshim drew near. When he mingled with the center of the army, he proclaimed "God is most great!" The Muslims followed suit, having taken up their positions. Hāshim said: "The beginning of the battle is individual combat, and then the shooting of arrows." He took his bow, put an arrow on the middle of the string, and pulled it, but [at the same time] his mare raised her head and the arrow pierced her ear. Hāshim said, laughing: "What a bad shot from a man who is being watched by everyone who sees him! What do you think, where would my arrow have reached?" They said: "[It would have reached] al-ʿAtīq!" Having dislodged the arrow, Hāshim spurred his mare on. Then he hit her until she reached al-ʿAtīq, and [2320]
he hit her again until she rushed with him and broke through the Persian lines.[376] Hāshim then returned to his position, while the groups of horsemen continued to arrive and join the first ones.

The polytheists spent the night repairing the litters of their elephants and putting them back in place. By morning they were in their positions. The elephants moved forward, accompanied by infantrymen, who protected them against the possibility of their girths' being cut again.[377] The infantrymen were, in turn, accompanied by horsemen, who protected them. When the Persians

374. A village in the vicinity of al-Kūfah. See Yāqūt, *Muʿjam*, II, 456.

375. For a suggestion that *ra'y* be interpreted in this way, see Fries, *Heereswesen*, 64.

376. *Takhruquhum* is to be understood in light of the expression *kharaqa ṣaffahum*; see Balādhurī, *Futūḥ*, 258.

377. Cf. p. 2301, above.

wanted to attack a military unit, they moved toward it with an elephant and its escort in order to scare the horses of the Muslims. But they did not succeed in doing this as they had done on the previous day, because the elephant is more ferocious when he is alone and there is no one with him; when he is accompanied, he is more gentle.

The battle went on in this manner till the end of daylight. The battle on the Day of ʿImās was heavy throughout the day, the Arabs and the Persians being equal. When the smallest thing occurred between them, the Persians would shout the information to each other until it reached Yazdagird,[378] and he would send to them the reinforcements that he still had so that the Persians were strengthened by them. He had reinforcements at the postal stations, keeping them [for such an eventuality as] he had faced on the previous day. If God had not favored the Muslims by inspiring al-Qaʿqāʿ in the two days of battle, and if He had not made things easier for them by the arrival of Hāshim, the Muslims would have been routed.

According to al-Sarī — Shuʿayb — Sayf — Mujālid — al-Shaʿbī:
[2321] Hāshim b. ʿUtbah came from the direction of Syria with seven hundred men after the victories at al-Yarmūk and at Damascus, accompanied by Qays b. Makshūḥ al-Murādī. He hastened with seventy men, among who was Saʿīd b. Nimrān al-Hamdānī.

According to Mujālid: Qays b. Abī Ḥāzim was in Hāshim's vanguard with al-Qaʿqāʿ.

According to al-Sarī — Shuʿayb — Sayf — Jakhdab b. Jarʿab — ʿIṣmah al-Wābilī, who took part in the battle of al-Qādisiyyah: Hāshim came from Syria with the Iraqis. He hastened forward with men, almost all of whom were from Iraq, except for very few. Ibn Makshūḥ was among these. When he drew near [al-Qādisiyyah], he hastened forward with three hundred men and reached the Muslims when they were in their positions. His men joined the Muslim battle lines.

According to al-Sarī—Shuʿayb—Sayf—Mujālid—al-Shaʿbī: The third day [of the battle of al-Qādisiyyah] was the Day of ʿImās. Among the battle days of al-Qādisiyyah there was none like this, and the two armies emerged from it equal. Everybody endured his suffering patiently; whatever the Muslims inflicted upon the infidels, the infidels inflicted upon the Muslims, and whatever the in-

378. Cf. p. 2287, above.

fidels inflicted upon the Muslims, the Muslims inflicted upon the infidels.

According to al-Sarī—Shuʿayb—Sayf—ʿAmr b. al-Rayyān—Ismāʿīl b. Muḥammad b. Saʿd: Hāshim b. ʿUtbah reached al-Qādisiyyah on the Day of ʿImās. He always fought on a mare and never on a male horse. When he stood among the Muslims, he shot an arrow, which hit the ear of his own mare, and said: "What a bad shot it is! What do you think, where would my arrow have reached if it had not hit the horse's ear?" They said: "Such-and-such a place!" He wheeled around, dismounted, left his horse, and went forth hitting the Persians until he reached the place that they mentioned. According to al-Sarī—Shuʿayb—Sayf—Muḥammad, Ṭalḥah, and Ziyād: Hāshim was in the right wing. [2322]

According to al-Sarī—Shuʿayb—Sayf—ʿAmr b. al-Rayyān—Ismāʿīl b. Muḥammad: We saw that Hāshim b. ʿUtbah was in charge of the right wing. Most of the Muslims were shielded only with saddle cloths across which they fastened leafless palm branches; those who did not have any protection bound their heads with girths.

According to al-Sarī—Shuʿayb—Sayf—Abu Kibrān—al-Ḥasan b. ʿUqbah: Qays b. al-Makshūḥ said upon his arrival from Syria with Hāshim, standing among those who were next to him:

> O Arabs! God has favored you with Islam and has honored you with Muḥammad; may God pray for him and grant him peace! By the grace of God you have become brethren. Your call is one and you are united. [All this happened] after you had been attacking each other like lions and violently abducting each other like wolves. Help God, so that He may help you! Ask God to grant you victory over the Persians, because He has already fulfilled His promise to give your brethren victory over Syria and to wrest [from their enemies] the excellent castles and palaces [there].

According to al-Sarī—Shuʿayb—Sayf—al-Miqdām al-Ḥārithī—al-Shaʿbī: ʿAmr b. Maʿdīkarib said:

> I am about to attack the elephant and those who are around it [meaning the elephant in front of the Muslims]. Do not leave me alone longer than is necessary to slaughter a camel,

> for should you be late, you will lose Abū Thawr,[379] and where
> [2323] are you going to find for yourselves again someone like Abū Thawr? When you reach me, you will find me with a sword in my hand.

He launched an attack, started fighting them without delay, and was kept out of sight by the dust. His companions said: "What are you waiting for? You are not likely to reach him in time, and, if you lose him, the Muslims will have lost their [choice] horseman." They launched an attack, following which the polytheists let ʿAmr b. Maʿdīkarib loose after they had thrown him down and stabbed him. He was fighting them, holding the sword in his hand, his horse having been stabbed. When he saw his companions and the Persians disengaged themselves from him, he seized the leg of a Persian soldier's horse. The rider spurred him on, but the horse was agitated [and did not move]. The Persian turned toward ʿAmr and intended to kill him. When the Muslims saw this, they struck him. The Persian dismounted from his horse and hastened to join[380] his companions. ʿAmr said: "Let me have his reins," and they gave the reins to him and he mounted the horse.

According to al-Sarī—Shuʿayb—Sayf—ʿAbdallāh b. al-Mughīrah al-ʿAbdī—al-Aswad b. Qays—their elders who participated in the battle of al-Qādisiyyah: On the Day of ʿImās, a Persian went forth, stood between the battle lines, and called out in a sonorous voice: "Who is going to fight me?" A man from among us, whose name was Shabr b. ʿAlqamah, and who was short, slender, and ugly, said: "Oh Muslims! This man has dealt with you fairly, but nobody has responded to him and nobody has gone forth to fight him." Then he said: "By God, if it were not that you would treat me with contempt, I would go forth to fight him." When he saw that no one was preventing him from taking his sword and his shield,[381] he went forward. When the Persian saw Shabr, he roared, dismounted near him,
[2324] bore him down, and then sat on his chest and grasped his sword in order to slay him. The halter of the Persian's horse was tied to his

---

379. This was the *kunyah* of ʿAmr b. Maʿdīkarib.

380. I am translating *ḥāḍara* according to the gloss in note *h* to this page in the Leiden edition.

381. *Ḥajafah* is a shield made of camel skins sewed one over another. See Lane, *Lexicon*, s.v.

belt, and when the Persian drew his sword, the horse swerved so that the halter pulled him and overturned him. While the Persian was being dragged, Shabr trampled upon him. Shabr's companions shouted at him. Shabr said: "Shout as much as you like, but by God I shall not leave him until I kill him and plunder his possessions." Then Shabr slew the Persian, took his possessions, and brought the corpse to Saʿd, who said: "Come to me at the time of the noon prayer." Shabr brought the spoils to Saʿd, who praised God, glorified Him, and said: "I see fit to give him the spoils; whoever actually takes spoils, they are his." Shabr sold [the spoils] for twelve thousand [dirhams].

According to al-Sarī—Shuʿayb—Sayf—Muḥammad, Ṭalḥah, and Ziyād: When Saʿd saw the elephants' driving a wedge between the Muslim units and doing again what they had done on the Day of Armāth, he sent for Ḍakhm, Muslim, Rāfiʿ, ʿAshannaq, and their Persian companions who had embraced Islam. When they came to him, he asked them whether the elephants have vital organs where a wound would cause death (*maqātil*). They said: "Yes, the trunks and the eyes; when these are gone, the elephants are of no use." Saʿd sent a message to al-Qaʿqāʿ and ʿĀṣim, the two sons of ʿAmr, saying: "Take care of the white elephant for me." All the elephants were following[382] the white one, which was stationed opposite al-Qaʿqāʿ and ʿĀṣim. Saʿd sent a message to Ḥammāl (b. Mālik) and to al-Ribbīl (b. ʿAmr), saying: "Take care of the scabby elephant for me." All the elephants were following the scabby one, which was opposite Ḥammāl and al-Ribbīl. Al-Qaʿqāʿ and ʿĀṣim took two solid but flexible spears, moved forward with the horsemen and footmen, and said: "Surround the elephant in order to confuse him." Meanwhile, al-Qaʿqāʿ and ʿĀṣim were intermingling with the Persians, and [2325] Ḥammāl and al-Ribbīl did the same. When they came close to the elephants and surrounded them, each elephant looked right and left, preparing to hit the ground with his feet, and while the elephant was distracted by those around him al-Qaʿqāʿ and ʿĀṣim launched an attack and simultaneously pierced the eyes of the white elephant with their spears. The elephant roared, shook his head, threw off his rider, and let his trunk hang down. Al-Qaʿqāʿ struck him and threw

382. This translation takes into account the version of Ibn Ḥubaysh, mentioned in note *l* to this page in the Leiden edition: *al-fiyalah tatbaʿuhu*.

him down. The elephant fell on his side, and the Muslims killed those who were riding him.

Ḥammāl launched an attack, saying to al-Ribbīl: "You have the choice: either strike his trunk and I shall pierce his eye, or you will pierce his eye and I shall strike his trunk." Al-Ribbīl chose to strike the trunk, and while the elephant was distracted by those who surrounded him, Ḥammāl attacked him, his rider fearing only for the girth.[383] These [two Muslims] dealt with the elephant alone. [Ḥammāl] pierced his eye; the elephant sat down on his hindquarters and then stood up. Al-Ribbīl struck him and severed his trunk. The elephant rider noticed al-Ribbīl, however, and slit his nose and forehead with an axe.

According to al-Sarī—Shuʿayb—Sayf—Mujālid—al-Shaʿbī: Two men belonging to the Banū Asad, whose names were al-Ribbīl and Ḥammāl, said: "O Muslims, which is the most painful death?" They replied, "To attack this elephant!" Hence al-Ribbīl and Ḥammāl urged their horses on. When the horses rose on their feet, they made them dash at the elephant opposite them. One of them pierced the elephant's eye, so that it trampled upon those who were behind it. The other struck the elephant's trunk, but the elephant's rider dealt him a crippling blow in his face with an axe. Both he and Ribbīl
[2326] escaped. Al-Qaʿqāʿ and his brother attacked the elephant opposite them, putting out its eyes and cutting its trunk. The elephant wandered, bewildered, between the two battle lines. When he came to the Muslim line, they stabbed him, and when he came to the polytheists' line, they goaded him and drove him away.

According to al-Sarī — Shuʿayb — Sayf — ʿAmr — al-Shaʿbī: Among the elephants there were two who were leading the rest. On the Day of al-Qādisiyyah, the Persians sent them to attack at the center of their army. Saʿd ordered al-Qaʿqāʿ and ʿĀṣim from the tribe of Tamīm and Ḥammāl and al-Ribbīl from the tribe of Asad to deal with the two elephants. [This tradition is identical with the previous one, except that it says:] He [survived and] lived afterward.[384] The two elephants screamed like pigs. Then the scabby one, who had been blinded, turned around and jumped into al-ʿAtīq. The other el-

383. Probably because of the Muslim tactics employed on the previous days; cf. p. 2301, above.

384. This seems to refer to the fact that al-Ribbīl survived the injuries that he had sustained while attacking the elephant.

ephants followed him, broke through the Persian lines, and crossed al-ʿAtīq in his wake. They reached al-Madāʾin with their litters, but those who were in the litters perished.

According to al-Sarī—Shuʿayb—Sayf—Muḥammad, Ṭalḥah, and Ziyād: When the elephants departed and the Muslims remained alone with the Persians and the day drew to its end, the Muslims marched forward, protected by the horsemen who had fought earlier in the day. They fought with the swords, with determination and fury, until the evening.[385] [In this fight] the two armies were equal. When the Muslims did what they did to the elephants, the units of the armored camels went into formation, hamstrung the elephants, and repelled them. Concerning this, al-Qaʿqāʿ b. ʿAmr recited:

Maḍraḥī b. Yaʿmar roused my tribe;
how excellent is my tribe when they brandish the spears!
He did not refrain from using them on the day when our troops
protected the clients of the people of Qudays.
When I fought the enemy, I routed him, [2327]
and I encountered great calamities in war:
[I encountered] elephants resembling houses charging forward,
and I put out their eyes!

According to al-Sarī—Shuʿayb—Sayf—Muḥammad, Ṭalḥah, and Ziyād: When the Muslims reached the end of the day and entered upon the night, the fighting intensified. Both sides endured and emerged equal, with battle cries being heard on both sides. The night was called the Night of Howling (*laylat al-harīr*). After it, there was no night battle in al-Qādisiyyah.

Abū Jaʿfar (al-Ṭabarī) has said: According to al-Sarī—Shuʿayb—Sayf—ʿAmr b. Muḥammad b. Qays—ʿAbd al-Raḥmān b. Jaysh: On the Night of the Howling, Saʿd sent Ṭulayḥah and ʿAmr (b. Maʿdīkarib) to a crossing [of al-ʿAtīq?] downstream from the camp. He wanted them to stay at the crossing for fear lest the Persians come [and attack him] from there and said to them: "If you find that the Persians have arrived at the crossing ahead of you, stay in front of them. If you find that they do not know about it, stay there until you receive my orders."

385. De Goeje's text reads *fa-ijtaladū bihā ḥattā amsaw ʿalā hardin bi-al-suyūfi*; *bi-al-suyūfi* is in apposition to *bihā* and has been omitted from the Cairo edition.

ʿUmar had instructed Saʿd not to put the [former] leaders of the apostates (*ahl al-riddah*) in charge of a hundred men,[386] but when they arrived at the crossing and did not see anybody at it, Ṭulayḥah said: "If only we could cross here [to attack] the Persians from behind!" but ʿAmr said: "Nay, we should cross farther downstream." Ṭulayḥah said: "What I suggest is more beneficial to the Muslims," but ʿAmr said: "You are asking me to do what I cannot do." So they parted company. Ṭulayḥah went alone in the direction of the [Persian] camp across al-ʿAtīq, and ʿAmr went downstream with the companions of both. They then attacked, and the Persians rushed against them.

[2328] Saʿd was apprehensive of what had happened between Ṭulayḥah and ʿAmr and sent after them Qays b. al-Makshūḥ with seventy men. Qays was one of the [former] leaders [of the apostates], and Saʿd was forbidden to put him in command of one hundred men. Saʿd said: "If you catch up with them, you are in command." So Qays went after them. When he arrived at the crossing, he found the Persians repelling ʿAmr and his companions, so the Muslims [who came with Qays] drove [the Persians away] from him. Qays however approached ʿAmr and rebuked him, and they reviled each other. The companions of Qays said to ʿAmr: "Qays has been made commander over you." ʿAmr fell silent, then said: "Is a man whom I fought in the Jāhiliyyah for a lifetime assuming command over me?"[387] and he returned to camp.

Ṭulayḥah moved forward, and when he was opposite the dam,[388] he proclaimed three times "God is most great!" and then he went away. The Persians went in pursuit but did not know which way he had taken. He went downstream, crossed [al-ʿAtīq], came to Saʿd, and reported to him. All this pressed hard on the polytheists. The Muslims were glad but did not know what had happened.

According to al-Sarī—Shuʿayb—Sayf—Qudāmah al-Kāhilī—the person who informed him: [There were] ten brothers from Banū Kāhil b. Asad, called the sons of Ḥarb. On that night one of them began to compose *rajaz* poems and said:

I am the son of Ḥarb, and my sword is with me,
    I shall hit them with a sharp, glittering sword.

386. See note 77, above.
387. See pp. 2259–60, above.
388. See p. 2285, above.

When Abū Isḥāq disliked death,[389]
    and the soul heaved, on the point of dying;[390]
Endure, ʿIfāq, because this is the passing away!

ʿIfāq was one of the ten brothers. The hip of the author of the poem was hurt on that day, and he recited: [2329]

Endure, ʿIfāq: these are the Persians horsemen;
    endure, and do not let a lost leg distract your attention![391]

He died of his wounds on the same day.

According to al-Sarī—Shuʿayb—Sayf—al-Naḍr—Ibn al-Rufayl—his father—Ḥumayd b. Abī Shajjār: Saʿd sent Ṭulayḥah on an errand, but he neglected it, crossed al-ʿAtīq, and went to the Persian camp. When he stood at the barrier in the canal,[392] he proclaimed "God is most great!" three times. He frightened the Persians, and the Muslims were amazed. The two armies disengaged from each other to investigate the matter; the Persians sent [someone] to do it, and the Muslims asked about it. Then [the Persians] returned and restored their battle order, starting to do things which they had not done during the three days of battle. The Muslims were also arrayed in their battle order. Ṭulayḥah started saying [to the Persians]: "May you never lack the man who [resolved] to destroy you!"[393]

---

389. Translating *idh kariha al-mawta* with the Cairo edition, rather than *adhkarahu al-mawta* of the Leiden text. This superior reading can also be found in Ibn Durayd, *Ishtiqāq*, 248. Ibn Durayd also says that the *kunyah* Abū Isḥāq refers to Saʿd b. Abī Waqqāṣ, who did not take an active part in the battle on account of his illness.

390. Literally "the soul heaved (and reached the clavicles)"; cf. Qur'ān 75:26, where "when [the soul] reached the clavicles" (*idhā balaqhat [al-nafs] al-tarāqī*) is taken to be a sign of imminent death. See Ṭabarī, *Tafsīr*, XIX, 121.

391. The poet seems to be asking his brother not to be distracted from the fighting by the desire to take care of his wound.

A very similar verse is attributed to Hayyāsh b. Qays al-Aʿwar b. Qushayr, who became famous for his reported bravery at the battle of Yarmūk. The verse reads;

aqdim khidāmu innahā al-asāwirah
    wa-lā taqhurrannaka sāqun nādirah.

Khidhām is the name of a horse; Hayyāsh is reported to have lost a leg without being aware of it. See Elad; "'And he who seeks his leg . . ." the verse is quoted on p. 244. See also Jawālīqī, *Muʿarrab*, 69; and Ibn Durayd, *Jamharat al-lughah*, II, 215.

392. See p. 2285, above.

393. By this expression Ṭulayḥah means himself.

Masʿūd b. Mālik al-Asadī, ʿĀṣim b. ʿAmr al-Tamīmī, Ibn Dhī al-Burdayn al-Hilālī, Ibn Dhī al-Sahmayn, Qays b. Hubayrah al-Asadī, and people like them went forth, fought the Persians, and hastened into battle. The Persians stood together, did not charge, and wanted to move only in formation. They sent forward a line with two "ears,"[394] followed by another and a third and a fourth, until their
[2330] lines numbered thirteen in the center and in the two wings. When the horsemen of the [Arab] army moved against the Persians, they shot at them, but this did not change the course in which they were riding. Then the [Persian] units caught up with the [Muslim] horsemen. Khalīd b. Yaʿmar al-Tamīmī al-ʿUmarī was killed on that night. Al-Qaʿqāʿ launched an attack advancing in the direction from which Khālid had been shot. The Muslims were in distress. Then al-Qaʿqāʿ recited:

O Khawṣāʾ, may God water the grave of Ibn Yaʿmar!
When those who were leaving departed, he did not depart.[395]
May God water the land where Khālid's grave is situated,
with rain pouring from thunderous morning clouds!
I took an oath that my sword will not stop slaying them,
and [even] if men withdraw, I shall not do the same.

With the Muslims under their flags, al-Qaʿqāʿ moved against the Persians, without Saʿd's permission. Saʿd said: "O God, forgive him and grant him victory! I have given him permission, though he did not ask for it."[396] The Muslims were in their positions, except those who were forming military units or were fighting the Persians. They were arrayed in three lines. The infantrymen, armed with spears and swords, constituted one line; the second line was made of the archers; and the third one of the horsemen who stood in front of the infantrymen. The right wing and the left wing were arrayed in the same way. Saʿd said: "By God, the thing to do is what al-Qaʿqāʿ did. When I proclaim 'God is most great!' three times, move forward." When he proclaimed "God is most great!" [for the first time], the Muslims prepared themselves, all of them being in agreement with Saʿd. The fiercest battle was raging around al-Qaʿqāʿ and around those who were with him.

---

394. *Lahu udhunāni*; see Fries, *Heereswesen*, 72 n. 5.
395. The verse praises Ibn Yaʿmar's perserverance on the battlefield.
396. See p. 2332, below.

According to al-Sarī — Shuʿayb — Sayf — ʿUbaydallāh b. ʿAbd al-Aʿlā — ʿAmr b. Murrah: Qays b. Hubayrah, who had not participated in any of the battles of al-Qādisiyyah except on this night, stood up among his followers and said: "Your enemy does not want anything except a battle. The sound tactic is that of your commander; it is not good that horsemen attack without being accompanied by infantry. If men move forward and are attacked by a mounted enemy who have [2331] no infantry with them, they will kill their horses, and the horsemen will then not be able to advance against them. Prepare yourselves, therefore, for the attack."[397] They prepared themselves, waiting for the proclamation "God is most great!" and for the attack of the Muslims,[398] while the arrows of the Persians were flying across the Muslim lines.

According to al-Sarī — Shuʿayb — Sayf — al-Mustanīr b. Yazīd — a man who transmitted the tradition to him: Durayd b. Kaʿb al-Nakhaʿī,[399] who held the standard of the tribe of al-Nakhaʿ, said: "The Muslims have prepared themselves for battle. Tonight be the first among the Muslims to reach God and to [engage in] holy war (*al-jihād*), because whoever is first tonight will receive his reward accordingly. Compete with the [other] Muslims for martyrdom and accept death cheerfully. This will more effectively save you from death, if you wish to live; and if not, then it is the hereafter which you wish to attain."

According to al-Sarī — Shuʿayb — Sayf — al-Ajlaḥ: Al-Ashʿath b. Qays said: "O Arabs, it is not fitting that these Persians should be more courageous in the face of death and more generous in giving up this world [than you are]. Compete with each other [in risking] your children and wives. Do not fear being killed, because being killed is the aspiration of the noble and the destiny of the martyrs." Then he dismounted.

According to al-Sarī — Shuʿayb — Sayf — ʿAmr b. Muḥammad: Ḥanẓalah b. al-Rabīʿ and the commanders of the military units (*al-aʿshār*) said: "Dismount, O Muslims, and do as we do. Do not fear the inevitable, for standing firm is safer than taking fright." Ṭulayḥah, Ghālib, Ḥammāl, and the brave men from all the tribes did the same.

397. "But do not attack yet"; see below.

398. Literally "and for the time that coincides (*muwāfaqah*) with the attack of the Muslims (*al-nās*)."

399. *See Ibn Saʿd, Ṭabaqāt*, V, 388; Ibn Ḥajar, *Iṣābah*, II, 387 no. 2397.

[2332] According to al-Sarī—Shuʿayb—Sayf—ʿAmr and al-Naḍr b. al-Sarī: Ḍirār b. al-Khaṭṭāb al-Qurashī[400] dismounted and all the (Muslim) troops hastily followed each other toward the Persians between Saʿd's proclamations "God is most great!" [They did this because] they thought that he was acting too slowly. When Saʿd proclaimed "God is most great!" for the second time, ʿĀṣim b. ʿAmr launched an attack and joined al-Qaʿqāʿ and the tribe of al-Nakhaʿ also launched an attack. All troops except the commanders disobeyed Saʿd and did not wait for his third proclamation, "God is most great!" However, when he proclaimed "God is most great!" for the third time, they moved forward, joined their companions, mingled with the Persians, and faced the night after performing the evening prayer.

According to al-Sarī—Shuʿayb—Sayf—al-Walīd b. ʿAbd Allāh b. Abī Ṭaybah—his father: On the Night of the Howling, all the Muslims attacked, without waiting with the attack for Saʿd['s instructions]. The first man to launch an attack was al-Qaʿqāʿ. Saʿd said: "O God, forgive him and grant him victory!"[401] Then he kept exclaiming: "O for Tamīm!" for the rest of the night. Then he said: "I see the situation. This is what it requires: When I proclaim "God is most great!" three times, launch the attack!" He proclaimed "God is most great!" once, and the tribe of Asad joined the attack. It was said [to Saʿd]: "Asad has launched an attack." Saʿd said: "O God, forgive them and grant them victory! O for Asad!" [and he kept on saying this] for the rest of the night. Then it was said: "The tribe of al-Nakhaʿ has launched an attack." Saʿd said: "O God, forgive them and grant them victory! O for Nakhaʿ!" [and he kept on saying this] for the rest of the night. Then it was said: "The tribe of Bajīlah has launched an attack." Saʿd said: "O God, forgive them and grant them victory! O for Bajīlah!" Then the Kindīs launched an attack. It was said: "Kindah has launched an attack." Saʿd said: "O for Kindah!" Then the commanders moved forward with those who were waiting for the [third] proclamation, "God is most great!"

---

400. Ḍirār b. al-Khaṭṭāb belonged to the tribe of Quraysh and was a poet of repute. He fought against the Muslims in the battles of Uḥud and the Ditch. He is reported to have boasted that he killed ten Companions of the Prophet and caused them "to wed the virgins of paradise" (*al-ḥūr al-ʿīn*). Ḍirār embraced Islam after the conquest of Mecca. See (ʿI.) Ibn al-Athīr, *Usd*, III, 40; Ibn Ḥajar, *Iṣābah*, III, 483–85 no. 4177.

401. Cf. p. 2330, ll. 8–9.

They fought vehemently until the morning; this was the Night of Howling.

According to al-Sarī — Shuʿayb — Sayf — Muḥammad b. Nuwayrah—his uncle Anas b. al-Ḥulays: I participated in [the battle of] the Night of the Howling. On that night the sound of the steel [swords hitting each other] was like the sound produced by locksmiths, and it went on until the morning. The Muslims were inspired with abundant endurance.[402] Saʿd spent a night the like of which he had never spent before, and the Arabs and the Persians saw things the like of which they had not seen before. The sounds of voices and information [about the events] had not reached Rustam and Saʿd,[403] and Saʿd began to pray, until at sunrise the Muslims proclaimed their tribal affiliation;[404] Saʿd inferred from this that they had the upper hand and that victory was theirs. [2333]

According to al-Sarī — Shuʿayb — Sayf — ʿAmr b. Muḥammad — al-Aʿwar b. Bayān al-Minqarī: The first thing that Saʿd heard on that night, the thing that was an indication that victory would be theirs in the second, remaining part of the night, was the voice of al-Qaʿqāʿ b. ʿAmr, who recited:

We have killed a crowd or more,
four, five, and one.
Above the horses' manes we are considered venomous snakes;
when they died, I prayed fervently.
God is my Lord, and I purposely guard myself from sin.[405]

According to al-Sarī—Shuʿayb—Sayf—ʿAmr—al-Aʿwar and Muḥammad — his uncle and al-Naḍr — Ibn al-Rufayl: They fought on that night from its beginning till sunrise. They did not speak: their speech was howling, and the night was therefore called the Night of Howling. [2334]

402. For the expression *afragha ʿalayhim al-ṣabra*, see Qurʾān 2:250, 7:126.

403. This seems to mean that the methods of transmitting information devised by the Persians and the Arabs broke down because of the fierce battle. See p. 2287, above.

404. It is difficult to decide what is the best version. The Leiden edition reads *ibtahā* in the sense of *iftakhara* "he boasted." In comparing this passage with p. 2312 ll. 9–13, it seems preferable to read *intamā* "he proclaimed his tribal affiliation," following (ʿI.) Ibn al-Athīr, *Kāmil*, II, 373 l. 7; this version is noted in the critical apparatus of the Leiden edition. For another example of this usage of *intamā*, see Ṭabarī, I, 2193 l. 5, and note 358, above.

405. This verse does not seem to be very coherent.

According to al-Sarī—Shuʿayb—Sayf—ʿAmr b. al-Rayyān—Muṣʿab b. Saʿd: On that night, Saʿd sent to the [battle] line Bijād, a boy, because he could not find another messenger and said: "See what their situation is." When Bijād returned, Saʿd asked him: "What have you seen, son?" and he replied, "I have seen them playing." Saʿd said: "Or, rather, exerting themselves."

According to al-Sarī — Shuʿayb — Sayf — Muḥammad b. Jarīr al-ʿAbdī — ʿĀbis al-Juʿfī — his father: A fully armed Persian unit (*katībah*) was in front of [the tribe of] al-Juʿfī on the Day of ʿImās. They moved toward the Persians and fought them with the swords, but they saw that the swords had no effect on the [Persian armor made of] iron, and they retreated. Ḥumayḍa said: "What is the matter with you?" and they replied, "The weapons do not penetrate into them." Ḥumayḍa said: "Stay where you are till I show you; look!" and he attacked a Persian and broke his back with a spear. Then he turned to his companions and said: "I am confident that they will die and you will survive." So then they attacked the Persians and drove them back to their lines.

[2335] According to al-Sarī — Shuʿayb — Sayf — Mujālid — al-Shaʿbī: Only seven hundred men from the tribe of Kindah proper participated in this battle, and Turk al-Ṭabarī was opposite them. Al-Ashʿath said: "O men, march against them!" and he marched against them with seven hundred men, drove them away, and killed Turk. Their *rajaz* poet (i.e., the poet of Kindah) said:

"We have left their Turk in the field,
dyed with the splendor of the vein."[406]

The Night of al-Qādisiyyah

According to al-Sarī — Shuʿayb — Sayf — Ṭalḥah and Ziyād: In the morning that followed the Night of al-Qādisiyyah [which is (also) the morning of the Night of Howling; of these battle days, this was the night called the Night of al-Qādisiyyah], the Muslims were exhausted, for they did not close their eyes throughout the night. Al-Qaʿqāʿ walked among the men, saying: "He who resumes the fight against the Persians will defeat them in an hour. Endure for [another]

406. That is to say, blood.

hour and launch the attack, because victory comes with endurance. Prefer endurance to fear." A group of commanders gathered around him and stood up against Rustam, until they became entangled at sunrise with the Persians who were protecting him. When the tribes saw this, some of their men rose [to speak]. Qays b. ʿAbd Yaghūth, al-Ashʿath b. Qays, ʿAmr b. Maʿdīkarib, Ibn Dhī al-Sahmayn al-Khathʿamī, and Ibn Dhī al-Burdayn al-Hilāli—all stood up and said: "Let not these men be more earnest than you in complying with God's orders, and let them [meaning the Persians][407] not be more daring when facing death. Let their souls not be more generous in giving up this world,[408] and compete with each other [for martyrdom]."[409]

They launched an attack from the area adjacent to them and became entanged with [the Persians] opposite them. A number of men rose up among the tribe of Rabīʿah and said: "You know the Persians best, and you were the most courageous against them in the past.[410] What is it, then, that prevents you from being [even] more courageous today?" The first Persians to retreat at noon were al-Hurmuzān and al-Bayruzān; they retreated but made a stand in the place that they reached. At noon a gap was opened in the center [of the Persian army] and dust covered them. A violent westerly[411] wind blew away the sunshade[412] from Rustam's throne, and it fell into al-ʿAtīq. The dust blew against the Persians. [2336]

Al-Qaʿqāʿ and his companions reached Rustam's throne and top-

407. Cf. (ʿI.) Ibn al-Athīr, *Kāmil*, II, 373 l. 19.

408. A similar exhortation is attributed, in Balādhurī, *Futūḥ*, 258, to Qays b. Makshūḥ.

409. The expression *tanāfasūhā* is difficult. The apparent antecedent of the feminine pronoun is *al-dunyā*, but this does not seem to make any sense. Cf. p. 2331 l. 8: *nāfisūhum fī al-shahādah*.

410. See p. 2223, above.

411. The removal of Rustam's sunshade foreshadows his imminent defeat. The choice of the *dabūr* wind for this purpose is significant: It is a wind that is frequently described as destructive, worthless, and bringing no rain with it. The wind that God sent to destroy the ancient nation of ʿĀd, called in the Qurʿān *al-rīḥ al-ʿaqīm*, is said to have been the *dabūr* (or the *janūb*); see *Tafsīr al-Jalālayn* on Qurʿān 51:41; and Ṭabarī, *Tafsīr*, XXVII, 4, on the same verse. The idea is also expressed in a tradition in which the Prophet is reported to have said: "I was helped by the easterly wind, while ʿĀd were destroyed by the westerly one (*nuṣirtu bi-al-ṣabā wa-uhlikat ʿĀd bi-al-dabūr*)." See Bukhārī, *Ṣaḥīḥ*, I, 263; and Wensinck *et al.*, *Concordance*, s.v. *dabūr*, for further references.

412. Cf. note 282, above.

pled it. Rustam vacated it when the wind had blown the sunshade away and transferred to some mules which had brought to him certain possessions on that day and were standing [nearby], taking shelter in the shade of one of the mules and of its litter. Hilāl b. ʿUllafah[413] hit the litter under which Rustam was (hiding) and cut its ropes. One of the half-loads fell on Rustam, so that Hilāl did not see him and did not notice him. The load hit Rustam and displaced a vertebra in his spine. His [sleeves][414] diffused scent. He moved toward al-ʿAtīq and threw himself into it, but without any hesita-
[2337] tion, Hilāl went after him and caught him after Rustam had already started to swim. Hilāl stood upright, seized Rustam's leg, and dragged him out to the river's bank, and then struck his forehead with the sword and killed him. Then he dragged him farther and threw him at the feet of the mules. He seated himself on Rustam's throne and exclaimed: "By the Lord of the Kaʿbah, I have killed Rustam! Come to me!" Men gathered around him without noticing or seeing the throne, proclaiming "God is most great!" and calling out to each other.

At this point the polytheists lost heart and were defeated. Al-Jālnūs stood on the barrier and called upon the Persians to cross it. The dust settled. As for those who were chained together, they panicked and threw themselves, one after the other, into al-ʿAtīq. The Muslims stabbed them with their spears, and none of them escaped to tell the story. They numbered thirty thousand. Ḍirār b. al-Khaṭṭāb seized the royal flag[415] and was given thirty thousand [dirhams] in exchange for it; its value was one million and two hundred thousand. The Muslims killed in the battle ten thousand men, over and above those whom they had killed on the previous day.

According to al-Sarī — Shuʿayb — Sayf — ʿAṭiyyah — ʿAmr b. Salamah: Hilāl b. ʿUllafah killed Rustam on the Day of al-Qādisiyyah.

According to al-Sarī—Shuʿayb—Sayf—Abu Mikhrāq—Abū Kaʿb

---

413. See (ʿI.) Ibn al-Athīr, *Usd*, V, 69.

414. I am translating *nafaḥat ardānuhu miskan* according to the version of Ibn Ḥubaysh, mentioned in the notes to the Leiden edition. Ṭabarī has *nafaḥat miskan*, without a subject for *nafaḥat*. Cf. Ṭabarī, I, 2194 l. 17.

415. For an explanation of the term *drafsh-i kavyān* (*kābiyān* in Ṭabarī's text), see Christensen, *Sassanides*, 212, 502–4; and *EI*², s.v. "Kāwah" (Ed). A brief description of the flag, which is said to have been made from panther skin and to have measured 8 by 12 cubits, is given in Ṭabarī, I, 2175. See also Balādhurī, *Futūḥ*, 252; Nuwayrī, *Nihāyat al-arab*, XIX, 215.

al-Ṭā'ī—his father: Before the Night of Howling, two thousand five hundred Muslims were hurt, and six thousand of them were killed on the Night of Howling and on the Day of al-Qādisiyyah; they were buried in the moat, opposite [the valley of] Musharriq.[416] [2338]

According to al-Sarī—Shuʿayb—Sayf—Muḥammad, Ṭalḥah, and Ziyād: When the Persians were defeated, none of them remained between the moat and al-ʿAtīq, and the dead covered the area between al-Qudays and al-ʿAtīq; Saʿd ordered Zuhrah to pursue the [fleeing] Persians. Zuhrah summoned the vanguard; he ordered al-Qaʿqāʿ to pursue those who fled downstream and ordered Shuraḥbīl to pursue those who fled upstream. He ordered Khālid b. ʿUrfuṭah to plunder the dead and to bury the martyrs. Two thousand five hundred martyrs who were killed on the Night of Howling and on the Day of al-Qādisiyyah were buried around Qudays, across al-ʿAtīq, opposite [the valley of] Musharriq, and the martyrs killed before the Night of Howling were buried in Musharriq. The spoils and the wealth were gathered; a quantity such as this had never been gathered, neither before al-Qādisiyyah nor after it.

Saʿd sent for Hilāl (b. ʿUllafah), blessed him, and said: "Where is your man?" He replied: "I threw him under [the feet of] the mules." Saʿd said: "Go and bring him here." When Hilāl brought the corpse, Saʿd said: "Strip it of everything, except that which you want to leave on it." Hilāl took Rustam's spoils and did not leave on him anything.

When al-Qaʿqāʿ and Shuraḥbīl returned, Saʿd told each one of them to pursue those who had been pursued before by the other. One went upstream, the other downstream,[417] until each covered the distance between al-Kharrārah and al-Qādisiyyah.[418]

Zuhrah b. al-Ḥawiyyah went after the Persians. He reached the barrier which the Persians had broken in order to thwart the pursuit. Zuhrah said: "Advance, O Bukayr!" Bukayr hit his mare—he fought only on mares—and said: "Jump, Aṭlāl!" She exerted herself and

416. Cf. pp. 2304, 2317, above.

417. Saʿd's intention seems to have been to check one more time the two escape routs of the Persians. This time, so it appears, al-Qaʿqāʿ went upstream and Shuraḥbīl downstream.

418. According to Yāqūt (*Muʿjam*, II, 409), al-Kharrārah is a place near al-Saylaḥūn, in the neighborhood of al-Kūfah. There is no indication of the distance between al-Qādisiyyah and al-Kharrārah.

[2339] said: "Jump, by the Sūrah of the Cow!"[419] Zuhrah, who rode a stallion, and the rest of the horsemen leaped forward[420] and waded the canal. Three hundred horsemen followed. When the horses were afraid [to advance], Zuhrah called out: "O men, take the way of the bridge and move along the opposite side." He set out and the Muslims went to the bridge following him. He then caught up with the Persians, with al-Jālnūs in their rear guard, protecting them. Zuhrah attacked him, they exchanged blows, and Zuhrah killed and plundered him. They killed [the Persians who were] between al-Kharrārah, al-Saylaḥūn, and al-Najaf. In the evening they returned and spent the night at al-Qādisiyyah.

According to al-Sarī—Shuʿayb—Sayf—ʿAbdallāh b. Shubrumah—Shaqīq: We forced our way into al-Qādisiyyah in the morning. When we retreated, the time of prayer came along, but the *mu'adhdhin* had been hit. The Muslims quarreled with each other for the right to pronounce the call to prayer, and almost fought it out with the swords. So Saʿd cast lots among them, and the man whose lot was drawn pronounced the call to prayers.

Another account: The Muslims who pursued the Persians upstream of al-Qādisiyyah and downstream returned. The time of prayer came, but the *mu'adhdhin* had been killed, and the Muslims quarreled with each other for the right to pronounce the call to prayer. Saʿd cast lots among them. They stayed [in their places] for the rest of the day and the [following] night, until Zuhrah returned. In the morning all of them gathered, and they did not expect anyone
[2340] else from the army [to return]. Saʿd wrote [to ʿUmar] about the victory, about the number of [the Persians whom the Muslims] killed, and about the number of the Muslims who had been hit. He sent to ʿUmar the names of those whom ʿUmar knew with Saʿd b. ʿUmaylah al-Fazārī.

According to al-Sarī—Shuʿayb—Sayf—al-Naḍr—Ibn al-Rufayl—his father: Saʿd summoned me and sent me to inspect the dead on his behalf and to provide him with the names of the chieftains

419. Bukayr was the nickname of Bakr b. Shaddākh (or Shaddād) al-Laythī, who was in his youth one of the Prophet's servants. The story of his mare Aṭlāl is related in slightly different versions in Ibn Ḥajar, *Iṣābah*, I, 324–5; Aʿrābī, *Asmā' al-khayl*, 83–84; Ghundijānī, *Asmā'*, 33–34; Ibn Manẓūr, *Lisān al-ʿArab*, s.v. *ṭ-l-l*.

420. Translating *wathaba* of the Cairo edition, instead of *awthaba* of the Leiden text.

among them. I came to him and gave him the information but I did not see Rustam in his place. Saʿd sent for a man from the tribe of Taym whose name was Hilāl and said to him: "Did you not inform me that you had killed Rustam?" Hilāl said: "Yes, I did." Saʿd said: "What did you do with him?" He replied, "I threw him under the feet of the mules." Saʿd said: "How did you kill him?" He gave him the information, saying: "I struck his forehead and his nose." Saʿd said: "Bring him to us." He gave Rustam's spoils to Hilāl. Rustam had thrown off some of his clothing when he rushed into the water. Hilāl sold what was found on Rustam's body for seventy thousand [dirhams]; the value of his headgear (*qalansuwah*)[421] would have been one hundred thousand if Hilāl had been able to take possession of it.[422]

A group of Christians (*al-ʿibād*) came to Saʿd and said: "O commander, we have seen the body of Rustam near the gate of your castle, but he had the head of another man; the blows have disfigured him [beyond recognition]." At this, Saʿd laughed.

According to al-Sarī—Shuʿayb—Sayf—Muḥammad, Ṭalḥah, and Ziyād: The Daylamīs[423] and the chiefs of the garrisons who re- [2341]
sponded to the Muslims and fought on their side without embracing Islam said: "Our brethren who became Muslims from the beginning have better judgment and are more virtuous than we are. By God, no Persian will prosper after Rustam's death except those who became Muslims."

The youngsters of the army went to inspect the dead. They had with them vessels of water. They gave water to the Muslims in whom there was a breath of life and killed the polytheists in whom there was a breath of life. They came down from al-ʿUdhayb at the time of the evening prayer.

Zuhrah went in pursuit of al-Jālnūs. Al-Qaʿqāʿ, his brother, and Shuraḥbīl went in pursuit of the Persians who had fled upstream and downstream. They killed them in every village, in every thicket, and on every river bank, and then returned in time for the noon

---

421. See Dozy, *Vêtements*, 365–71; *EI*², s.v. "Libās" (Y. K. Stillman and N. A. Stillman) at V, 734b–735a.

422. Rustam apparently threw away his *qalansuwah* when he made his way into the water.

423. See *EI*², s.v. "Daylam" (V. Minorsky).

prayer. The commander greeted the Muslims,[424] praised every clan, and mentioned it by name.

According to al-Sarī — Shuʿayb — Sayf — Saʿīd b. al-Marzubān: Zuhrah set out and caught up with al-Jālnūs, who was one of the Persian princes, between al-Kharrārah and al-Saylaḥūn. He was wearing two pairs of bracelets (*qulbāni, yāraqāni*) and two earrings (*qurṭāni*) and was riding an exhausted horse. Zuhrah attacked him and killed him. (Saʿīd b. al-Marzubān also) said: "By God, Zuhrah rode on that day a horse whose reins were made of nothing but twisted rope, like a halter, and its girth was of woven hair. He
[2342] brought the spoils of al-Jālnūs to Saʿd. The prisoners who were with Saʿd recognized the spoils and said: 'These are the spoils of al-Jālnūs.'" Saʿd said to Zuhrah: "Has anyone helped you to kill him?" He replied: "Yes." Saʿd said: "Who was it?" He replied: "God." Saʿd thereupon gave him the spoils of al-Jālnūs.

According to al-Sarī — Shuʿayb — Sayf — ʿUbaydah — Ibrāhīm: Saʿd thought that Zuhrah had received an excessive share of the spoils. He wrote to ʿUmar concerning this, and ʿUmar wrote back to him: "Whoever has killed a man, I have given him his spoils." Saʿd gave the spoils to Zuhrah, who sold them for seventy thousand [dirhams].

According to Sayf — al-Barmakān; and al-Mujālid — al-Shaʿbī: Zuhrah caught up with al-Jālnūs. A ball was held up for him, and he did not miss it with an arrow.[425] Zuhrah and al-Jālnūs faced each other. Zuhrah struck al-Jālnūs and threw him down. Now Zuhrah was a noble man;[426] he had been made a tribal chief in the Jāhiliyyah, had acquitted himself well in Islam, and had embraced it early.[427] He was [still] a young man. He put on the armor of al-Jālnūs, the value of which was seventy odd thousand, but when he returned to Saʿd,

---

424. The Cairo edition reads *hannaʾa al-nāsu amīrahum* "the Muslims greeted their commander." The word order favors this reading, but it is nevertheless unlikely in view of the rest of the sentence, where the commander is clearly the subject.

425. For another case in which the Muslims used a ball as a target, in order to impress the enemy with their marksmanship, see Ṭabarī, I, 2443 ll. 6–11; *pace* Juynboll, *Conquest*, 23. See also Ṭabarī, I, 2353 l. 4.

426. Literally: "He had a forelock (*dhuʾābah*)." *Dhuʾābah* is used metaphorically for nobility and honor. See Ibn Manẓūr, *Lisān al-ʿArab*, s.v. *dh-ʾ-b* (*ustuʿīra li-al-ʿizz wa-al-sharaf wa-al-martabah*); cf. de Goeje's *Glossary*, s.v.

427. It is unnecessary to add *lahu* and read *wa lahu sābiqah* with the Cairo edition. The main sentence is *li-Zuhrah dhuʾābah . . . wa sābiqah*; the phrase in between is parenthetical.

Saʿd took the spoils away from him and said: "[Why] did you not wait for my permission?" Saʿd and ʿUmar exchanged letters concerning this. ʿUmar wrote to Saʿd: "You will need men like Zuhrah. He endured a great deal and your war is not yet over. You will put him off his mettle[428] and spoil his spirit. Confirm him in the possession of his spoils and give him a stipend that is greater than that of his companions by five hundred [dirhams]."[429]

According to Sayf—ʿUbaydah—ʿIṣmah: ʿUmar wrote to Saʿd: "I know Zuhrah better than you do. He is not a man who would conceal anything from the spoils he has taken. If the man who slandered him to you is lying, let God confront him with a man like Zuhrah, with two bracelets on his arms.[430] To everybody who killed a man, I have awarded the dead man's spoils." Saʿd gave the spoils to Zuhrah, and the latter sold them for seventy thousand. [2343]

According to Sayf—ʿUbaydah—Ibrāhīm and ʿĀmir: Those who acquitted themselves well in the battle of al-Qādisiyyah were given a stipend greater by five hundred [dirhams]; these numbered twenty-five men and included Zuhrah, ʿIṣmah al-Ḍabbī, and al-Kalaj. As for the men who fought in the [former] battles (*ahl al-ayyām*), they received three thousand each and were given more than the people of al-Qādisiyyah.

According to Sayf—ʿUbaydah—Yazīd al-Ḍakhm: It was said to ʿUmar: "Would you put the people of al-Qādisiyyah on a par with them?" He replied: "I cannot put on a par with them anybody who did not [join the army early enough to] fight with them."[431] It was said to him concerning the people of al-Qādisiyyah: "Would you prefer those who live far away to those who fought the Persians close to their homes?" He replied:

> How can I prefer them because of the remoteness of their homes? [Those who live close to the battlefield] are a source

---

428. Literally "you will break his horn."

429. Ibn Khaldūn considers ʿUmar's decision an example of proper conduct, conducive to the self-reliance and high morale of the troops. See *Muqaddimah*, 126; tr. I, 259.

430. The bracelets are apparently considered a sign of a fearless warrior. Cf. p. 2341, where al-Jālnūs is described as wearing two pairs of bracelets and a pair of earrings.

431. One of the meanings of *adrakahu* is "he lived in someone's time, he lived long enough to reach his time." The suggested translation is derived from this meaning. The men concerned were of course alive at the time of the early battles of Iraq but had not yet joined the Muslim army.

of vexation for the enemy. I have not made both groups equal before I found them to be virtuous; and did the Emigrants (*al-Muhājirūn*) treat the helpers (*al-Anṣār*) in this way because they fought close to their homes?"[432]

According to Sayf—al-Mujālid—al-Shaʿbī and Saʿīd b. al-Marzubān—a man from the tribe of ʿAbs: When Rustam moved from his place, he rode a mule. When Hilāl came close to him, Rustam drew an arrow, pierced Hilāl's leg, fastened it to the stirrup [with the arrow] and said: "Stay where you are (*bi-pāye*)!"[433] Hilāl approached
[2344] him, and Rustam dismounted and got down under the mule. When Hilāl could not get to him, he cut off the mule's load. Then he dismounted and split Rustam's head.[434]

According to Sayf—ʿUbaydah—Shaqīq: On the Day of al-Qādisiyyah we all attacked the Persians, like one man. God defeated them. I found myself signaling to one of the Persian commanders, who came at me, fully armed. I killed him and took whatever was on him.

According to Sayf—Saʿīd b. al-Marzubān—a man from the tribe of ʿAbs: The Persians were afflicted after their defeat in the same way as the Muslims had been afflicted beforehand. They were killed. The situation was such that if a Muslim called a Persian, the Persian would come, stand in front of the Muslim, and the Muslim would kill him. The Muslim would even take the Persian's weapon and kill him with it or order two Persians to kill each other. This happened many times.

According to Sayf—Yūnus b. Abī Isḥāq—his father—a man who participated in the battle of al-Qādisiyyah: Salmān b. Rabīʿah al-Bāhilī saw some Persians sitting under a flag of theirs. They dug a hole for it in the ground, sat under it, and said: "We shall not move from here until we die." Salmān attacked them, killed those who were under the flag, and took their spoils. Salmān was the [choice]

---

432. The meaning seems to be that, though most battles of early Islam were fought close to Medina, the home of the Helpers, the Helpers did not receive a lesser share of the spoils than that of the Emigrants.

433. Cf. Ṭabarī, I, 2356 l. 14, where the expression is translated into Arabic: *kamā anta*. See de Goeje's *Glossary*, s.v. *ka*; and *WKAS*, I, 9a, for numerous references to this usage.

434. Cf. Ṭabarī, I, 2336 ll. 10ff. According to Kūfī, *Futūḥ*, I, 212, the killer of Rustam was Hilāl b. ʿAlqamah al-ʿUqaylī.

horseman of the Muslims on the Day of al-Qādisiyyah and was one of those who turned against the Persians who had showed further resistance after their defeat. The other one was ʿAbd al-Raḥmān b. Rabīʿah Dhū al-Nūr ("the man of light"); he turned against other Persians who had [regrouped], forming military units (*takattabū*) and rising up against the Muslims. He crushed them with his horsemen.

According to Sayf — al-Ghuṣn b. al-Qāsim — al-Bahī: al-Shaʿbī said: It used to be said: "Verily, Salmān is more knowledgeable about the joints [of horses] than the slaughterer about the joints of the slaughtered camel." The place that serves today as jail (in al-Kūfah) was the house of ʿAbd al-Raḥmān b. Rabīʿah. The house that is between this house and the house of al-Mukhtār is the house of Salmān. Al-Ashʿath b. Qays asked for a yard in front of it, and it was given to him. [This yard is included today in the house of al-Mukhtār.] Salmān protested to him: "O Ashʿath, what emboldened you [to act] against me? By God, if you take possession of it, I shall strike you with al-Junthī,"[435] meaning his sword. "Let us see what remains of you after that." Al-Ashʿath gave it up and did not attempt to claim it. [2345]

According to Sayf — al-Muhallab, Muḥammad, Ṭalḥah, and his companions: Thirty odd [Persian] military units showed resistance after the defeat. They courageously courted death and were ashamed to run away, hence God destroyed them. Thirty odd Muslim chieftains confronted them, rather than pursue the fleeing Persians. Salmān b. Rabīʿah confronted one unit, and ʿAbd al-Raḥmān b. Rabīʿah Dhū al-Nūr confronted another one. A Muslim chieftain confronted each of these units. The men of these Persian units fought in two ways: some of them were cowards[436] and fled, but others stood firm until they were killed. Among the commanders of the units who fled was al-Hurmuzān, who was facing ʿUṭārid;[437] Ahwad, [2346] who was facing Ḥanẓalah b. al-Rabīʿ, the secretary of the Prophet; Zād b. Buhaysh, who was facing ʿĀṣim b. ʿAmr; and Qārin, who was facing al-Qaʿqāʿ b. ʿAmr. Among those who courageously courted death were Shahriyār b. Kanārā, who was facing Salmān (b. Rabīʿah); Ibn al-Hirbidh, who was facing ʿAbd al-Raḥmān (b. Rabīʿah); al-

---

435. Cf. Schwarzlose, *Waffen*, 136.

436. For this meaning of *kadhdhaba* see Ibn Manẓūr, *Lisān al-ʿArab*, s.v. *k-dh-b*, I, 709a.

437. For ʿUṭārid b. Ḥājib b. Zurārah b. ʿAdas al-Tamīmī, see note 126, above.

Farrukhān al-Ahwazī, who was facing Busr b. Abī Ruhm al-Juhanī; and Khusrawshnūm al-Hamadhānī, who was facing Ibn al-Hudhayl al-Kāhilī. Saʿd afterward sent al-Qaʿqāʿ and Shuraḥbīl after the Persians who fled downstream and upstream from the camp. He sent Zuhrah b. Ḥawiyyah after al-Jālnūs.

The Account of Ibn Isḥāq

Abū Jaʿfar al-Ṭabarī has said: The narrative returns to the account
[2347] of Ibn Isḥāq. Al-Muthannā b. al-Ḥārithah died and Saʿd b. Abī Waqqāṣ married his wife Salmā bint Khaṣafah; this happened in the year 14/635–36. ʿUmar b. al-Khaṭṭāb conducted the pilgrimage in that year. Abū ʿUbaydah entered Damascus in that year and spent the winter there. In the summer Heraclius moved with the Byzantines and camped in Antioch, having with him people who had become assimilated among the Arabs[438] from the tribes of Lakhm,[439] Judhām,[440] Balqayn,[441] Balī,[442] and ʿĀmila.[443] These were tribes affiliated to Quḍāʿah[444] and Ghassān,[445] amounting to a great multitude, and a similar number of men from Armenia were also with him. When Heraclius halted in Antioch, he stayed there and sent out al-Ṣaqalār, who was his eunuch. He set out with one hundred thousand warriors, and he had with him twelve thousand men from Armenia, led by Jarajah,[446] and twelve thousand *mustaʿribah* Arabs affiliated with Ghassān and the tribes of Quḍāʿah, led by Jabalah b. al-Ayham al-Ghassānī.[447] This whole army was commanded by al-Ṣaqalār, the eunuch of Heraclius. The Muslims, numbering twenty-four thousand and commanded by Abū ʿUbaydah b. al-Jarrāḥ, marched toward them. They confronted each other in al-Yarmūk in the

438. For *al-ʿarab al-mustaʿribah*, as against *al-ʿarab al-ʿāribah*, see *EI²*, s.v. "al-ʿArab, Djazīrat al-" (G. Rentz), at I, 544b. For a discussion of the lineage of some of the tribes mentioned below, see Ibn Khaldūn, *Muqaddimah*, tr. I, 266.

439. See *EI²*, s.v. "Lakhm" (H. Lammens [I. Shahid]).

440. See *EI²*, s.v. "Djudhām" (C. E. Bosworth).

441. Balqayn is a contraction for Banū al-Qayn; see *EI²*, s.v. "al-Ḳayn" (W. M. Watt).

442. On Balī see *EI²*, s.v. "Ḳuḍāʿa" (M. J. Kister), at V, 317b–18a.

443. See *EI²*, s.v. "ʿĀmila" (H. Lammens [W Caskel]).

444. See *EI²*, s.v. "Ḳuḍāʿa" (M. J. Kister).

445. See *EI²*, s.v. "Ghassān" (J. Shahid).

446. Cf. Donner, *Conquests*, 132, 365.

447. The last ruler of the Ghassānid dynasty; see *EI²*, s.v. "Djabala b. al-Ayham" (I. Kawar).

month of Rajab of the year 15/July–August 636. The fighting was heavy and the camp of the Muslims was penetrated. When this happened, women from the tribe of Quraysh fought with the swords,[448] competing with the men. Among them was Umm Ḥakīm bint al-Ḥārith b. Hishām.[449]

When the Muslims went to confront the Byzantines, they were joined by men from the tribes of Lakhm and Judhām, but when these last saw the severity of the fighting, they fled and escaped to the neighboring villages and let the Muslims down. [2348]

According to Ibn Ḥumayd — Salamah — Muḥammad b. Isḥāq — Yaḥyā b. ʿUrwah b. al-Zubayr—his father: An [anonymous] Muslim recited when he saw what Lakhm and Judhām did:

The men of Lakhm and Judhām are in flight,
while we and the Byzantines in the meadow fight.
We shall not associate with them if they return after the fight.

According to Ibn Ḥumayd — Salamah — Ibn Isḥāq — Wahb b. al-Qaysān — ʿAbdallāh b. al-Zubayr: I was with my father, al-Zubayr, during the year of the battle of al-Yarmūk. When the Muslims arrayed themselves for battle, al-Zubayr put on his breast-plate, mounted his horse, and said to two clients of his: "Keep ʿAbdallāh b. al-Zubayr in the camp with you because he is a small boy." Al-Zubayr then set out and took his place among the Muslims. When the Muslims and the Byzantines were engaged in battle, I saw people standing on the hill and not fighting together with the Muslims. I took a horse of al-Zubayr which he had left behind in the camp, mounted it, and rode to these people. I stood with them and said [to myself]: "I shall look and see what are these men doing." And, behold, Abū Sufyān b. Ḥarb was standing there with elders from the tribe of Quraysh who [had embraced Islam] and emigrated [only after] the conquest of Mecca (*muhājirat al-fatḥ*). They were not fighting. When they saw me, they saw only a young boy and did not take any precautions. By God, when the Muslims floundered and the war was going against them and in favor of the Byzantines, they began to [2349]

448. Cf. Balādhurī, *Futūḥ*, 135.

449. Umm Ḥakīm bint al-Ḥārith b. Hishām was for a time a wife of ʿUmar b. al-Khaṭṭāb and gave birth to Fāṭimah, one of his daughters. She had also participated in the battle of Marj al-Ṣuffar. See Ibn Saʿd, *Ṭabaqāt*, III/i, 190; IV/i, 71.

say: "Go on, O Banū al-Aṣfar!"[450] And when the Byzantines floundered and the Muslims pressed them hard, they said: "Woe to you, O Banū al-Aṣfar!" I became puzzled by what they said. When God defeated the Byzantines and al-Zubayr returned, I told him their story. Al-Zubayr started laughing and said: "May the curse of God befall them! They want only enmity. Will they gain anything if the Byzantines overcome us? We are better for them than they are."

Then God the Exalted granted victory [to the Muslims]. The Byzantines and the armies gathered by Heraclius were defeated. Seventy thousand of the Armenians and of the people who were assimilated among the Arabs (*mustaʿribah*) were killed. God killed al-Ṣaqalār and Bāhān,[451] whom Heraclius had sent forward with al-Ṣaqalār when Bāhān joined him. When the Byzantines were defeated, Abū ʿUbayda sent ʿIyāḍ b. al-Ghanm[452] in their pursuit. He crossed al-Aʿmāq[453] and reached Malaṭyah.[454] The inhabitants of Malaṭyah concluded a treaty with him, agreeing to pay the *jizyah*, and after this, ʿIyāḍ b. al-Ghanm went back. When Heraclius heard of this, he sent for the fighting men [of Malaṭyah] and for the rest of its inhabitants and banished them to his region. He then gave orders for Malaṭyah to be burned.

The following Muslims were killed in the battle of al-Yarmūk: from Quraysh, Banū Umayyah b. ʿAbd Shams: ʿAmr b. Saʿīd b. al-ʿĀṣī, Abān b. Saʿīd b. al-ʿĀṣī; from Banū Makhzūm: ʿAbdallāh b. Sufyān b. ʿAbd al-Asad; from Banū Sahm: Saʿīd b. al-Ḥārith b. Qays.

At the end of the year 15/636–37 God killed Rustam in Iraq.

---

450. For this appellation of the Byzantines, see Goldziher, *Muslim Studies*, I, 243; and *EI²*, s.v. "Aṣfar" (I. Goldziher).

451. Bāhān was a commander in the Byzantine army, bearing the title *biṭrīq*, "patricius." See Ṭabarī, I, 2081–82, 2088–89, 2091, 2146.

452. ʿIyāḍ b. Ghanm was a Companion of the Prophet who participated in the conquest of Syria. After the death of Abū ʿUbaydah b. al-Jarrāḥ in A.H. 18/639 he was appointed governor of Ḥimṣ, Qinnasrīn, and al-Jazīrah. See Balādhurī, *Futūḥ*, 172, and index; Ibn Saʿd, *Ṭabaqāt*, VII, 122; (ʿI.) Ibn al-Athīr, *Usd*, IV, 164–66.

453. Aʿmāq is mentioned in the *ḥadīth* in connection with the eschatological wars against the Byzantines: "The Hour will not come until the Byzantines camp at al-Aʿmāq." See Muslim, *Ṣaḥīḥ*, IV, 2221. Yāqūt (*Muʿjam*, I, 316) says that the plural form Aʿmāq may stand for the singular ʿAmq, the alluvial plain of northern Syria, for which see *EI²*, s.v. "al-ʿAmḳ" (D. Sourdel).

454. An ancient city near the upper Euphrates, now situated in eastern Turkey. See the detailed article in *EI²*, s.v. "Malaṭya" (E. Honigmann [J. Faroghi]). Yāqūt (*Muʿjam*, IV, 633–35) does not provide any information about the city in the early Islamic period.

When the troops who fought in the battle of al-Yarmūk finished the battle, they participated in the battle of al-Qādisiyyah with Saʿd b. Abī Waqqāṣ. The reason for this was that Saʿd moved from Sharāf in the direction of al-Qādisiyyah after the winter was over. When Rustam heard this, he himself set out against Saʿd; when this came to Saʿd's knowledge, he wrote to ʿUmar, asking for reinforcements. Hence ʿUmar sent to him al-Mughīrah b. al-Shuʿbah al-Thaqafī [2350] with four hundred men as reinforcements from Medina. He also reinforced him with Qays b. Makshūḥ al-Murādī with seven hundred men, who came to him from al-Yarmūk. ʿUmar wrote to Abū ʿUbaydah saying: "Help Saʿd b. Abī Waqqāṣ, the *amīr* of Iraq, with one thousand of the troops at your disposal." Abū ʿUbaydah complied and appointed ʿIyāḍ b. Ghanm al-Fihrī as their commander.

ʿUmar b. al-Khaṭṭāb conducted the pilgrimage of the Muslims in the year 15/636–37.

The Persian king (*kisrā*) had a garrison in Qaṣr Banī Muqātil.[455] Its commander was al-Nuʿmān b. al-Qabīṣah, who was Ibn Ḥayyah al-Ṭāʾī, the paternal cousin of Qabīṣah b. Iyās b. Ḥayyah al-Ṭāʾī, the governor of al-Ḥīrah. He was in a lookout (*manẓarah*) of his, and when he heard about [the coming] of Saʿd b. Abī Waqqāṣ, he asked ʿAbdallāh b. Sinān b. Jarīr al-Asadī al-Ṣaydāwī about him. He was told: "He is a man from the tribe of Quraysh." Al-Nuʿmān b. Qabīṣah commented: "If he is a man from the tribe of Quraysh, he is nothing. By God, I shall vigorously fight him. The Quraysh are nothing except slaves of those who hold superior power. By God, they do not protect those whom they should protect and do not leave their land without a protector."[456] ʿAbdallāh b. Sinān al-Asadī was enraged when al-Nuʿmān said this. After some time, he entered upon him while he was asleep, thrust his spear between his two shoulders, and killed him. Then he joined Saʿd and embraced Islam. He recited concerning the killing of al-Nuʿmān b. Qabīṣah:

---

455. Yāqūt (*Muʿjam*, IV, 121–22) mentions Qaṣr Muqātil, which was situated, according to one version, near al-Quṭquṭānah (see note 19, above).

456. This passage is difficult because most dictionaries have *khafīr* only in the active sense of protector, and the first part of the sentence is not intelligible if *khafīr* is understood in this sense. I have followed al-Fayrūzābādī, who says in *Qāmūs*, II, 23): *al-khafīr al-mujār al-mujīr* "the *khafīr* is the protected and the protector."

When the people set out at night,
    they left the man of great deeds knocked down in the palace of the Christian;
I approached him under the cover of dust and stabbed him.
    In the morning he was lying, blood-stained, in a pool of blood.
[2351] With the spear in his shoulder blade, I am telling him:
    "Oh Abū ʿĀmir, you are free from fulfilling your oath!"
By stabbing him, I gave al-Nuʿmān to drink a cup full to the brim;
    I served him, with the spear, a potent poison.
I left the beasts of the desert (?)[457] around him,
    after he had been a refuge from them for Ibn Ḥayyah.
I have taken care of the duty of Quraysh because their army is not here,
    and I have destroyed a long-standing glory of al-Nuʿmān!

When al-Mughīrah b. Shuʿbah, Qays b. Makshūḥ, and those who were with them reached Saʿd, he marched in the direction of Rustam, of whom he had heard [news].[458] He halted at Qādis, a village near al-ʿUdhayb, and the Muslim troops encamped there. Saʿd stayed in the castle of al-ʿUdhayb. Rustam approached with the armies of Persia, sixty thousand men plus the dependents and the slaves. [This was the number counted for us in his register.] He encamped at al-Qādisiyyah with its bridge[459] between him and Muslims. Saʿd was in his dwelling, full of pain; he was afflicted with severe ulcers. Abū Miḥjan b. Ḥabīb al-Thaqafī was imprisoned in the castle, where Saʿd had jailed him because he drank wine.

When Rustam established camp near them, he sent [a messenger to the Muslims], saying: "Send to me a steadfast man and I shall speak with him." The Muslims sent to him al-Mughīrah b. Shuʿbah, who came to Rustam after he had divided his hair into four sections. He separated it [by a line running] from the forehead to the neck, and [another one] between his ears. Then he plaited his hair, put on a

---

457. I am unable to explain *yaʿrifna* in this context.

458. This is the literal meaning. The sense of the passage seems to be that Saʿd marched toward Rustam, of whose preparations to engage him in battle he had heard.

459. The Leiden edition reads, with the manuscripts, *wa-baynahu wa-bayna al-nās al-ʿAtīq jisr al-Qādisiyyah*, as if al-ʿAtīq were the name of the bridge. Since al-ʿAtīq is the name of a canal (see pp. 2268 l. 8; 2285 l. 15; 2286 ll. 2, 11; 2366 l. 9), it is difficult to interpret the Leiden text. I have translated according to the Cairo edition, which omits al-ʿAtīq.

cloak, and approached Rustam, who was beyond the bridge of al-ʿAtīq[460] on the Iraqi side. The Muslims were on the other side, close to al-Ḥijāz, between al-Qādisiyyah and al-ʿUdhayb. Rustam addressed al-Mughīrah, saying: [2352]

> O Arabs, you were people afflicted with misery and adversity. You used to come to us as merchants, hirelings, and messengers. You ate from our food, drank from our drink, and took shelter in our shade. Then you went back, invited your companions, and brought them to us. Your case is similar to that of a man who possessed a walled vineyad and saw a fox in it. He said: "What is one fox?"[461] The fox went away and invited [numerous] foxes to the vineyard. When they gathered in it, the man closed the hole through which they had entered and killed them all.[462] O Arabs, I know that the reason which caused you to do this is the adversity which had afflicted you. Return this year [to your land], because you have distracted us from building our country and from dealing with our enemy. We shall load your riding beasts with wheat and dates and shall issue an order to provide you with clothing. Leave our land, and may God keep you well!

Al-Mughīrah b. Shuʿbah replied:

> Whatever you have mentioned, we were afflicted with an adversity like it or greater. The person whose life was the most virtuous in our mind was one who killed his cousin, took his property, and consumed it. We were eating carrion, blood, and bones. Our situation did not change until God sent to us a Prophet and revealed to him a book, and the Prophet summoned us to God and to the message with which he had been sent. Some of us believed in him and oth- [2353]
> ers denied him. Those who believed in him fought those who denied him. We [all] entered his religion either out of conviction or by coercion when it became clear to us that he spoke the truth and that he was the Messenger of God. He

---

460. The Leiden edition has *al-jisr al-ʿatīq,* which is difficult. I have translated according to the emendation suggested by the editor in note *l.*

461. Meaning that one fox can do no harm.

462. Cf. Ṭabarī, I, 2281–82.

ordered us to fight those who opposed us and informed us that those of us who would be killed for the sake of his religion would be given Paradise and those who would survive would rule and overcome those who opposed them. We therefore call upon you to believe in God and in His messenger and to embrace our religion. If you do this, your country will be yours. None will enter it except those whom you wish to admit. You will be obliged to pay the alms tax (*zakāt*) and the fifth of the booty (*khums*).[463] If you refuse, you will have to pay the poll tax; if you refuse this as well, we shall fight you until God decides between us.[464]

Rustam said to him: "I did not think that I would live to hear such things from you. O Arabs, before tomorrow evening falls, I shall finish with you and kill you all." Then he ordered al-ʿAtīq to be filled up and spent the night filling it with saddle clothes,[465] soil, and reeds until by morning, it had become a beaten road. The Muslims arrayed themselves against Rustam. Saʿd placed Khālid b. ʿUrfuṭah, confederate of the Banū Umayyah b. ʿAbd Shams, in command of the Muslims, appointing Jarīr b. ʿAbdallāh al-Bajalī to command the right wing and Qays b. Makshūḥ al-Murādī the left wing. Rustam moved against the Muslims and the Muslims moved against Rustam.

According to Ibn Ḥumayd — Salamah — Muḥammad b. Isḥāq — ʿAbdallāh b. Abī Bakr: Most Muslims were shielded only with sad-
[2354] dle cloths across which they fastened leafless palm branches in order to protect themselves. What they put on their heads was in most cases only saddle girths: A man would bind his head with the girth of his saddle in order to protect himself. The Persians were clad in iron mail and coats. The fighting was heavy. Saʿd was in the castle, observing [the battlefield], with Salmā bint Khaṣafah, who had been before the wife of al-Muthannā b. Ḥārithah. The [Muslim] horsemen were wheeling around, and Salmā was terrified when she saw them do this. She said: "Alas for Muthannā! I have no Muthannā today!" Saʿd became jealous and slapped her face. She said: "Are you

---

463. Islamic law stipulates that one-fifth of the booty taken in *jihād* is managed by the state treasury (*bayt al-māl*). For a discussion of the ways in which the *khums* is to be used, see *EI*², s.v. "Bayt al-māl" (N. J. Coulson *et al.*), at I, 1142a.

464. Cf. p. 2283 ll. 12ff., above.

465. Reading *al-barādhiʿ* with the Cairo edition, and with another version of this tradition in Ṭabarī, I, 2286 l. 3, rather than *al-zarʿ*. Cf. de Goeje's note in *Addenda et Emendanda*, DCXVIII.

both jealous and cowardly?"[466] Abū Miḥjan was with Saʿd in the castle of al-ʿUdhayb and observed [the battlefield]. When he saw the horsemen wheel around, he recited:

It is grievous enough that the horsemen gallop with the spears,
while I am left tied up, with my fetters on.
When I stand up, the iron hurts; the doors
are closed behind me and do not respond to the caller.
In the past I was a man of much wealth and brothers;
now they have left me alone, having no brother.[467]

He spoke to Zabrāʾ, the concubine[468] of Saʿd, at whose place he was jailed. Saʿd was on the top of the castle, observing the people [on the [2355]
battlefield]. Abū Miḥjan said: "O Zabrāʾ, set me free! I swear by God and I pledge to you that if I am not killed, I shall certainly return to you, so that you can put the iron back on my feet." She untied him, allowed him to ride Saʿd's horse Balqāʾ, and let him go. Abū Miḥjan set out attacking the enemy. Saʿd was looking on, not sure whether the horse was his or not.[469] When they had finished the battle and God had defeated the armies of Persia, Abū Miḥjan returned to Zabrāʾ and placed his foot in his fetter. When Saʿd came down from the top of the castle, he saw his horse sweating. He understood that she had been ridden. He asked Zabrāʾ about it and she told him Abū Miḥjan's story, whereupon Saʿd set him free.

According to Ibn Ḥumayd — Salamah — Ibn Isḥāq: ʿAmr b. Maʿdīkarib participated in the battle of al-Qādisiyyah on the side of the Muslims.

According to Ibn Ḥumayd—Salamah—Ibn Isḥāq—ʿAbd al-Raḥmān b. al-Aswad al-Nakhaʿī—his father: I participated in the battle of al-Qādisiyyah. I saw a young man from among us, from the tribe of al-Nakhaʿ, leading away sixty or eighty Persians.[470] I said: "God has indeed humiliated the Persians."

---

466. Cf. note 327, above.

467. See above, pp. 2313–14.

468. *Umm walad*, "mother of a child," is a concubine who has borne a child to her master. See *EI²*, s.v. "Umm al-Walad" (J. Schacht).

469. Literally "Saʿd began to recognize his horse and to deny [that] it [was his]" *jaʿala Saʿd yaʿrifu farasahu wa yunkiruhā*), oscillating between the two.

470. *Abnāʾ al-aḥrār*, or *abnāʾ*, was an epithet for the descendants of Persians who emigrated into the Yemen and married there. This passage indicates that it was also used for Persians in general. See J. ʿAlī, *Mufaṣṣal*, III, 528; IV, 556–57.

According to Ibn Ḥumayd — Salamah — Muḥammad b. Isḥāq — Ismāʿīl b. Abī Khālid, a client of Bajīlah — Qays b. Abī Ḥāzim al-Bajalī, who participated in the battle of al-Qādisiyyah on the side of the Muslims: A man from the tribe of Thaqīf was with us on the day
[2356] of al-Qādisiyyah. He joined the Persians as a renegade (*murtadd*) and informed them that the Muslims in the area held by Bajīlah had (the most) courage and valor. We were [only] one-quarter of the Muslims, but they sent against us sixteen elephants and sent only two elephants against the rest. They scattered iron spikes under the feet of our horses and sprayed us with arrows, so that it was as if rain were falling upon us. They tied their horses to each other so that they could not run away.[471]

ʿAmr b. Maʿdīkarib used to pass by and say: "O Emigrants, be lions! A lion is a man who takes care of his affairs on his own. When a Persian drops his spear, he is nothing but a stupid goat." There was a Persian commander whose arrow never missed the target. We said to ʿAmr b. Maʿdīkarib: "O Abū Thawr, beware of this Persian, because his arrow never misses the target." ʿAmr turned toward him. The Persian shot at him an arrow which hit his bow. ʿAmr fell upon him, seized him by the neck, and slew him, taking from him two golden bracelets, a gold-plated belt, and a brocade coat.

God killed Rustam and restored[472] to the Muslims his camp and everything in it. The Muslims numbered only six or seven thousand. The man who killed Rustam was Hilāl b. ʿUllafah al-Taymī, who saw Rustam and turned toward him. While Hilāl was going after him, Rustam shot him with an arrow, hit his leg, and fastened it to the stirrup of his saddle, and said in Persian *bi-pāye*, which means in Arabic "Stay where you are!"[473] Hilāl b. ʿUllafah attacked him,
[2357] struck him, and killed him. Then he cut off his head and hung it up. The Persians retreated and the Muslims went in their pursuit, killing them. When the Persians reached al-Kharrārah, they halted, drank wine, and ate. Then they started to wonder why their archery

---

471. Cf. note 206, above.

472. The verb *afāʾa* is said to express the idea that, when Muslims take booty, God restores to them only what belongs to them by right. While it is not certain that this was the original significance of the Qurʾānic usage, "restore" seems to approximate the meaning of *afāʾa* in this and similar passages in our text. See *EI*², s.v. "Fayʾ" (F. Løkkegaard).

473. Cf. note 433, above.

was not effective against the Arabs. Al-Jālnūs stepped forward; they raised a ball for him and he started shooting at it and piercing it with arrows. Muslim horsemen caught up with them while they were in this place, and Zuhrah b. Ḥawiyyah al-Tamīmī attacked al-Jālnūs and killed him. The Persians were defeated and fled to Dayr Qurrah[474] and beyond. Saʿd rushed with the Muslims[475] and encamped in Dayr Qurrah facing the Persians who were there. While in Dayr Qurrah they were joined by ʿIyāḍ b. Ghanm with his Syrian reinforcements, numbering one thousand men. Saʿd gave ʿIyāḍ and his companions a share in the spoils which the Muslims had taken at al-Qādisiyyah.

Saʿd was in pain because of his ulcers. Jarīr b. ʿAbdallāh (al-Bajalī) recited:

I am Jarīr, and my agnomen (*kunyah*) is Abū ʿAmr;
God granted victory while Saʿd was in the castle!

A[nother] Muslim said also:

We were fighting until God granted His victory,
while Saʿd took refuge at the gate of al-Qādisiyyah.
We returned after many women had been widowed,
but there is no widow among the wives of Saʿd!

[Qays b. Abī Ḥāzim al-Bajalī] said: When the verses came to Saʿd's knowledge, he went out to the Muslims, excused himself and showed them the ulcers which he had on his thighs and on his buttocks. Consequently, the Muslims excused him; I swear by my life [2358]
that Saʿd was not considered a coward. Saʿd recited in response to the verses of Jarīr:

I do not wish Bajīlah anything except
that they be rewarded on the Day of Reckoning.
Their horses were confronted with horses,
and [their] horsemen were engaged in combat.
The elephants drew near the ground held by them,
looking like scabby camels.

---

474. On the outskirts of al-Kūfah. See Yāqūt, *Muʿjam*, II, 685, 652.

475. The expression *nahaḍa Saʿd bi-ʾl-muslimīn* seems to indicate that Saʿd himself went to the battlefield for the first time in the battle of al-Qādisiyyah.

The Persians fled from Dayr Qurrah to al-Madā'in, on their way to Nihāwand.[476] They took with them the gold, the silver, the brocade, the clothes, the silk, the weapons, the garments of the king and his daughters. They left everything else behind. Saʿd sent after them Muslim troops in order to seek them out. He dispatched Khālid b. ʿUrfuṭah, who was a confederate of the Banū Umayyah, and sent with him ʿIyāḍ b. Ghanm and his companions. He appointed Hāshim b. ʿUtbah b. Abī Waqqāṣ to lead the Muslim vanguard, Jarīr b. ʿAbdallāh al-Bajalī to lead the right wing, and Zuhrah b. Ḥawiyyah al-Tamīmī to lead the left wing. Saʿd himself remained behind because of the pain with which he was afflicted. When he partially recovered, he followed the troops together with the Muslims who had been with him and caught up with them on this side of the Tigris, near Bahurasīr.[477] When they encamped on the bank of the Tigris and put down their luggage, they looked for a crossing point but
[2359] could not find it. Then a Persian from the people of al-Madā'in came to Saʿd and said: "I will show you a way by which you can catch up with them before they go far," and he took them to a crossing point at Qaṭrabbul.[478] The first man to cross was Hāshim b. ʿUtbah with his infantrymen. Having crossed the river, he was followed by his horsemen. Then Khālid b. ʿUrfuṭah crossed with his horsemen, followed by ʿIyāḍ b. Ghanm and his horsemen. Then the Muslims followed one after the other, waded through the river, and crossed it. It has been claimed that this crossing point was not used afterward.

The Muslims then marched on and reached Muẓlim Sābāṭ[479] but were apprehensive that an enemy ambush might be located there. Hence they hesitated and were afraid to enter it. The first person to enter it with his troops was Hāshim b. ʿUtbah. When he moved across it, he made a sign with his sword to the Muslims; they learned thereby that there was nothing to be afraid of. Khālid b. ʿUr-

---

476. See *EI*¹, s.v. "Nihāwand" (V. Minorsky). See also Yāqūt, *Muʿjam*, IV, 827–30; Le Strange, *Lands*, 196–97.

477. A city on the western bank of the Tigris; one of the seven cities constituting al-Madā'in. See Yāqūt, *Muʿjam*, I, 768–69; *EI*², s.v. "Madā'in" (M. Streck [M. Morony]); Oppenheimer *et al.*, *Babylonia*, 190–91, and index.

478. A village between Baghdad and ʿUkbarah, known for its wine and wine sellers. See Yāqūt, *Muʿjam*, IV, 133–35; Morony, *Iraq*, 145–46.

479. Sābāṭ Kisrā is one of the cities of al-Madā'in. According to Yāqūt (*Muʿjam*, III, 3–4; IV, 569) Muẓlim Sābāṭ is related to it, but he does not provide any information as to why it was so called.

fuṭah led them across. Then Saʿd joined the army and they reached Jalūlāʾ,[480] where a Persian unit was situated. There the battle of Jalūlāʾ took place, and God defeated the Persians. In Jalūlāʾ the Muslims took more valuable spoils than in al-Qādisiyyah. A daughter of the Persian king whose name was Manjānah was killed there, but according to another account, it was his son's daughter.

A poet of the Muslims recited:

Many a nice, well-shaped foal,
carries the loads of a Muslim boy.
He takes refuge from hell in the Merciful God,
on the day of Jalūlāʾ and the day of Rustam.
On the day of the march on al-Kūfah he is in the vanguard,
on the day he encounters adversity he is defeated.
The religion of the infidels fell down, lying on its face.

Then Saʿd wrote to ʿUmar about the victory that God granted to the Muslims. ʿUmar wrote to him: "Halt and do not seek further conquest." Saʿd wrote back to him: "This is nothing but a small band of horsemen whom we have pursued;[481] the land is before us.[482] [2360]
ʿUmar wrote again to Saʿd: "Stay where you are and do not follow them. Establish for the Muslims a place where they can migrate [and settle] (*dār hijrah*)[483] and from which they can wage holy war. Do not place a great river (*baḥr*) between me and the Muslims."[484] Saʿd set-

480. Jalūlāʾ was a city located to the northeast of al-Madāʾin, on the Diyala river. See *EI*², "Djalūlāʾ" (M. Streck); Yāqūt, *Muʿjam*, II, 107. On the crucial battle of Jalūlāʾ, see Morony, *Iraq*, 193–94, 197.

481. See *Glossary*, s.v. *s-r-b*.

482. The meaning seems to be that the Muslims will encounter no difficulty in conquering the land beyond the Euphrates.

483. Cf. Donner, *Conquests*, 227 n. 28 (where "Muslims" should replace "Bedouins").

484. To understand ʿUmar's instructions, one has to keep in mind that the battle of al-Qādisiyyah took place west of the Euphrates and the Muslims were therefore not required to cross any major waterway in order to reach the battlefield. After victory was attained, military logic dictated an advance into the lowlands (*sawād*) of Iraq. Nevertheless, ʿUmar expressed his opposition to the crossing of the Euphrates and the Tigris.

See also Balādhurī, *Futūḥ*, 275; Ṭabarī, I, 2483; and Ibn Saʿd *Ṭabaqāt*, VII/i, 2 l. 3. Yāqūt (*Muʿjam*, I, 637) reports that ʿUmar opposed the building of a city across the Tigris, saying: "There is no use to build a city in a place separated from me by the Tigris" (*lā ḥājata fī shayʾin baynī wa-baynahu Dijlah an tattakhidhūhu miṣran*). It is noteworthy that ʿUmar is also described as opposed to naval expeditions. According to a tradition, he developed this attitude after a Muslim unit that he had sent on

tled the Muslims in al-Anbār,[485] but they did not like it. They were afflicted with fever, and the place was not suitable for them. Saʿd wrote to ʿUmar informing him of this, and ʿUmar replied thus to Saʿd: "No place is suitable for the Arabs except grassland that suits their camels and sheep. Find a plain next to the river and seek a place for the Muslims in it." So Saʿd went forth and halted at Kuwayfat ʿUmar b. Saʿd,[486] but it was not suitable for the Muslims because of the flies and the fever. Saʿd sent a man from the Helpers, whose name was al-Ḥārith b. Salamah [according to another account, he sent ʿUthmān b. Ḥunayf, a confederate of Banū ʿAmr b. ʿAwf]. He chose for them the place in which al-Kūfah stands today and established the mosque and the settlement quarters (*khiṭaṭ*) for the Muslims.

ʿUmar b. al-Khaṭṭāb set out this year for Syria and encamped at al-Jābiyah.[487] He was given victory overy Iliyā, the city of Jerusalem (*madīnat bayt al-maqdis*). In the same year Abū ʿUbaydah b. al-Jarrāḥ sent Ḥanẓalah b. al-Ṭufayl al-Sulamī to Ḥimṣ; God enabled him
[2361] to conquer this city. Saʿd b. Abī Waqqāṣ appointed a man from Kindah, whose name was Shuraḥbīl b. al-Simṭ, to be the governor of al-Madāʾin. He is the man about whom a poet recited:

I wish I were with Saʿd b. Mālik,[488]
with Zabrāʾ,[489] and with Ibn al-Simṭ in the midst of the sea.[490]

---

an expedition to Abyssinia was wiped out. See Ṭabarī, I, 2546, 2548, 2595; Ibn Ḥajar, *Iṣābah*, IV, 561. For a brief note on this topic, with regard to early Muslim incursions into the Indian province of Sind, see Friedmann, "Minor Problems," 253–55. See also Noth, *Studien*, 24–25.

485. Al-Anbār is located on the eastern bank of the Euphrates, and Saʿd's choice therefore does not strictly conform to ʿUmar's instructions. See *EI²*, s.v. "al-Anbār" (M. Streck [A. A. Duri]).

486. Yāqūt (*Muʿjam*, IV, 331) says that Kuwayfat ʿUmar b. Saʿd was situated near Bāziqiyā, in the vicinity of Ḥillah and between the two branches of the Euphrates. For Bāziqiyā, see Yāqūt, *Muʿjam*, I, 608.

487. A city in the Jawlān (Golan), 80 kilometers south of Damascus. It became famous because of the meeting that ʿUmar is said to have held there with his governors. See *EI²*, s.v. "al-Djābiya" (H. Lammens [J. Sourdel-Thomine]); Yāqūt, *Muʿjam*, II, 3–4.

488. Saʿd b. Mālik and Saʿd b. Abī Waqqāṣ are one and the same person; see note 16, above.

489. Zabrāʾ was one of the wives of Saʿd b. Abī Waqqāṣ; see Ibn Saʿd, *Ṭabaqāt*, V, 126.

490. Probably meaning that with these persons he would feel safe, even in the middle of the sea.

An Account of the People of the Lowlands (ahl al-sawād)

According to al-Sarī — Shuʿayb — Sayf — ʿAbd al-Malik b. ʿUmayr— Qabīṣah b. Jābir: A man from among us recited on the Day of al-Qādisiyyah, when victory was attained:

We were fighting until God granted His victory,
while Saʿd took refuge at the gate of al-Qādisiyyah.
We returned after many women had been widowed,
but there is no widow among the wives of Saʿd!

The poem spread among the people and came to Saʿd's knowledge. He said: "O God, the poet is a liar; or he has said what he said out of hypocrisy, out of desire for fame and out of falsehood. [I pray you], cut off his tongue and hand, so that he does not harm me anymore!" Qabīṣah said: "By God, one day the poet was standing between the battle lines. An arrow flew at him in response to Saʿd's prayer and hit his tongue. Half of his tongue withered and he did not utter another word till his death."

According to al-Sarī—Shuʿayb—Sayf—al-Miqdām b. Shurayḥ al-Ḥārithī—his father: Jarīr recited on that day:

I am Jarīr and my agnomen (*kunyah*) is Abū ʿAmr;
God granted victory while Saʿd was in the castle!

Saʿd looked at him and said: [2362]

I do not wish Bajīlah anything except
that they be rewarded on the Day of Reckoning.
Their horses were confronted with horses,
and [their] horsemen were engaged in combat.
Had it not been for the troops of Qaʿqāʿ b. ʿAmr
and Ḥammāl,[491] they would have been inexorably drawn into retreat.
They defended your troops by stabbing
and hitting, ripping the skin open.
Had it not been for that, you would have been branded as riffraff,
and your troops disabled like flies!

491. B. Mālik; cf. p. 2308.

According to al-Sarī — Shuʿayb — Sayf — al-Qāsim b. Sulaym b. ʿAbd al-Raḥmān al-Saʿdī — ʿUthmān b. Rajāʾ al-Saʿdī: Saʿd b. Mālik[492] was the most courageous and the bravest man. He stayed in an unfortified castle between the battle lines and observed the Muslims. If [those in] the battle lines had exposed it even for a short while, it would have been captured in its entirety, but by God, the terror of these days did not cause him distress nor anxiety.

According to al-Sarī — Shuʿayb — Sayf — Sulaymān b. Bashīr — Umm Kathīr, the wife of Hammām b. al-Ḥārith al-Nakhaʿī: We were present at the battle of al-Qādisiyyah with Saʿd and with our
[2363] husbands. When he heard that the Muslims had finished [the fighting], we fastened our clothes and armed ourselves with sticks. Then we came to the mortally wounded men[493] [lying on the battlefield]. To those who were Muslims we gave water and we lifted them; those who were polytheists, we finished them off. The youngsters followed us. We charged them with this task and gave them a free hand to do it.

According to al-Sarī — Shuʿayb — Sayf — ʿAṭiyyah, who is Ibn al-Ḥārith — a person who lived through these events: No Arab tribe had more women present on the Day of al-Qādisiyyah than Bajīlah and al-Nakhaʿ. In the tribe of al-Nakhaʿ there were seven hundred unmarried women; in Bajīlah there were one thousand. One thousand men from the Arab tribes married the latter and seven hundred the former. Al-Nakhaʿ and Bajīlah were called the kinsmen of the Emigrants. The fact that Khālid, followed by al-Muthannā, Abū ʿUbayd, and the participants of the former battles, prepared the way encouraged them to travel with their belongings. Then after that they encountered great adversity.

According to al-Sarī — Shuʿayb — Sayf — Muḥammad, al-Muhallab, and Ṭalḥah: Bukayr b. ʿAbdallāh al-Laythī and ʿUtbah b. Farqad al-Sulamī and Simāk b. Kharashah al-Anṣārī (who is not the man known as Abū Dujānah) asked a woman in marriage on the Day of al-Qādisiyyah. (The women of the Muslims were with them: seven hundred women were with the tribe of al-Nakhaʿ. They were called the kinsmen of the Emigrants. The Emigrants married them im-

---

492. See note 16, above.

493. This meaning of *qatīl*, pl. *qatlā*, does not seem to be listed in the dictionaries, but it is unavoidable.

mediately before[494] the victory and after it. They married all of them. [2364]
Seven hundred men from various tribes became attached to them.)

When all the marriages were over,[495] these three men sought the same woman in marriage. She was Arwā bint ʿĀmir al-Hilāliyyah (from the clan of Hilāl, belonging to the tribe of al-Nakhaʿ.) She was the sister of Hunaydah, the wife of al-Qaʿqāʿ b. ʿAmr al-Tamīmī. Arwā said to her sister: "Consult your husband and ask him which one of them he deems a suitable match for us." Hunaydah did it after the battle, while they were still in al-Qādisiyyah. Al-Qaʿqāʿ said: "I shall describe them in a poem. Help your sister," then he recited:

If you are desirous of money, marry
Simāk, who is from the Helpers, or Ibn Farqad.
If you desire a fighter,[496] set your eyes
on Bukayr, when the horses wheel away from death.
All of them have a place on the peak of glory;
it is up to you—the matter will become clear tomorrow.

The Arabs between al-ʿUdhayb and ʿAdan Abyan,[497] between al-Ubullah and Aylah,[498] were expecting a battle between them and the Persians at al-Qādisiyyah. They understood that the continued existence of their dominion or its disappearance depended on it. In every town they were attentively listening to [information about] it and were trying to find out what was happening with regard to it. They were so preoccupied with this that when a man wanted to do something, he used to say: "I shall not consider it before I see what is happening with the affair of al-Qādisiyyah." When the battle of al-Qādisiyyah took place, it was the *jinn* who brought the news about it to humans; the news brought by the *jinn* had arrived before that which was brought by men.

A woman appeared one night on a mountain in Ṣanʿāʾ (it is not known who she was) and recited:

---

494. For *ḥattā kāna qarīban*, see Reckendorf, *Syntax*, 215.

495. Literally "when the people finished, . . ."

496. Literally "a fight" *ṭiʿān*.

497. According to Muqaddasī (*Aḥsan al-taqāsīm*, 113), Abyan was located three *farsakhs* from ʿAdan in the Yemen. ʿAdan was related to Abyan because it used to receive its agricultural products from there (Muqaddasī, *Aḥsan al-taqāsīm*, 85). For other explanations of ʿAdan Abyan, see Yāqūt, *Muʿjam*, I, 110; III, 621–22.

498. A port city at the northern end of the gulf of ʿAqabah; modern Eilat. See *EI²*, s.v. "Ayla" (H. W. Glidden).

[2365] May you be blessed on our behalf, O ʿIkrimah bint Khālid!
the best provisions are not the few, the insufficient.
May the rising sun bless you on my behalf
and every swift and solitary camel
And a group of men from the tribe of al-Nakhaʿ,
with beautiful faces, believing in Muḥammad.
They stood up to Kisrā, dealing blows to his soldiers,
with every thin-bladed, Indian sword.
When the call for help was sounded time and again,[499] they laid down the bare chest
of death,[500] and the night became black.

The people of al-Yamāmah[501] heard a passerby sing the following verses:

We found the Banū Tamīm, who were numerous,
the most steadfast of men on the morning of battle.
They set out with a huge army,[502] dense in formation,
against a tumultuous [enemy army] and drove it away, dispersed.
They are seas [of generosity], but for the Persian kings they are men
like lions of the forests; you would think they were mountains.
They left[503] in Qādis glory and honor

499. For *thawwaba* in this sense, see Bevan, *Naqāʾiḍ*, III, 302.

500. This verse calls for an explanation. When a camel kneels down, he puts his heavy chest on the ground and bears down on it (see Bevan, *Naqāʾiḍ*, III, 540). In classical Arabic poetry war is metaphorically described in a similar way; it is putting its chest down and crushing whatever happens to be underneath it. See Abū Tammān, *Ḥamāsah*, I, 120:

anakhtum ʿalaynā kalkala ʾl-ḥarbi marratan
fa-naḥnu munīkhūhā ʿalaykum bi-kalkali,

and Yāqūt, *Muʿjam*, IV, 144 l. 5. For the connection between the kneeling camel and this description, see Abū Tammām, *Ḥamāsah*, I, 145. See also Abū Tammām, *Naqāʾiḍ*, 66 l. 10; and Ibn Kathīr, *Bidāyah*, VII, 47. In this verse the Nakhaʿīs are described as responding to the repeated calls for help and as bearing down on the enemy with the bare chest of death.

501. Al-Yamāmah was a district in central Arabia. See Yāqūt, *Muʿjam*, IV, 1026–34; *EI*[1], s.v. "al-Yamāma" (A. Grohmann).

502. For *arʿan* in this sense, see de Goeje's *Glossary*, referring to al-Masʿūdī, *Tanbīh*, 280 l. 15.

503. Reading *humū tarakū*, a variant mentioned in the Leiden edition, instead of *taraknā*. For a slightly different version of the poem, see Ibn Kathīr, *Bidāyah*, VII, 47.

and long battle days on the two mountain slopes.
[They left the Persians'] hands and feet crushed to pieces [2366]
with a rock where they encountered the men.

Poems like this were heard in the entire land of the Arabs.

According to al-Sarī — Shuʿayb — Sayf — Muḥammad, al-Muhallab, and Ṭalḥah: Saʿd wrote [to ʿUmar] about the victory, informing him of the number of the Persians whom they had killed and of the number of Muslims who had been killed. He sent to ʿUmar the names of his acquaintances by the hand of Saʿd b. ʿUmaylah al-Fazārī.

According to the previous chain of transmission, and also according to al-Naḍr b. al-Sarī — Ibn al-Rufayl b. Maysūr: Saʿd's letter read as follows:

> Now, then (*ammā baʿdu*), God granted us victory over the Persians and treated them in the way in which He had treated their coreligionists who preceded them.[504] [Victory came] after a long fight and violent upheaval. They confronted the Muslims with an army such as had never been seen before. God did not allow them to benefit from this, but rather, He deprived them of it and gave it over to the Muslims. The Muslims pursued them on the canals, on the edge of the thicket (*ʿalā ṭufūf al-ājām*), and on the roads. Saʿd b. ʿUbayd, the Qurʾān reader,[505] and so-and-so and so-and-so were killed from among the Muslims. Also killed were Muslims whom we do not know, but God knows them.[506] When night fell, they were whispering the Qurʾān, humming like bees. They were lions among men, and the [real] lions did not resemble them. Those who died from among [2367] them were not superior to those who survived, except by the virtue of martyrdom, which had not been decreed for the latter.

504. De Goeje understands *sunana man kāna qablahum* against the background of *sunnat al-awwalīn* in Qurʾān 18:56; this was interpreted as divine punishment or annihilation. See Ṭabarī, *Tafsīr*, XV, 173; Bayḍāwī, *Anwār*, III, 228–29; and de Goeje's *Glossary*, s.v. *m-t-ḥ*.

505. Saʿd b. ʿUbayd was an Anṣārī Companion and fought in the early battles of Islam. He is said to have been engaged in the collection of the Qurʾān during the Prophet's lifetime. See Ibn Saʿd, *Ṭabaqāt*, III/ii, 30; (ʿI.) Ibn al-Athīr, *Usd*, II, 285–86; Ibn Ḥajar, *Iṣābah*, III, 68.

506. And will reward them.

According to al-Sarī—Shuʿayb—Sayf—Mujālid b. Saʿīd: When ʿUmar b. al-Khaṭṭāb learned that Rustam had established camp at al-Qādisiyyah, he gathered information from the riders about the people of al-Qādisiyyah from morning till midday. Then he went back to his family and home. When ʿUmar met the bearer of news, he asked him: "From where [are you coming]?" The bearer of news replied. ʿUmar said: "O ʿAbdallāh,[507] tell me." The bearer of news said: "God has defeated the enemy!" ʿUmar was jogging along while the other man was riding his she-camel without having recognized ʿUmar. When they entered Medina, the people began to greet ʿUmar as the Commander of the Faithful. The man said: "May God have mercy upon you, why did you not tell me that you were the Commander of the Faithful?" ʿUmar said: "O my brother, you are not to blame."

According to al-Sarī—Shuʿayb—Sayf—Muḥammad, Ṭalḥah, al-Muhallab, and Ziyād: The Muslims were expecting the arrival of the news bearer and of ʿUmar's orders. They were evaluating the spoils, estimating the numbers of their troops, and putting their affairs in order.

The Iraqi participants in previous battles who fought at al-Yarmūk and Damascus followed one another and returned to reinforce the people of al-Qādisiyyah. They came to al-Qādisiyyah on the next day and on the day following it.[508] The first of them came on the Day of al-Aghwāth and the last on the second day after victory. Reinforcements including [men from] Murād, Hamdān, and other tribes arrived. The Muslims in al-Qādisiyyah wrote about them to ʿUmar
[2368] and asked him what was the proper treatment which should be given to these people;[509] this was the second letter after victory, sent with Nadhīr b. ʿAmr.

When the news of victory reached ʿUmar, he stood in the midst of the Muslims, read to them the letter in which victory was announced,[510] and said:

---

507. The name ʿAbdallāh is used for any Muslim whose name is not known to his interlocutor.

508. The following sentence indicates that the "next day" (*al-ghad*) is the second day of the battle, the Day of Aghwāth.

509. Probably about the question whether or not these men were entitled to a share in the spoils.

510. For *fatḥ* in this sense, see *Glossary*, s.v. *f-t-ḥ*.

> I am eager to provide for every need as long as the means are sufficient for everyone. Should this not be possible, we shall share our food so that we are equal in the means of subsistence. I wish you to know my feelings with regard to you. I am not your teacher except by what I do. By God, I am not a king so that I should enslave you; I am only a servant of God to whom a trust was offered. If I were to refuse to take it and were to return it to you, and if I were to follow you until you eat and drink to your satisfaction in your homes, I would be happy. If I were to take the trust and invite you to follow me into my home, I would be miserable. I would experience little happiness and feel a great deal of grief. I shall not be forgiven, nor shall I be restored [to my former condition][511] so that I could ask you a favor.

They wrote to ʿUmar [sending the letter] with Anas b. al-Ḥulays:

> Some inhabitants of the *sawād* claim to have treaties. Nobody except the people of Bāniqyā,[512] Basmā,[513] and Ullays al-ākhirah[514] stayed [on their land] according to the treaty agreed upon with the Muslims who had fought in the previous battles (*ahl al-ayyām*) and nobody fulfilled it.[515] The inhabitants of the *sawād* have claimed that the Persians forcibly recruited them into the army.[516] They did not come to us and did not migrate. [2369]

Saʿd wrote [to ʿUmar, sending the letter] with Abū al-Hayyāj al-Asadī [also known as Ibn Mālik]:

> The inhabitants of the *sawād* migrated from their land. With regard to those who held fast to their treaty and did not

511. In which I held no public office. The translation of this sentence is tentative.

512. Bāniqyā was a village in the vicinity of al-Kūfah. See Yāqūt, *Muʿjam*, I, 483–84; Oppenheimer *et al.*, *Babylonia*, index.

513. Basmā was a village in the vicinity of al-Kūfah. See Donner, *Conquests*, 180; Morony, *Iraq*, 151.

514. For Ullays, see Donner, *Conquests*, 329 n. 66.

515. For the treaty concluded by Khālid b. al-Walīd (or by Jarīr b. ʿAbdallāh al-Bajalī on Khālid's behalf) with the people of Bāniqyā, Basmā, and Ullays, see Ṭabarī, I, 2019, 2049; Balādhurī, *Futūḥ*, 244–45; and Donner, *Conquests*, 180, for additional sources.

516. For this meaning of *ḥasharūhum* see de Goeje's *Glossary* to Balādhurī, *Futūḥ*; and Kister, "Some Reports," 3, 6 (n. 22: *nuslimu ʿalā an lā nuḥshara*), 10–11.

help [the enemy] against us,[517] we implemented the agreements made between them and the Muslims who had been here before us. They claimed that [some] inhabitants of the *sawād* proceeded to al-Madā'in. Make a new ruling for us with regard to those who remained [in their abodes],[518] for those who migrated, and for those who claim to have been forcibly recruited into the [Persian] army, fled away, did not fight, or surrendered. We are in a desirable land; it is empty of its inhabitants and we are few. Those who want to make peace with us are numerous. To gain their goodwill will bring prosperity to us and weakness to our enemy.[519]

ʿUmar stood up in the midst of the people and said:

Those who act according to their passions and are disobedient, their fortune will collapse and they will harm only themselves. Those who follow the *sunnah*, abide by the laws of religion, and adhere to the manifest way—out of desire to obtain what God has in store for people who obey Him—will do the right thing and will be fortunate. This will be so because God the Exalted says: "And they will find what they did present and your Lord will not treat anybody with injustice."[520] The people who fought in the previous battles and those who fought in al-Qawādis[521] took hold of the area close to them. Its inhabitants migrated. Those who stayed [on their land] according to the treaty agreed upon with the Muslims who had fought in the previous battles came to the Muslims [who fought in al-Qādisiyyah]. What is your view of those who claim that they were forcibly recruited into the [Persian] army; of those who did not claim this, did not stay, and migrated; of those who stayed, did not claim anything, and did not migrate; and of those who surrendered?

---

517. See de Goeje's *Glossary* to Balādhurī, *Futūḥ*, s.v. *j-l-b*; and Lane, *Lexicon*, 439b.

518. For this meaning of *tamma*, see Dozy, *Supplément*, s.v.

519. Cf. Donner, *Conquests*, 260.

520. Qur'ān 18:47.

521. It seems that this term means the three days of battle in al-Qādisiyyah.

The Muslims unanimously decided that the treaty should be fulfilled with regard to those who had stayed and had refrained [from fighting the Muslims]; their being overwhelmed would only improve their position. Those who made a claim which was accounted genuine or who fulfilled [the conditions of their treaty] would have the status of the former group.[522] If their claim is considered false, the treaty will be revoked and the Muslims will make a new peace treaty with them. [They also decided] that the matter of those who [2370] migrated should be decided at the discretion of the Muslims. If they wish, they will make a treaty with them and [the migrants] will become *ahl al-dhimmah;* if the Muslims wish [otherwise], they will persevere in preventing them from returning to their land and offer them nothing except war. Those who have stayed and have surrendered will be offered the choice between paying the poll tax and exile. The same applies to the peasants.

ʿUmar wrote a reply to the letter brought by Anas b. al-Ḥulays, saying:

> Now, then, God the Exalted has granted in certain cases a dispensation (*rukhṣah*)[523] in every matter, except in just conduct and in the remembrance of God (*dhikr*). As for the remembrance of God there can be no dispensation with regard to it in any event, and only abundance of it is satisfactory.[524] As for justice, there can also be no dispensation with regard to it, neither for relative nor for stranger, neither in adversity nor in prosperity. Even if justice seems to be lenient, it is stronger and more effective in suppressing injustice and falsehood than injustice, even if it seems harsh. It is [also] more effective in uprooting infidelity.
>
> Those inhabitants of *sawād* who held fast to their treaty and did not help the enemy against you in any way have the protection (*dhimmah*) and must pay the poll tax. As for

522. Those who claimed that they had been forcibly recruited but had otherwise fulfilled the conditions of their treaty will be treated in the same way as those who stayed on their land and did not fight the Muslims.

523. For the concept of *rukhṣah* in early Islam, see Kister, "Concessions."

524. Alluding to Qur'ān 33:41: "Oh those who believe, remember God in abundance." The *dhikr* later became an important ritual of Muslim mystics. See *EI*², s.v. "Dhikr" (L. Gardet).

> those who claim that they were forced [to leave the land] and did not come to you after the Persians had gone or migrated, do not believe what they have claimed, unless you wish to. If you do not so wish, revoke the treaty and escort them to a place which is secure for them.[525]

ʿUmar replied to the letter brought by Abū al-Hayyāj, saying:

> As for those who stayed and did not migrate without having a treaty, they will have the same rights as those who have a treaty because they stayed for your sake and refrained from fighting you, in response to your call. The same applies to the peasants, if they behaved in the same manner. Those who have claimed [to have been forcibly evicted or recruited] will have protection if their claim is considered true. If it is considered false, their treaty will be revoked. As
> [2371] for those who assisted [the Persians] and migrated, this is a matter placed by God at your discretion. If you wish, invite them to stay on their land for your sake. They will have protection and will be obliged to pay the poll tax. Should they dislike this, divide among yourselves their property which God has restored to you.[526]

When ʿUmar's letters reached Saʿd b. Mālik[527] and the Muslims, they made offers to those who had migrated from the areas close to them and left the *sawād* to return: They would have protection and would be obliged to pay the poll tax. They returned and became *ahl al-dhimmah* like those who had stayed and held fast to their treaty, but their land tax (*kharāj*) was made heavier. The Muslims gave the same status to those who claimed to have been forcibly evicted and fled; they made a treaty with them, giving those who stayed the status of those who had treaties. The same applied to the peasants.

The Muslims did not include in the peace conditions the property of the royal family, of those who had left [the *sawād*] with them and had not accepted the alternative offer of embracing Islam or paying the poll tax. This property became immovable booty (*fay*ʾ) of those

---

525. Alluding to Qurʾān 8:58 and 9:6.
526. Cf. note 471, above.
527. He is Saʿd b. Abī Waqqāṣ; cf. note 16, above.

to whom God had restored it. This and the first state domains (*ṣawāfī*)[528] became the property of those to whom Allāh had restored them.

The rest of the *sawād* [inhabitants] became *ahl al-dhimmah*. The Muslims imposed upon them the land tax (*kharāj*) which had previously been levied by the Persian king. It was to be paid by every man,[529] proportionately to the property and the land which he possessed. The property that God restored to the Muslims included the property of the Persian royal family and of those who had gone with them, the families of those who had fought on the side of the Persians and their property, the property of the fire temples, the thicket, the marshes, the property of the mail service,[530] and the property of the Persian royal family.[531] It was not feasible to divide the booty that had belonged to the Persian king and to those who had gone with him because it was scattered all over the entire *sawād*. It was administered for those who were entitled to it (*ahl al-fay'*) by [2372]
people whom they trusted and agreed upon. This is what was debated between the *ahl al-fay'*, not the greater part of the *sawād*. When the *ahl al-fay'* were in dispute among themselves, the administrators deemed its division between them easy. This is what made the ignorant people confused about the affair of the *sawād*, and, if the intelligent people had supported the ignorant who asked the administrators to divide the *fay'*, they would have divided it between them. But the intelligent ones refused [to support the idea], and the administrators followed (the advice of) the intelligent and neglected the views of the ignorant. ʿAlī (b. Abī Ṭālib) and everyone who was asked to divide the *fay'* acted in the same way, followed [the advice] of the intelligent, and neglected the views of the ignorant. They said: "[We refrain from dividing the *fay'*] so that you do not hit each other in the face."[532]

---

528. See Løkkegaard, *Taxation*, index; Duri, "Taxation," 139. It is not clear what is meant by the "first" *ṣawāfī*.

529. Literally "The *kharāj* of Kisrā was [imposed] on the heads of men. . . . "

530. *Mā kāna li-'l-sikak* should be understood in light of a parallel passage in Ṭabarī, I, 2468: *mā kāna . . . li-sikak al-burūd*. Cf. Løkkegaard, *Taxation*, 168, 224.

531. In this form the last part of the sentence is redundant: The property of the royal family has already been mentioned. As de Goeje pointed out in his notes, some description of this property seems to be missing.

532. In order to get the better portion. The question whether it was more advisable to divide the conquered lands of Iraq between the warriors or to keep them as a per-

According to al-Sarī — Shuʿayb — Sayf — Muḥammad b. Qays — ʿĀmir al-Shaʿbī: I (Muḥammad b. Qays) said to ʿĀmir al-Shaʿbī:[533] "What is the status of the *sawād*?" He replied: "It was conquered by force (*ʿanwatan*) and so was the entire land except for the fortresses. The inhabitants migrated and were then invited to make peace and receive protection. They responded, returned, and became *ahl al-dhimmah*. They are obliged to pay the poll tax, and they enjoy protection. This is the *sunnah*, and this is what the Messenger of God did in Dūmah."[534] The property of the Persian royal family and of those who migrated with them remained the *fay*ʾ of those to whom God had restored it.

According to al-Sarī — Shuʿayb — Sayf — Ṭalḥah — Sufyān — Māhān: God conquered the *sawād* by force; the same applies to the entire land between the *sawād* and the river of Balkh,[535] except for the fortresses. The inhabitants were invited to make peace and became *ahl al-dhimmah*, and their land remained in their possession. The property of the royal family and of their followers was not included
[2373] in this arrangement; this became the *fay*ʾ of those to whom God had restored it. Nothing of the conquests becomes *fay*ʾ until it is divided,[536] as is meant by His saying: "Whatever booty you take,[537] i.e., of what you divide among yourselves.

According to al-Sarī — Shuʿayb — Sayf — Ismāʿīl b. Muslim — al-Ḥasan b. Abī Ḥasan: Most of what the Muslims conquered is land taken by force (*ʿanwah*); then they invited the inhabitants to return and receive protection. They made them the offer of paying the poll

---

petual source of income for the community was debated between ʿUmar and leading Muslims. The view of ʿUmar, who opposed the division, prevailed. See Abu Yūsuf, *Kharāj*, 67–72, 86–87; Ibn Sallām, *Amwāl*, 57–59.

533. Cf. Ṭabarī, I, 2062 l. 1.

534. See note 541, below. For the issue of the status of the *sawād* lands, see also Ṭabarī, *Ikhtilāf*, 220.

535. *Nahr Balkh* is the Oxus, in Arabic Jayḥūn. See Yāqūt, *Muʿjam*, I, 713; Le Strange, *Lands*, 434.

536. Those parts of the *sawād* that were not divided among the Muslims but remained the property of the original inhabitants, who were subject to the payment of the poll tax, were therefore not considered part of the *fay*ʾ.

537. The first words are part of Qurʾān 8:41, which reads: "Whatever booty you take, one-fifth of it is God's and the Messenger's. . . ." The verse is adduced because it speaks about the division of the booty; it is taken to be a proof that only things that are divided among the Muslims can be considered *fay*ʾ. In his commentary on the Qurʾān Ṭabarī also maintains that the verse speaks about booty that is being divided. See Ṭabarī *Tafsīr*, X, 3 ll. 10–11.

tax, and when the inhabitants agreed to this, they extended protection to them.

According to Sayf — ʿAmr b. Muḥammad — al-Shaʿbī: I said to him: "Some people claim that the people of the *sawād* are slaves."[538] He replied:

> On what basis would poll tax be taken from slaves? The *sawād* was taken by force. The same applies to all the land you know, except some fortresses on the mountains and the like. The inhabitants were invited to return, they came back, the poll tax was accepted from them, and they became *ahl al-dhimmah*. Whatever was taken as spoils can be divided, but that which was not taken as spoils whose owners had agreed to pay the poll tax beforehand belongs to them. This is the *sunnah* with regard to it.

According to al-Sarī — Shuʿayb — Sayf — Abū Ḍamrah — ʿAbdallāh b. al-Mustawrid — Muḥammad b. Sīrīn: All lands were taken by force, except a few fortresses whose inhabitants concluded a treaty before they were allowed to leave. They — meaning the people who were conquered by force — were invited to return and to pay the poll tax, and they became *ahl al-dhimmah*, both the people of the *sawād* and those of the mountains. This was the way in which the *ahl al-fayʾ* were treated.[539] ʿUmar and the Muslims acted with regard to the poll tax and protection according to the custom enacted by the Messenger of God in this matter. He sent Khālid b. al-Walīd from [2374]
Tabūk[540] to Dūmat al-Jandal and conquered it by force. He took its king Ukaydir b. ʿAbd al-Malik captive. He invited him to receive protection and pay the poll tax, after his land had been conquered by force and he himself had been taken prisoner.[541] Khālid did the same

538. In Ṭabarī's *Ikhtilāf*, 225, this view is attributed to the jurisprudent Sharīk b. ʿAbdallāh al-Nakhaʿī; for information about him, see Ibn Ḥajar, *Tahdhīb*, IV, 333–37; and Schmucker, *Untersuchungen*, 149.

539. If the text is correct, it means that those entitled to the booty were consistently treated in this way; the land was left in the possession of the inhabitants and not divided among them.

540. Tabūk is a city in the northern part of the Arabian peninsula. See Yāqūt, *Muʿjam*, I, 824–25; and *EI²*, s.v. "Tabūk" (F. Buhl).

541. Dūmat al-Jandal is located in the northwestern part of the Arabian peninsula, at the head of Wādī Sirhān. See *EI²*, s.v. "Dūmat al-Djandal" (L. Veccia Vaglieri); and *EI¹*, s.v. "Djawf al-Sirḥān" (H. von Wissmann *et al.*); for its geographic location, see also *EI²*, s.v. "Badw" (J. Schleifer), map. According to one tradition, the Prophet sent

with the two sons of ʿArīḍ, after they had been captured and claimed to be Ukaydir's friends. He concluded a treaty with them, stipulating payment of the poll tax and protection. In the same way he handled the affair of Yuḥannah b. Ru'bah, the ruler of Aylah.[542] [The things which are customarily done are not according to the traditions transmitted by the few. Whoever relates things other than those done by the just imāms and the Muslims is lying about them and staining their honor.]

According to Sayf—Ḥajjāj al-Ṣawwāf—Muslim, the client of Ḥudhayfah: The Emigrants and the Helpers married women from the *sawād* who belonged to the People of the two Books. If the people of the *sawād* were slaves, the Muslims would not have been permitted to do this. It would not have been permissible for them to marry slave girls belonging to the People of the Book, because God the Exalted says: "Those of you who do not have the means [to marry free, believing women, let them marry your believing slave girls who have come into your possession]."[543] He did not say "their slave girls" [which would mean slave girls] from among the People of the two Books.[544].

According to Sayf—ʿAbd al-Malik b. Abī Sulaymān—Saʿīd b. Jubayr: After ʿUmar b. al-Khaṭṭāb appointed Ḥudhayfah to be gover-

---

Khālid b. al-Walīd on an expedition against it in the year 9/630–31. The town was ruled by Ukaydir b. ʿAbd al-Malik, who was a Christian from the tribe of Kindah. Khālid won the battle, took Ukaydir prisoner, and brought him before the Prophet. The Prophet spared his life, concluded with him a treaty stipulating payment of the poll tax, and set him free. See Ṭabarī, I, 1702–3; Ibn Saʿd, *Ṭabaqāt*, II/i, 119–20; Yāqūt, *Muʿjam*, II, 626. Ukaydir was then killed after an attack launched against Dūmat al-Jandal by Khālid b. al-Walīd in 12/633–34. See Ṭabarī, I, 2065–66, 2077.

It should be noted, however, that, according to another tradition recorded by Balādhurī (*Futūḥ*, 61–62, quoted by Yāqūt, *Muʿjam*, II, 627) and Ibn Saʿd (*Ṭabaqāt*, I/ii, 36), Ukaydir embraced Islam; in that case his story would be irrelevant to the issue at hand.

542. For Aylah, see note 498, above. Muslim historians are not aware of any fighting that preceded the conclusion of a treaty and the imposition of the poll tax on Yuḥannah b. Ru'bah. Ṭabarī himself says (I, 1702) that, when the Prophet reached Tabūk, Yuḥannah b. Ru'bah came to him, concluded a treaty, and agreed to pay the poll tax. See Balādhurī, *Futūḥ*, 59; Ibn Saʿd, *Ṭabaqāt*, I/ii, 28–29, 37.

543. The part of the verse that is in parentheses is not quoted by Ṭabarī.

544. See Qur'ān 4:24. The commentators are not in agreement on whether the verse really forbids Muslims to marry Jewish and Christian slave girls. See Ṭabarī, *Tafsīr*, V, 12–13. Ṭabarī's own view in favor of this interpretation is on p. 13 ll. 9–17. Ṭabarī mentions the legality of marriages between Muslims and the *sawād* women in order to prove that the inhabitants of the *sawād* were free *dhimmīs* and not slaves.

nor of al-Madā'in and the number of (unmarried) Muslim women increased, he sent him a message saying: "It came to my knowledge that you have married a woman from al-Madā'in, belonging to the [2375] People of the Book. Divorce her." Ḥudhayfah wrote back to him: "I shall not do it until you inform me whether it is permissible or forbidden, and what is the intention of this [order]." ʿUmar wrote to Ḥudhayfah: "It is indeed permissible, but the non-Arab women are captivating, and if you draw near to them they will wrest you from your wives." Ḥudhayfah said: "[I shall do it] now," and he divorced her.

According to al-Sarī—Shuʿayb—Sayf—Ashʿath b. Siwār—Abū al-Zubayr—Jābir: I participated in the battle of al-Qādisiyyah with Saʿd. We married women from the People of the Book, as we did not find many Muslim women. When we returned, some of us divorced them and some of us kept them.

According to Sayf—ʿAbd al-Malik b. Abī Sulaymān—Saʿīd b. Jubayr: The *sawād* was conquered by force. The inhabitants were invited to return and became *ahl al-dhimmah*, but the property of the royal family and of their followers became booty of those who were entitled to it (*fay' li-ahlihi*). This was what the people of al-Kūfah understood; when this understanding was forgotten, their view was taken as referring to the entire *sawād*. But the status of their *sawād* is like that.[545]

According to Sayf—al-Mustanīr b. Yazīd—Ibrāhīm b. Yazīd al-Nakhaʿī: The *sawād* was taken by force. The inhabitants were invited to return, and those who responded were obliged to pay the poll tax and received protection, while the property of those who refused became *fay'*. It is not permissible to sell anything of this *fay'* between al-ʿUdhayb and the Mountains (*al-jabal*), neither in the *sawād* nor in the Mountains.[546]

According to Sayf—Muḥammad b. Qays—al-Shaʿbī: The same tradition: It is not permissible to sell anything of this *fay'* between the Mountains and al-ʿUdhayb. [2376]

According to Sayf—ʿAmr b. Muḥammad—ʿĀmir: al-Zubayr,

545. If the text is correct, it probably means that, in contradistinction to the property of the royal family, which became *fay'*, most of the *sawād* remained in the possession of its inhabitants, in the way described (see, e.g., p. 2372, below).

546. Meaning the province of Jibāl ("the Mountains"), situated to the east of the Iraqi lowlands. See Le Strange, *Lands*, 185ff.

Khabbāb,[547] Ibn Masʿūd,[548] Ibn Yāsir,[549] and Ibn Habbār received fiefs in the days of ʿUthmān. If ʿUthmān committed an error, then those who accepted the error from him committed a greater one; they are the people from whom we have received our religion.[550] ʿUmar gave a fief to Ṭalḥah,[551] to Jarīr b. ʿAbdallāh, and to al-Ribbīl b. ʿAmr. He gave the Dār al-Fīl[552] to Abū Mufazzir and to others from whom we took [our religion]. All the fiefs were freely divided from out of the fifth of the *fay*ʾ.

ʿUmar wrote to ʿUthmān b. Ḥunayf[553] (sending the letter) with Jarīr: "Now, then, give Jarīr a fief sufficient for his sustenance, no less and no more." ʿUthmān wrote to ʿUmar: "Jarīr brought to me a letter in which you allocated to him a fief sufficient for his sustenance. I did not want to put it into effect before I could contact you in this matter." ʿUmar wrote to him: "Jarīr spoke the truth. Carry out my instructions, but you did well to consult me." ʿUmar [also] gave a fief to Abū Mūsā.[554] ʿAlī gave al-Kurdūsiyyah to Kurdūs b. Hāniʾ and gave a fief to Suwayd b. Ghafalah al-Juʿfī.[555]

---

547. Khabbāb b. al-Aratt beloned to the tribe of Tamīm. A blacksmith and sword maker by trade, he was taken prisoner in the Jāhiliyyah and was sold into slavery in Mecca. He was one of the first Muslims and is said to have been severely tortured by the Meccans because of his conversion. After the *hijrah* he participated in the early battles of Islam. He died as a rich man in al-Kūfah in 37/657–58. See Ibn Saʿd, *Ṭabaqāt*, III, 116–18; (ʿI.) Ibn al-Athīr, *Usd*, II, 106–8; Ibn Ḥajar, *Iṣābah*, II, 258–59 no. 2212; Ibn Ḥajar, *Tahdhīb*, III, 133–34; Goldziher, *Introduction*, 118.

548. See *EI²*, s.v. "Ibn Masʿūd" (J. C. Vadet).

549. ʿAmmār b. Yāsir was born in Mecca to his father (who belonged to the tribe of Madhḥij and had moved to Mecca from the Yemen) and Sumayyah, a slave girl, or *mawlāt* attached to the clan of Makhzūm. After embracing Islam, he was tortured by the Meccans, who tried to force him to renege on his new religion. Tradition makes him the first man to build a mosque in Islam. Having emigrated to Medina with the Prophet, he participated in the battles of nascent Islam. He was killed in the battle of Ṣiffīn at the age of ninety-three. See Ibn Saʿd, *Ṭabaqāt*, III/i, 176–89; VI, 7–8; (ʿI.) Ibn al-Athīr, *Usd*, IV, 43–47; Ibn Ḥajar, *Iṣābah*, IV, 575–76 no. 5707; Ibn Ḥajar, *Tahdhīb*, VI, 408–10.

550. It was therefore their responsibility to act properly and not to accept fiefs in a way incompatible with the rules mentioned above.

551. See *EI¹*, s.v. "Ṭalḥah" (G. Levi della Vida).

552. Balādhurī (*Futūḥ*, 358) mentions a place called Dār al-Fīl in al-Baṣrah.

553. ʿUthmān b. Ḥunayf belonged to the tribe of Aws and was one of the Helpers (*anṣār*). ʿUmar put him in charge of the *sawād* lands. He is said to have imposed the poll tax and the land tax on its inhabitants. He died during the reign of Muʿāwiyah. See (ʿI.) Ibn al-Athīr, *Usd*, III, 371; Ibn ʿAbd al-Barr, *Istīʿāb*, 483; Ibn Ḥajar, *Iṣābah*, IV, 449 no. 5439; Ibn Ḥajar, *Tahdhīb*, VII, 112–13.

554. For Abū Mūsā al-Ashʿarī, see *EI²*, s.v. "al-Ashʿarī, Abū Mūsā" (L. Veccia Vaglieri).

555. Suwayd b. Ghafalah belonged to the tribe of Madhḥij. He embraced Islam and

According to Sayf—Thābit b. Huraym—Suwayd b. Ghafalah: "I asked ʿAlī for a fief. He said: Write the following: This is a fief given by ʿAlī to Suwayd: the land of Dādhawayhi[556] between this and that point and what God has willed."

According to Sayf—al-Mustanīr—Ibrāhīm b. Yazīd: ʿUmar said: [2377]
"If you conclude a peace treaty with a people, state that you are not responsible to them for the excesses committed by the troops without authorization." So they were writing to those with whom they concluded a peace treaty: "We are not responsible to you for the excesses committed by the troops without authorization."[557]

Al-Wāqidī said: The battle of al-Qādisiyyah and its conquest took place in the year 16/37–38. Some of the people of al-Kūfah say that the battle of al-Qādisiyyah took place in the year 15/636–37. [Al-Ṭabarī] has said: The correct version in our view is that it occurred in the year 14/635–6. Muḥammad b. Isḥāq said: It took place in the year 15/636–37. His account of this has been related.

The Building of al-Baṣrah

Abū Jaʿfar (al-Ṭabarī) has said: According to al-Wāqidī's account, ʿUmar b. al-Khaṭṭāb ordered the Muslims in the year 14/635–36 to worship during the nights of Ramaḍān in the mosques of Medina. He wrote to the newly established garrison towns (*al-amṣār*) and ordered the Muslims to do the same.

In this year—meaning the year 14/635–36—ʿUmar b. al-Khaṭṭāb dispatched ʿUtbah b. Ghazwān to al-Baṣrah and ordered him to encamp in it with those who accompanied him and to cut off the supplies of the Persians in al-Madāʾin and the vicinity. This is according to the version of al-Madāʾinī. Sayf maintained that al-Baṣrah was es-

---

paid the poor tax during the lifetime of the Prophet but came to Medina only after his death. He participated in the battles of Yarmūk and al-Qādisiyyah and was ʿAlī's supporter in the battle of Ṣiffīn. He claimed to have been born in the "Year of the Elephant" (ca. A.D. 570) and is said to have died more than 120 years old in 80, 81, or 82/699–702. See Ibn Saʿd, *Ṭabaqāt*, VI, 45–46; (ʿI.) Ibn al-Athīr, *Usd*, II, 379–80; Ibn Ḥajar, *Iṣābah*, III, 270 no. 3723; Ibn Ḥajar, *Tahdhīb*, IV, 278–79.

556. Dādhawayhi al-Isṭakhrī was of Persian extraction and an inhabitant of the Yemen (cf. note 470, above). In the Islamic tradition he is mentioned as one of the killers of al-Aswad al-ʿAnsī, the Yemeni claimant to prophethood. He was killed by Qays b. Makshūḥ during the *riddah* rebellion. See Ibn Saʿd, *Ṭabaqāt*, V, 390; Ṭabarī, I, 1990–91 and index; (ʿI.) Ibn al-Athīr, *Usd*, II, 129.

557. For this meaning of *maʿarrat al-juyūsh* see Lane, *Lexicon*, s.v. *ʿ-r-r*; Ibn Manẓūr, *Lisān, al-ʿArab*, s.v. *ʿ-r-r* (IV, 556b); and Blachère *et al.*, *Dictionnaire*, s.v. *b-r-ʾ*.

tablished in the spring of the year 16/637–38 and that ʿUtbah b. Ghazwān set out for al-Baṣrah from al-Madāʾin after Saʿd had finished [the battles] of Jalūlāʾ,[558] Takrīt,[559] and al-Ḥiṣnān.[560] He was sent there by Saʿd according to ʿUmar's orders.

According to al-Sarī — Shuʿayb: according to ʿUmar b. Shabbah; according to ʿAlī b. Muḥammad — Abū Mikhnaf — Mujālid — al-
[2378] Shaʿbī: Mihrān[561] was killed in the month of Ṣafar in the year 14/ March–April 635. ʿUmar said to ʿUtbah — meaning Ibn Ghazwān:

> God the Exalted has conquered at the hand of your brethren al-Ḥīrah and its vicinity. One of the chieftains of al-Ḥīrah was killed. I do not feel safe that their Persian brethren will not help them. I therefore wish to send you to [al-Ubullah, known as] "the land of India"[562] in order that you may prevent the people of that area from assisting their brethren against your brethren and in order to fight them; it may be that God will grant you victory. So go with the blessing of God. Fear God as much as you can, rule with justice, perform the prayer at the appointed time, and remember God frequently.[563]

ʿUtbah set off with three hundred and ten odd men and was joined by some Bedouins and inhabitants of the desert. He reached al-Baṣrah with five hundred men, more or less, and encamped there in the month of Rabīʿ al-Awwal or Rabīʿ al-Ākhir of the year 14/635–36. At that time al-Baṣrah was called "the land of India,"[564] and there

---

558. See note 480, above.

559. On Takrīt and its conquest in the year 16/637–38, see *EI*¹, s.v. "Takrīt" (J. H. Kramers); Ṭabarī, I, 2474–77; Yāqūt, *Muʿjam*, I, 861–63.

560. The conquest of al-Ḥiṣnān is mentioned in conjunction with that of Takrīt (see Ṭabarī, I, 2476–77, 2481–82). The exact location of al-Ḥiṣnān is not given by Yāqūt (*Muʿjam*, II, 275), who devotes his entry to the grammatical form of the *nisbah* of al-Ḥiṣnān. See, however, (ʿI.) Ibn al-Athīr, *Kāmil*, II, 408 (and cf. Juynboll, *Conquest*, 55 n. 188), where al-Ḥiṣnān ("the two fortresses") are said to be Nīnawā (= Nineveh) and al-Mawṣil.

561. Mihrān b. Bādhān al-Hamadhānī was a commander in the Persian army. According to another account, he was killed in the battle of Buwayb in the year 13/634–35 (see Ṭabarī, I, 2192, 2199, and index).

562. See Ṭabarī, I, 2223 l. 11, where al-Ubullah is called *farj al-Hind*; cf. note 57, above. For *arḍ al-Hind* as an epithet for al-Ubullah, see Yāqūt, *Muʿjam*, I, 641.

563. Cf. Qurʾān 33:41.

564. See note 57, above.

were white, coarse stones in it.[565] ʿUtbah encamped in al-Khuraybah.[566] [In the area of al-Baṣrah] there were seven villages (*dasākir*): in al-Zābūqah,[567] in Khuraybah, in the area of Banū Tamīm, and in the area of al-Azd. Two were in al-Khuraybah, two in the area of al-Azd, two in the area of Banū Tamīm, and one in al-Zābūqah. ʿUtbah wrote to ʿUmar and described for him the area in which he had encamped. ʿUmar wrote back to him: "Gather the people together in one place and do not scatter them." ʿUtbah stayed there for several months without making any raids and without confronting anyone.

According to Muḥammad b. Bashshār—Ṣafwān b. ʿĪsā al-Zuhrī—ʿAmr b. ʿĪsā Abū Naʿāmah al-ʿAdawī—Khālid b. ʿUmayr and Shuwaysh Abū al-Ruqqād: ʿUmar b. al-Khaṭṭāb dispatched ʿUtbah [2379] b. Ghazwān and said to him: "Set out, you and those who are with you. When you reach the farthest part of the Arab land and the closest part of the non-Arab land, then halt." They marched out. When they reached al-Mirbad,[568] they found soft stones (*kadhdhān*) and said: "What are these soft stones (*al-baṣrah*)?"[569] Then they moved on and reached a place in front of a small bridge. There were tall grass and sprouting reeds. They said: "This is the place where you were ordered (to halt),"[570] so they halted short of [crossing into the territory of] the governor of the city of al-Furāt (*ṣāḥib al-Furāt*).[571] Some people came to the governor and said: "A group of men with a banner are here. They are heading toward you." The gov-

565. This is a reference to one of the etymologies of the name al-Baṣrah. See Lane, *Lexicon*, s.v. *b-ṣ-r*; Ibn Manẓūr, *Lisān al-ʿArab*, s.v. *b-ṣ-r* (IV, 66–7); Yāqūt, *Muʿjam*, I, 636–37.

566. See Yāqūt, *Muʿjam*, II, 429–31.

567. See Yāqūt, *Muʿjam*, II, 905.

568. Al-Mirbad, situated to the west of al-Baṣrah, was the town market. Later it became a large residential area of the city, where poets and orators used to have their assemblies. Numerous political meetings were also held there. Yāqūt (*Muʿjam*, I, 484) says that in his day al-Mirbad was three miles from al-Baṣrah and was a separate town. The area between al-Baṣrah and al-Mirbad, which had been inhabited in the past, was in ruins in Yāqūt's days. For a history of al-Mirbad, with extensive bibliography, see S. A. ʿAlī, "Khiṭaṭ," 282–86; cf. *EI*², s.v. "al-Mirbad" (Ch. Pellat).

569. See Yāqūt, *Muʿjam*, I, 637, where al-Kadhdhān and al-Baṣrah are glossed by each other. See note 565, above.

570. The vegetation indicated that they had reached the boundary between the desert land of the Arabs and the fertile land of the Persians, as commanded by ʿUmar. See above; and p. 2384, below.

571. A city in the vicinity of al-Ubullah, on the eastern bank of the Euphrates. See Balādhurī, *Futūḥ*, 341–42; and Donner, *Conquests*, 159–60 and index.

ernor moved out with four thousand horsemen. He said: "They are nothing except what I see.[572] Tie their necks with ropes and bring them to me." ʿUtbah raised his voice and said: "I have participated in warfare together with the Prophet."[573] When the sun declined, ʿUtbah gave the order: "Attack!" They attacked the Persians and killed them all; nobody survived except the governor of al-Furāt, whom they took prisoner. ʿUtbah b. Ghazwān said: "Seek for us a halting place more salubrious than this." It was a hot and humid day. A pulpit was erected for ʿUtbah. He stood up to deliver a sermon and said:

> This world is coming to an end, quickly turning back and passing away. Nothing but a small part of it remains, like a small quantity of water in a vessel.[574] You are about to move from it to the Abode of Permanence.[575] Move with the best things in your possession.[576] I was told that if a rock were to
> [2380] be hurled from the brink of Hell, it would be falling for seventy years. [Nevertheless,] Hell will be filled.[577] Do you wonder at it? I was also told that a walk between two of the gates of Paradise would take forty years, but a day will come when it will be crammed full. In a dream I saw myself as one of seven men in the company of the Prophet. We did not have anything to eat except for leaves of acacia trees, so that our mouths became ulcerated. I picked up a mantle and shared it with Saʿd. There was none among us who has not become

572. Apparently meaning that the Muslims are nothing but ordinary people and the Persians should not be intimidated by them.

573. The rest of ʿUtbah's speech seems to have been omitted.

574. A slightly different version of these sentences is quoted and explained in Ibn Manẓūr, *Lisān al-ʿArab*, s.v. *ḥ-dh-dh*. See also Blachère *et al.*, *Dictionnaire*, s.v. *ḥ-dh-dh*, but the meaning given there does not seem to be correct.

The sermon reflects the feeling that the end of the world and the Day of Judgment are imminent. This feeling is frequently expressed in the literature describing the early period of Islam. One of the most widely quoted prophetic traditions that reflects this feeling reads: "I and the Hour have been sent like ... these two—and he joined his index and middle fingers (*buʿithtu anā wa-al-sāʿah ... ka-hātayni—wa-qarana bayna al-sabbābah wa-al-wusṭā*). See Bukhārī, *Ṣaḥīḥ*, III, 473 (*Kitāb al-ṭalāq*, 25).

575. Cf. Qurʾān 40:39: "The Hereafter is the Abode of Permanence" (*inna al-ākhirah hiya dār al-qarār*).

576. Meaning the best deeds that one performed in this world and that would serve him well in the Hereafter.

577. With the infinite numbers of infidels and sinners. See Qurʾān 7:17: "I shall fill Hell with all of you."

amīr of a newly established garrison town (*miṣr*). The people will have experience of the amīrs who will follow us.[578]

According to Sayf — Muḥammad, Ṭalḥah, al-Muhallab, and ʿAmr: When ʿUtbah b. Ghazwān al-Māzinī [from the Banū Māzin b. Manṣūr] set out from al-Madāʾin to the "opening of India" (*farj al-Hind*),[579] he halted at the shore, facing the Arabian peninsula. He stayed there for a while, then moved elsewhere. The people then complained about this until finally, after three attempts at settlement, ʿUmar ordered him to halt in the desert because they disliked the clayey ground. At the fourth time they halted in a stony tract (*al-baṣrah*) (*al-baṣrah* is used for any land of which the stones are gypsum). He ordered them to dig a canal through which water could be made to flow from the Tigris, so they dug a canal for drinking water to al-Baṣrah. The people of al-Baṣrah settled where al-Baṣrah is today, and the people of al-Kūfah settled where al-Kūfah is today, in the same month. As for the people of al-Kūfah they stayed in al-Madāʾin [2381]
before settling in al-Kūfah. As for the people of al-Baṣrah they stayed on the bank of the Tigris but then moved several times until they settled in the desert.[580] Then they went back the distance of a *farsakh*[581] and dug a canal; then they repeated this until they reached the desert and extended the canal [as far as the site of al-Baṣrah].[582] Al-Baṣrah was planned in the same way as al-Kūfah. Abū al-Jarbāʾ ʿĀṣim b. al-Dulaf, of the Banu Ghaylān b. Mālik b. ʿAmr b. Tamīm, was in charge of the settlement of al-Baṣrah.

According to ʿUmar [b. Shabbah?] — al-Madāʾinī — al-Naḍr b. Is-

---

578. The Leiden text reads *wa-sa-yujarrabūna al-nāsa baʿdanā*. I have translated *al-nās* as "amīrs" in light of a version of ʿUtba's sermon recorded in Muslim, *Ṣaḥīḥ*, IV, 2278–79 (*Kitāb al-zuhd wa-al-raqāʾiq*, 14). The relevant portion reads there: *wa-sa-takhburūna wa-tujarribūna al-umarāʾa baʿdanā*. Another, and much longer, version of the sermon is recorded by Ibn Saʿd (*Ṭabaqāt*, VII/i, 2), whose text reads: *wa-sa-tujarribūna al-umarāʾa baʿdanā wa-tujarrabūna fa-taʿrifūna wa-tunkirūna*; ll. 27–28. ʿUtbah expresses the idea that the way in which the Muslim community is governed will deteriorate. Prophecy will disappear and will be replaced by kingship (*mulk*). The Muslims will in the future experience rulers worse than those of the early period.

579. An epithet for al-Ubullah. See note 57, above.

580. Reading *badaw* with the Cairo edition, instead of *badaʾū* of the Leiden text.

581. A *farsakh* is approximately 6 kilometers; see Hinz, *Masse*, 62.

582. Literally "Then they went back another *farsakh* and extended the canal; then another *farsakh* and extended the canal; then another *farsakh* and extended the canal; then they reached the desert and extended the canal [to al-Baṣrah]."

ḥāq al-Sulamī — Quṭbah b. Qatādah al-Sadūsī: Quṭbah b. Qatādah[583] was raiding the vicinity of al-Khuraybah, which was a part of al-Baṣrah, just as al-Muthannā b. Ḥārithah al-Shaybānī was raiding the vicinity of al-Ḥīrah. Quṭbah wrote to ʿUmar informing him of his location and telling him that, if he had a small number of men at his disposal, he would defeat the Persians who were in front of him and banish them from their land. The Persians of the area dreaded him because of the battle which had been fought by Khālid (b. al-Walīd) at Nahr al-Marʾah.[584] ʿUmar wrote to him: "I have received your letter saying that you were raiding the Persians in front of you. You did the right thing and have been vouchsafed success. Stay in your place and take good care of your companions until you
[2382] receive my orders." ʿUmar sent Shurayḥ b. ʿĀmir, who belonged to the tribe of Saʿd b. Bakr, to al-Baṣrah and said to him: "Reinforce the Muslims in this area." He came to al-Baṣrah, left Quṭbah there, and set out for al-Ahwāz.[585] When he reached Dāris,[586] which was a Persian garrison, he was killed. Then ʿUmar dispatched ʿUtbah b. Ghazwān.[587]

According to ʿUmar (b. Shabbah?)—ʿAlī—ʿĪsā b. Yazīd—ʿAbd al-Malik b. Ḥudhayfah and Muḥammad b. al-Ḥajjāj—ʿAbd al-Malik b. ʿUmayr: ʿUmar (b. al-Khaṭṭāb) said to ʿUtbah b. Ghazwān when he dispatched him to al-Baṣrah:

> O ʿUtbah, I have appointed you to rule "the land of India,"[588] which is a stronghold of the enemy. I wish that God would spare you the trouble of having to deal with what is around it and that He would help you to overcome it. I wrote to al-ʿAlāʾ b. al-Ḥaḍramī[589] asking him to reinforce you with ʿAr-

583. See (ʿI.) Ibn al-Athīr, *Usd*, IV, 206; Ibn Ḥajar, *Iṣābah*, V, 445–46 no. 7125.

584. See Balādhurī, *Futūḥ*, 242; Yāqūt, *Muʿjam*, IV, 484; Donner, *Conquests*, 179, 329.

585. Ahwāz refers both to the whole province of Khūzistān and to the city the full name of which is Sūq al-Ahwāz. See Yāqūt, *Muʿjam*, I, 410–14; Le Strange, *Lands*, 232–34; *EI²*, s.v. "Ahwāz" (L. Lockhart).

586. See Donner, *Conquests*, 213.

587. See Ibn Saʿd, *Ṭabaqāt*, VII/i, 1–3; (ʿI.) Ibn al-Athīr, *Usd*, III, 363–65; Ibn Ḥajar, *Iṣābah*, 438–39; Ibn Ḥajar, *Tahdhīb*, VII, 100.

588. An epithet of al-Baṣrah; see Ṭabarī, I, 2378; cf. note 57, above.

589. Al-ʿAlāʾ b. al-Ḥaḍramī was an early convert to Islam. The Prophet sent him to govern al-Baḥrayn and to collect the poor tax there. He participated in the suppression of the *riddah* rebellion in this region. ʿUmar appointed him governor of al-Baṣrah, but al-ʿAlāʾ died on his way to Iraq. The date of his death is variously given as 14/

fajah b. Harthamah.[590] ʿArfajah is a man who knows how to fight the enemy and how to use stratagems against him. When he comes, consult him and let him be your close associate.[591] Summon the people to God; those who respond to your call, accept it from them,[592] but those who refuse must pay the poll tax out of humiliation and lowliness.[593] If they refuse this, it is the sword without leniency. Fear God with regard to what you have been entrusted. Beware lest your soul lures you into haughtiness which will render your brethren[594] disaffected toward you. You have been a companion of the Messenger of God, and through him you became noble after you had been lowly, and through him you became strong after you had been weak until you became an amīr to whom governmental power is entrusted and a ruler to whom obedience is due. Whatever you say is listened to; you command and your order is obeyed. This is, indeed, a blessing if it does not cause you to overstep your limits and does not cause you to behave insolently with those who are inferior to you. Beware of ease of circumstances as you [2383]
would beware of sin. In my view, the former is, indeed, the more fearful of the two; it may lead you astray and deceive you. As a result, you may fall into error and end up in Hell. I invoke the protection of God from this upon you and upon myself. People hasten to God, but when this world comes into their view, they seek after it. Seek God, do not seek the world, and beware of the places into which the wrongdoers are hurled down.

According to ʿUmar b. Shabbah—ʿAlī—Abū Ismāʿīl al-Hamdānī [2384]
and Abū Mikhnaf—Mujālid b. Saʿīd—al-Shaʿbī: ʿUtbah b. Ghaz-

635–36 or 21/641–42; the earlier date is incompatible with the tradition regarding his appointment as governor of al-Baṣrah. See Ibn Saʿd, *Ṭabaqāt*, IV, 76–79; (ʿI.) Ibn al-Athīr, *Usd*, IV, 7–8; Ibn Ḥajar, *Iṣābah*, IV, 541 no. 5646.

590. For ʿArfajah b. Harthamah (or b. Khuzaymah) see (ʿI.) Ibn al-Athīr, *Usd*, III, 400; Ibn Ḥajar, *Iṣābah*, V, 271 no. 6781.

591. Reading *wa-qarribhu* for *wa-farribhu*, an evident typographical error.

592. This is to say, accept their conversion as genuine and refrain from fighting them.

593. Cf. Qurʾān 9:29.

594. A possible emendation would be *ākhirataka*, instead of *ikhwataka*: "... which will ruin your Hereafter." Cf. Ibn Kathīr, *Bidāyah*, VII, 48 l. 18.

wān came to al-Baṣrah with three hundred men. When he saw a field of reeds and heard the croaking of frogs, he said: "The Commander of the Faithful ordered me to halt at the most distant edge of the Arab desert land and at the nearest point of the cultivated Persian land. This is the place where we must obey the orders of our imām." So he halted at al-Khuraybah. At that time, five hundred Persian horsemen (*asāwirah*) were in al-Ubullah defending the city. Al-Ubullah was a port for ships from China and from less distant places. ʿUtbah moved forward and halted before al-Ijjānah[595] and stayed there for about a month. Then the garrison of al-Ubullah came out to [fight] him, and ʿUtbah stood up against them. He put Quṭbah b. Qatādah al-Sadūsī and Qasāmah b. Zuhayr al-Māzinī[596] in charge of ten horsemen and said to them: "Stay behind us, drive back those (Muslims) who run away, and ward off those [Persians] who may attack us from our rear." Then the two armies confronted each other. They did not fight longer than is necessary to slaughter a camel and divide it; God routed the Persians;[597] they took to flight and withdrew into the city. ʿUtbah returned to his camp and stayed there for a few days. God put fear in the hearts of the people of al-Ubullah; they left the city, carried their light belongings with them, crossed [the Tigris] to the city of al-Furāt, and abandoned al-Ubullah. The Muslims entered the city, captured various goods, weapons, prisoners, and money. They divided the money between them,
[2385] and every man received two dirhams. ʿUtbah put Nāfiʿ b. al-Ḥārith[598] in charge of the spoils of al-Ubullah; he set aside the fifth[599] and divided the rest among those to whom God restored it.[600] He wrote about it [to ʿUmar, sending the letter] with Nāfiʿ b. al-Ḥārith.

According to Bashīr b. ʿUbaydallāh: Nāfiʿ b. al-Ḥārith killed nine men in the battle of al-Ubullah, and Abū Bakrah[601] killed six.

---

595. Al-Ijjānah was a lagoon (*qhawr*) at the end of a natural canal (*khawr*) leading to al-Baṣrah from the Tigris estuary. See Balādhurī, *Futūḥ*, 356–57; and Le Strange, *Lands*, 43–44.

596. See Ibn Ḥajar, *Iṣābah*, V, 527 no. 7291; Ibn Ḥajar, *Tahdhīb*, VIII, 378.

597. For *manaḥahum Allāh aktāfahum*, see Dozy, *Supplément*; and *WKAS*, s.v. *k-t-f*.

598. See Ibn Saʿd, *Ṭabaqāt*, V, 372; (ʿI.) Ibn al-Athīr, *Usd*, V, 8.

599. See note 463, above.

600. See note 472, above.

601. Abū Bakrah was a slave in al-Ṭāʾif and embraced Islam when the Prophet laid siege to the city. He died in al-Baṣrah in 51 or 52/671–72. See Ibn Saʿd,

According to Dāwūd b. Abī Hind: The Muslims seized in al-Ubullah six hundred dirhams. Each man took two dirhams, and ʿUmar allocated to the men who took two dirhams at the conquest of al-Ubullah a stipend of two thousand dirhams; these numbered three hundred men.

The conquest of al-Ubullah took place in the month of Rajab or in the month of Shaʿbān of this year.

According to al-Shaʿbī: Two hundred and seventy men participated in the conquest of al-Ubullah. Among them were Abū Bakrah, Nāfiʿ b. al-Ḥārith, Shibl b. Maʿbad,[602] al-Mughīrah b. Shuʿbah, Mujāshiʿ b. Masʿūd,[603] Abū Maryam al-Balawī, Rabīʿah b. Kaladah b. Abī al-Ṣalt al-Thaqafī, and al-Ḥajjāj.

According to ʿAbāyah b. ʿAbd ʿAmr: I participated in the conquest of al-Ubullah with ʿUtbah. ʿUtbah sent Nāfiʿ b. al-Ḥārith to ʿUmar with the news of the conquest. The people of Dast-i Maysān[604] gathered [an army] against us. ʿUtbah said: "I think that we should march against them." We marched and confronted the governor (*marzubān*) of Dast-i Maysān. We fought him; his companions were defeated and he was taken prisoner, his mantle and belt being seized. ʿUtbah sent him [to ʿUmar] with Anas b. Ḥujayyah al-Yashkurī. [2386]

According to Abū al-Malīḥ al-Hudhalī: ʿUtbah sent Anas b. Ḥujayyah to ʿUmar with the belt of the governor of Dast-i Maysān. ʿUmar said to him: "What is the condition of the Muslims?" Anas said: "The [wealth of this] world has engulfed them, and they are dripping with gold and silver." The people became attracted by al-Baṣrah and came to live there.

According to ʿAlī b. Zayd: When ʿUtbah finished with al-Ubullah, the governor of Dast-i Maysān gathered an army against him. ʿUtbah marched against him from al-Ubullah and killed him. Then he sent Mujāshiʿ b. Masʿūd to the city of al-Furāt. ʿUtbah went to ʿUmar and ordered al-Mughīrah to lead the prayers until Mujāshiʿ returned from al-Furāt. Upon his return, Mujāshiʿ was to be the amīr. Mujāshiʿ defeated the people of al-Furāt and returned to al-Baṣrah.

Ṭabaqāt, VII/i, 8–9; (ʿI.) Ibn al-Athīr, *Usd*, V, 38, 151; Ibn Ḥajar, *Iṣābah*, VI, 467–j68; Ibn Ḥajar, *Tahdhīb*, X, 469–70; Ibn ʿAbd al-Barr, *Istīʿāb*, 628–29.

602. See (ʿI.) Ibn al-Athīr, *Usd*, II, 385; Ibn Ḥajar, *Iṣābah*, III, 377–79 no. 3961.

603. See Ibn Saʿd, *Ṭabaqāt*, VII/i, 19; (ʿI.) Ibn al-Athīr, *Usd*, IV, 300; Ibn Ḥajar, *Iṣābah*, VI, 325 no. 8499; Ibn Ḥajar, *Tahdhīb*, X, 38.

604. For the district of Dast-i Maysān, situated on the lower Tigris, see Yāqūt, *Muʿjam*, IV, 714–15; Morony, *Iraq*, 159ff.

Faylakān, a chieftain of Abazqubādh,[605] gathered an army against the Muslims. Al-Mughīrah b. Shuʿbah set out against him, confronted him at al-Marghāb,[606] and defeated him. He wrote to ʿUmar about the victory. ʿUmar asked ʿUtbah: "Whom did you appoint as governor of al-Baṣrah?" He replied: "Mujāshiʿ b. Masʿūd." ʿUmar said: "You are appointing a bedouin (*rajul min ahl al-wabar*) to rule over town dwellers (*ahl al-madar*)? Do you know what has happened?" ʿUtbah said: "No." ʿUmar informed him of the affair of al-Mughīrah and ordered him to return to his city.[607] ʿUtbah died on his way, and ʿUmar appointed al-Mughīrah b. Shuʿbah [in his stead].

According to ʿAbd al-Raḥmān b. Jawshan: ʿUtbah went away after he killed the governor of Dast-i Maysān, sent Mujāshiʿ to the city of al-Furāt, and appointed him to govern [al-Baṣrah] in his place; after he ordered al-Mughīrah b. Shuʿbah to lead the prayers until the return of Mujāshiʿ from al-Furāt; and after the people of Maysān gathered an army, al-Mughīrah confronted them, defeated them before the coming of Mujāshiʿ from al-Furāt, and informed ʿUmar of the victory.

According to al-Ṭabarī's *isnād*—Qatādah: The people of Maysān gathered an army against the Muslims. Al-Mughīrah set out against them, leaving the heavy luggage behind. He confronted the enemy on
[2387] this side of the Tigris. Ardah bint al-Ḥārith b. Kaladah said: "I wish we could join the Muslim men and be with them," and she made a banner of her veil. The other women [also] used their veils as flags and set out in the direction of the Muslims. When they reached the Muslims, the polytheists were fighting them. But when the polytheists saw the approaching flags, they thought that reinforcements were coming to the Muslims and took to flight. The Muslims pursued them and killed many of them.

According to Ḥārithah b. Muḍarrib: Al-Ubullah was taken by force, and then ʿUtbah distributed white bread (*kakkah*)[608] to the troops. The same tradition was transmitted by Muḥammad b. Sīrīn.

Al-Ṭabarī has said: Among the prisoners taken at Maysān were

---

605. See Yāqūt, *Muʿjam*, I, 90–91; and Morony, *Iraq*, 188–89.

606. A canal in the vicinity of al-Baṣrah; see Yāqūt, *Muʿjam*, IV, 499 (deals also with other places bearing the same name); Balādhurī, *Futūḥ*, 364.

607. The text has *ʿamal*, which denotes any area under a governor, *ʿāmil*.

608. See *Glossary*, s.v. and Dozy, *Supplément*, s.v. *kaʿk*, and the sources quoted there.

Yasār, the father of Ḥasan al-Baṣrī,[609] and Arṭabān, the grandfather of ʿAbdallāh b. ʿAwn b. Arṭabān.

According to al-Muthannā b. Mūsā b. Salamah b. al-Muḥabbiq—his father—his grandfather: I participated in the conquest of al-Ubullah. A copper pot fell within my share [of the spoils]. When I looked at it closely, I suddenly noticed that it was of gold and contained eighty thousand *mithqāls*.[610] A letter concerning this was sent to ʿUmar, who replied: "Let Salamah swear by God that on the day when he took it he thought that it was of copper. If he takes the oath, the pot will be given to him. If not, it will be divided among the Muslims." I took the oath and the pot was given to me. Al-Muthannā said: "This is the source of the property which we own today."

According to ʿAmrah bint Qays: When the Muslims set out to fight the people of al-Ubullah, my husband and my son went with them. They took two dirhams and a *makkūk*[611] of raisins each. They marched and when they came opposite al-Ubullah they said to the enemy: "Shall we cross to your side, or will you cross to ours?" The enemy said: "Cross to our side." They took pieces of wood from the *ʿushar*[612] tree, tied them together, and crossed to the enemy side. The [2388]
polytheists said: "Do not take on the first of them until the last makes the crossing." When the Muslims reached land, they proclaimed "God is most great!" Then they proclaimed it for the second time, whereupon their mounts rose on their feet. Then they proclaimed it for the third time, and the mounts (of the Persians) began to throw their riders to the ground. We saw heads falling, but we did not see who was striking them off. God granted victory to the Muslims.

According to al-Madāʾinī: Ṣafiyyah bint al-Ḥārith b. Kaladah was the wife of ʿUtbah, and her sister Ardah bint al-Ḥārith was the wife

---

609. Ḥasan al-Baṣrī (21–110/642–728) was one of the most famous mystics of early Islam. See *EI²*, s.v. "Ḥasan al-Baṣrī" (H. Ritter).

610. The *mithqāl* is a unit of weight, used for gold and other precious metals. See Hinz, *Masse*, 1–8.

611. The *makkūk* is a measure of weight. According to Ibn Manẓūr (*Lisān al-ʿArab*, s.v. *m-k-k*), it was best known among the people of Iraq. The weight of the *makkūk* was not fixed; it changed according to the usage agreed upon in each area (*yakhtalifu miqdāruhu bi-'khtilāfi iṣṭilāḥ al-nās ʿalayhi fī al-bilād*). See Hinz, *Masse*, 44; *EI²*, s.v. "Makāyīl" (E. Ashtor), at VI, 118b, 119b.

612. See Lane, *Lexicon*, s.v.

of Shibl b. Maʿbad al-Bajalī. When ʿUtbah was appointed governor of al-Baṣrah, the relatives of his wife—Abū Bakrah, Nāfiʿ, and Shibl b. Maʿbad—came with him. Ziyād (b. Abī Sufyān) also joined them. When they conquered al-Ubullah, they did not find anyone who would divide [the spoils] between them, and eventually Ziyād divided the spoils between them. He was fourteen years old and possessed nobility.[613] They allocated for him two dirhams a day.

It was said: The governorship of ʿUtbah in al-Baṣrah was in the year 15/636–37. According to another version, it was in the year 16/637–38, but the first version is more correct. His governorship of al-Baṣrah lasted six months. [Then] ʿUmar appointed al-Mughīrah b. Shuʿbah as governor of al-Baṣrah. He remained two years in this position, and then certain accusations were directed against him[614] and ʿUmar then appointed Abū Mūsā (al-Ashʿarī). According to another version, ʿUmar appointed after ʿUtbah Abū Mūsā, and after him al-Mughīrah.

In this year, meaning the year 14/635–36, ʿUmar flogged his son ʿUbaydallāh and his companions because they drank wine, and he flogged Abū Miḥjan as well.[615]

In this year ʿUmar b. al-Khaṭṭāb led the Muslims in pilgrimage. The governor of Mecca was, according to one version, ʿAttāb b. al-Asīd;[616] Yaʿlā b. Munyah was governor of the Yemen; Saʿd b. Abī Waqqāṣ was governor of al-Kūfah; Abū ʿUbaydah b. al-Jarrāḥ was
[2389] governor of Syria; ʿUthmān b. Abī al-ʿĀṣ[617] was governor of Baḥrayn, although according to another version it was al-ʿAlāʾ b. al-Ḥaḍramī; and Ḥudhayfah b. Miḥṣan was governor of ʿUmān.

---

613. For *lahu dhuʾābah* see note 426, above.

614. Al-Mughīrah was accused of fornication. For ʿUmar's investigation, which resulted in al-Mughīrah's acquittal and in the punishment of his three accusers, see Ṭabarī, I, 2529–33.

615. See Ibn al-Jawzī, *Manāqib*, 240–43.

616. See Ibn Saʿd, *Ṭabaqāt*, V, 330; (ʿI.) Ibn al-Athīr, *Usd*, III, 358–59; Ibn Ḥajar, *Iṣābah*, IV, 429–30; Ibn Ḥajar, *Tahdhīb*, VI, 89–90.

617. ʿUthmān b. Abī al-ʿĀṣ, of the tribe of Thaqīf, was appointed governor of al-Ṭāʾif by the Prophet and confirmed in his position by Abū Bakr and ʿUmar. He is said to have been instrumental in keeping his tribe loyal to Islam during the *riddah* rebellion. He served also as governor of ʿUmān. The date of his death is given variously as 50/670–71, 51/671–72, or 55/672. See (ʿI.) Ibn al-Athīr, *Usd*, III, 371–73; Ibn Ḥajar, *Iṣābah*, IV, 451–52 no. 5445; Ibn Ḥajar, *Tahdhīb*, VII, 128–29.

The Events of the Year 15

(FEBRUARY 14, 636–FEBRUARY 1, 637)

Ibn Jarīr (al-Ṭabarī) has said: Some traditionists said that in this year Saʿd b. Abī Waqqāṣ established al-Kūfah. Ibn Buqaylah[618] led the Muslims there and said to Saʿd: "I shall lead you to a land free of mosquitoes[619] and beyond the desert."[620] He then led them to the place where al-Kūfah is located today.

---

618. For Ibn Buqaylah, see note 201, above.

619. Cf. Ṭabarī, I, 2360, where it is related that Saʿd abandoned an attempt to establish a city at Kuwayfat ʿUmar b. Saʿd because the area was infested with flies.

620. Literally "a land higher than [where] the mosquitoes [live] and lower than the desert." This phrasing can be understood in view of the Arabic linguistic usage in which travel from the Ḥijāz to Iraq, Syria, and ʿUmān is considered descent (*inḥidār*), whereas movement in the direction of Najd, Ḥijāz, and Yemen is considered ascent (*iṣʿād*). See Ibn Manẓūr, *Lisān al-ʿArab*, s.v. *ṣ-ʿ-d* (III, 253). The place suggested by Ibn Buqaylah is therefore "higher," to the south of the mosquito-infested Iraqi lowlands, and "lower," to the north of the Arabian desert. It is another expression of the idea that the Muslims should establish themselves at the beginning of their northward expansion in the borderland between Iraq and the desert. Cf. Balādhurī, *Futūḥ*, 276.

The Battle of Marj al-Rūm[621]

In this year the battle of Marj al-Rūm took place. It so happened that Abū ʿUbaydah set out with Khālid b. al-Walīd from Fiḥl[622] to Ḥimṣ. He marched together with men from al-Yarmūk who had joined them.[623] All of them halted at the camp of Dhū al-Kalāʿ.[624] The news of this reached Heraclius, who dispatched Theodore the Patricius, who established his camp on the plain of Damascus and to the west of the city. Abū ʿUbaydah attacked first Marj al-Rūm and this Byzantine army. The winter took its toll on the Byzantines and many were wounded. When Abū ʿUbaydah established his camp near the Byzantines in Marj al-Rūm, he was opposed on the day of his arrival by Shanas al-Rūmī, who had cavalry similar in size to that of Theodore; it was to serve as a reinforcement to Theodore and as assistance to the people of Ḥimṣ. Shanas established a separate camp, but
[2390] when night descended, the camp was deserted by Theodore. Khālid stood opposite Theodore and Abū ʿUbaydah opposite Shanas. Khālid was informed that Theodore had gone to Damascus, so Khālid and Abū ʿUbaydah agreed that Khālid should pursue him. Khālid pursued him that night with light cavalry. Yazīd b. Abī Sufyān was informed of what Theodore had done and confronted him, and they fought each other. Khālid caught up with them while they were fighting and attacked the Byzantines from the rear so that they were killed from all directions[625] and only those who escaped survived. The Muslims seized whatever they wanted: mounts, weapons,[626] and clothes. Yazīd b. Abī Sufyān divided this among his companions and the companions of Khālid. Then Yazīd set out for Damascus and Khālid returned to Abū ʿUbaydah after he had killed Theodore. Khālid recited:

We have killed Theodore and Sheodore,

621. See Donner, *Conquests*, 134, 138.

622. Fiḥl, or Pella, was a town on the east bank of the Jordan, across from Baysān (Bet Sh'an, Scythopolis). See Yāqūt, *Muʿjam*, II, 853; and Donner, *Conquests*, 130 and index.

623. See Donner, *Conquests*, 138.

624. See Donner, *Conquests*, 136, 138, 367 no. 58.

625. Literally "from the front and from the rear."

626. *Adāt* could mean any instrument or tool but is probably used here in the sense of *adāt al-ḥarb* "tools of war."

And before him we killed Ḥaydar,[627]
And made Ukaydir meet his death.[628]

After Khālid set out to pursue Theodore, Abū ʿUbaydah confronted Shanas. They fought in Marj al-Rūm, and Abū ʿUbaydah killed a great number of the Byzantines, also killing Shanas, and the valley was filled with fallen Byzantines. The ground was stinking because of them. Some Byzantines fled, but Abū ʿUbaydah did not let them escape and pursued them to Ḥimṣ.[629]

The Conquest of Ḥimṣ

Al-Ṭabarī has related according to Sayf (in his book)—Abū ʿUthmān: When the news about the rout of the Byzantines at Marj al-Rūm reached Heraclius, he ordered the commander of Ḥimṣ to march upon Ḥimṣ[630] and said to him: "I have been informed that the food of the Arabs is camel meat and that their drink is camel milk. It is winter now. Do not fight them except on cold days, for none of [2391]
those whose principal food and drink is this will survive until the summer." Heraclius set out from his camp to al-Ruhāʾ[631] and ordered his governor to defend Ḥimṣ.[632] Abū ʿUbaydah drew near and encamped around Ḥimṣ, and Khālid came after him and encamped around it as well. The Byzantines attacked the Muslims on every cold day, in the morning and in the afternoon. The Muslims experienced severe cold and the Byzantines experienced a long siege. The Muslims stood firm in their positions; God inspired them with endurance[633] and rewarded them with victory when the winter had lost its grip. The Byzantines on the other hand held fast to the city, hoping that the winter would destroy the Muslims.

---

627. Shūdhara is an artificial name, created in order to rhyme with Tūdhara. Although Ḥaydar is a real (Arab) name, it is also used here only for purposes of rhyme.

628. Translating *fayḍa* instead of *ghayḍa*, accepting de Goeje's conjecture in *Glossary*, s.vv. *z-w-r*, and *f-y-ḍ*. About the killing of Ukaydir, see Ṭabarī, I, 2077, cf. note 541, above.

629. For *rakiba aksāʾahum*, see *WKAS*, I, 169, s.v. *kusʾun*.

630. It is not clear where the amīr was at the time.

631. This is Arabic for Edessa; see Le Strange, *Lands*, 103–4.

632. For this meaning of *akhadhahu bi-*, see de Goeje's *Glossary*, p. CVIII; and his *Glossary* to Balādhurī, *Futūḥ*, s.v. *a-kh-dh*.

633. For the expression *afragha ʿalayhim al-ṣabra*, cf. Qurʾān 2:250, 7:126.

According to Abū al-Zahrā' al-Qushayrī — a man from his tribe: The people of Ḥimṣ enjoined each other: "Hold fast, because they are barefooted. When the cold afflicts them, their feet will be cut; this in addition to their (meager) food and drink." The situation of the Byzantines worsened; the feet of some fell off in their shoes. As for the Muslims, not even a toe of theirs was hurt, though they were wearing sandals.[634]

When the winter was over, an old man stood up among the Byzantines and called upon them to make peace with the Muslims. They said: "How can we do this while the king (Heraclius) is powerful and glorious? There is nothing between us and between them."[635] The man left them alone. Then another stood up among them, saying: "The winter is over and hope is lost. What are you waiting for?" They said: "We are waiting for the inflammation of the brain (*al-birsām*),[636] which is latent in the winter and appears in the summer." He said: "These are people who will receive [divine] help. It is better to come to them with an agreement and a covenant than to be taken by force. Accept my suggestion [now] and be praised for it, before you [will have to] accept it and receive blame." But they said: "He is a senile old man, having no knowledge of warfare."

According to elders from Ghassān[637] and Balqayn,[638] God rewarded the endurance of the Muslims during the battle days of Ḥimṣ by sending an earthquake which struck the people of the city. This is how it happened. The Muslims confronted them and proclaimed
[2392] "God is most great!," whereupon the Byzantines in the city were struck with an earthquake. The walls cracked, hence the Byzantines fled in fear to their leaders and men of judgment and to those who called upon them to make peace and had been rejected and humili-

---

634. For *khuff* (pl. *khifāf*) "shoe" and *naʿl* (pl. *niʿāl*) "sandal," see Dozy, *Vêtements*, 155–59, 421–24.

635. Probably meaning that no fighting that obliges the Byzantines to sue for peace has occurred. In the account of Ibn Kathīr (*Bidāyah*, VII, 52), the Byzantines say here: "Are we to make peace while the king is near to us?" (*a-nuṣāliḥu wa-al-malik minnā qarīb!*)

636. This seems to be the meaning intended here; see Rufus, *Krankenjournale*, 121. I am grateful to Professor Ullmann for his communication on this matter. For other meanings of *birsām*, see Ullmann, *Medizin*, 245 (pleurisy); and Blachère, *et al.*, *Dictionnaire*, s.v. (I, 542b; pleurisy or sunstroke). In Ibn Manẓūr, *Lisān al-ʿArab* (s.vv. *b-r-s-m*, *m-w-m*), it is glossed by *mūm*, which may mean a kind of smallpox.

637. See *EI²*, s.v. "Ghassān" (I. Shahīd).

638. See *EI²*, s.v. "Ḳayn" (J. Chelhod).

ated because of this. The Muslims then proclaimed "God is most great!" for the second time. As a result many buildings and walls caved in and the Byzantines fled in fear to their leaders and men of judgment, saying: "Do you not see the punishment of God?" The leaders replied: "Only you can sue for peace." They looked [toward the Muslims] and called out: "Peace, peace!" The Muslims were not noticing what had happened among the Byzantines. They complied and agreed to make peace on the condition that they would receive half of their houses,[639] that they would let the Byzantines retain their property and [the rest of] their buildings[640] and would not occupy them. The Muslims left the buildings for the Byzantines. Some of them made peace according to the conditions included in the peace treaty of Damascus: to pay one dīnār and to provide [to the Muslims a certain quantity of] food for every *jarīb*[641] forever, whether they were prosperous or poor. Others made peace [and agreed to pay] according to their ability. If their property should increase, their payment would grow; if it should decrease, the payment would decrease as well. The peace treaty with Damascus and al-Urdunn was the same; some of them agreed to pay a fixed amount whether they were prosperous or poor, while others agreed to pay according to their ability. They were allowed to take over the area which their rulers had abandoned.

Abū ʿUbaydah dispatched al-Simṭ b. al-Aswad[642] with the Banū Muʿāwiyah, al-Ashʿath b. Miʾnās[643] with the tribe of Sakūn (Ibn ʿĀbis was also with him), al-Miqdād[644] with the tribe of Balī, Bilāl[645] and Khālid with the army, and al-Ṣabbāḥ b. Shutayr, Dhuhayl b.

---

639. A very literal translation of *anṣāf dūrihim* would read "half of each of their houses."

640. *ʿAlā an yatruka al-muslimūna amwāl al-Rūm* cannot mean "and that they handed over the treasure of the Greeks"; *pace* Hill, *Termination*, 66 no. 141.

641. *Jarīb* is a measure of land. For its various uses, see Sauvaire, "Matériaux," 485–88; Hinz, *Masse*, 65–66.

642. See Ibn Ḥajar, *Iṣābah*, I, 264 no. 3703.

643. See Ibn Ḥajar, *Iṣābah*, I, 201 no. 465.

644. Al-Miqdād b. ʿAmr was an early convert to Islam. After the *hijrah* he participated in the battles of the Prophet. In the battle of Badr he earned the reputation of being the first Muslim to fight on horseback. He died near Medina in 33/653–54 at the age of 70. See Ibn Saʿd, *Ṭabaqāt*, III/i, 114–16; (ʿI.) Ibn al-Athīr, *Usd*, IV, 409–11; Ibn Ḥajar, *Iṣābah*, VI, 202–4 no. 8189; Ibn Ḥajar, *Tahdhīb*, X, 285–87.

645. For Bilāl b. Rabāḥ, best known as the *muʾadhdhin* of the Prophet, see *EI²*, s.v. "Bilāl b. Rabāḥ" (W. ʿArafat).

ʿAṭiyyah, and Dhū Shamistān. They were inside the city of Ḥimṣ. Abū ʿUbaydah stayed in his camp and wrote to ʿUmar, informing him of the victory, sending fifths of the booty with ʿAbdallāh b. Masʿūd. After
[2393] Abū ʿUbaydah had sent him, he was informed that Heraclius had crossed the river into the Jazīrah and was in al-Ruhāʾ and was alternating between going into hiding and coming out of it. Ibn Masʿūd came to ʿUmar, who ordered him to return and then sent him to Saʿd in al-Kūfah. Later he wrote to Abū ʿUbaydah: "Stay in your city and summon the strong and sturdy Arabs in Syria. God willing, I shall not neglect sending to you men who will help you."

The Story of Qinnasrīn[646]

According to Abū ʿUthmān and Jāriyah: After the conquest of Ḥimṣ, Abū ʿUbaydah sent Khālid b. al-Walīd to Qinnasrīn. When he camped in the populated area [around it],[647] the Byzantines lead by Mīnās marched against them. Mīnās was a Byzantine chieftain, the greatest man among them after Heraclius. They confronted each other in this area and Mīnās and his companions were killed; they had never suffered a defeat like this.[648] All the Byzantines died together following the death of Mīnās,[649] with none of them surviving. As for the people who lived around Qinnasrīn, they sent a message to Khālid, saying that they were Arabs and had been [forcibly] recruited;[650] it was not their idea to fight Khālid. Khālid accepted this and left them alone.[651] When this came to ʿUmar's knowledge, he said: "Khālid has made himself amīr! May God have mercy on Abū

646. A town in northern Syria, south of Aleppo. See *EI*², s.v. "Ḳinnasrīn" (N. Elisséeff); Yāqūt, *Muʿjam*, IV, 184–87.

647. For *al-ḥāḍir*, see Lane, *Lexicon*, s.v.; Balādhurī, *Futūḥ*, 173 l. 3; 144 l. 2; Yāqūt, *Muʿjam*, II, 184.

648. The Arabic text reads *fa-qutila Mīnās wa-man maʿahu maqtalatan lam yuqtalū mithlahā*. Although the text states that all Byzantine troops were killed in the battle, the second part of the sentence evidently refers to defeat rather than killing. In the sentence there is a shift in the meaning of *qatala* from "kill" to "subdue." Cf. de Goeje's *Glossary*, s.v. *q-t-l*.

649. For *mātū ʿalā damin wāḥidin*, see Dozy, *Supplément*, s.v. *d-m-w*.

650. For this meaning of *ḥashara*, see note 516, above.

651. Ibn al-ʿAdīm (*Zubdat al-ḥalab*, I, 26) reports this tradition in a significantly different version, which ends with the words: "[Khālid] killed some of them and left the rest alone (*qatala minhum wa-taraka al-bāqīn*). I tend to prefer Ṭabarī's version; *qabila minhum* is frequent in similar contexts, whereas *qatala minhum*, without an object for the verb, sounds awkward.

Bakr! He had better understanding of people than I have."[652] ʿUmar had dismissed Khālid and al-Muthannā when he assumed office[653] and had said: "I have not dismissed them because of suspicion, but the people venerated them excessively and I was afraid that they would put their trust in them."[654] ʿUmar changed his opinion after the conduct of Khālid at Qinnasrīn.[655]

Khālid marched to Qinnasrīn and encamped there. The people of Qinnasrīn fortified themselves against him. He said: "[Even] if you were in the clouds, God would carry us to you or would bring you down to us." [2394]

The people of Qinnasrīn considered their situation. They remembered the treatment meted out to the people of Ḥimṣ and wanted to make peace on the conditions of Ḥimṣ, but Khālid agreed only on the condition that the city be destroyed, so he destroyed it. Both Ḥimṣ and Qinnasrīn were leveled to the ground.

This time Heraclius retreated. The reason for his retreat was the following: Khālid killed Mīnās and all the Byzantines died with him. When he made an agreement with the people who lived around Qinnasrīn and left the city, ʿUmar b. Mālik appeared from the direction of al-Kūfah and Qarqīsiyā,[656] ʿAbdallāh b. al-Muʿtamm from the direction of Mosul, and Walīd b. ʿUqbah[657] from the land of the

---

652. The reference is to Abū Bakr's defense of Khālid b. al-Walīd against ʿUmar's criticism. See Ṭabarī, I, 1926.

653. For the dismissal of Khālid b. al-Walīd, see Balādhurī, *Futūḥ*, 116, 178; Ṭabarī, I, 2148, 2526–27.

654. Rather than in God, as de Goeje correctly observed in *Mémoire*, 126. See a slightly different version of this tradition in Ṭabarī, I, 2528.

655. See Ṭabarī, I, 2527.

656. A town near the confluence of the Khābūr river and the Euphrates. See Le Strange, *Lands*, 105 (read "on the left bank of the Euphrates") and index; Yāqūt, *Muʿjam*, IV, 65–66.

657. Al-Walīd b. ʿUqbah belonged to a leading Qurashī family. His father fought against the Muslims at Badr and was killed after the battle on the Prophet's orders. Al-Walīd embraced Islam after the conquest of Mecca. He served as a collector of the poor tax under the Prophet and under ʿUmar, but the tradition maintains that he did not discharge his duties wholeheartedly. ʿUthmān b. ʿAffān, who was his half-brother, appointed him governor of al-Kūfah in 25/645–46 but had to dismiss him after he was accused of drunkenness. In addition to his participation in the conquest of Syria, he led an expedition to Ādharbayjān in 28/648–49 (or 24/644–45 or 26/646–47). When the struggle between ʿAlī and Muʿāwiyah erupted, he did not take an active part in it and retired to al-Raqqah in the Jazīrah. Some traditions maintain, however, that in his poems and letters he incited Muʿāwiyah to fight. He died in al-Raqqah during Muʿāwiyah's reign. See Ibn Saʿd, *Ṭabaqāt*, VI, 15; VII/ii, 176–77; Ṭabarī, in-

Banū Taghlib with [men from] Taghlib and Arabs from the Jazīrah.[658] They passed by the cities of the Jazīrah, avoiding the direction of Heraclius. The people of the Jazīrah from[659] Ḥarrān,[660] al-Raqqah,[661] Naṣībīn,[662] and neighboring towns could not know[663] their intention without returning to their people [in the Jazīrah]. The Muslims left in the Jazīrah al-Walīd b. ʿUqbah so that they were not in danger of being attacked from the rear.[664]

Khālid and ʿIyāḍ (b. Ghanm) penetrated the Byzantine territory from the direction of Syria, and ʿUmar (b. Mālik) and ʿAbdallāh (b. al-Muʿtamm) penetrated it from the direction of the Jazīrah. This had never been done before. Then they returned. This was the first penetration of the Byzantine territory in Islamic times; it took place in the year 16/637–38.

Khālid returned to Qinnasrīn and settled in it, and his wife joined him. When [ʿUmar] dismissed him, he said: "ʿUmar put me in charge of Syria. When it became wheat and honey, he dismissed me."[665]

---

dex; (ʿI.) Ibn al-Athīr, *Usd*, IV, 90–92; Ibn Ḥajar, *Iṣābah*, VI, 614–18; Ibn Ḥajar, *Tahdhīb*, XI, 142–44.

658. Al-Jazīrah, "the island," was a term used for the area between the upper courses of the Euphrates and the Tigris. See Le Strange, *Lands*, 86ff.; *EI²*, s.v. "Djazīra" (M. Canard).

659. Reading *min* instead of *fī*; see note 664, below. The sentence refers to troops from the Jazīrah who participated in the Byzantine siege of Ḥimṣ. See Yāqūt, *Muʿjam*, II, 73 ll. 19–20.

660. For the city of Ḥarrān in the Jazīrah, see Le Strange, *Lands*, 103; Yāqūt, *Muʿjam*, II, 230–32.

661. For al-Raqqah, see Le Strange, *Lands*, 101–2; Yāqūt, *Muʿjam*, II, 802–4.

662. For Naṣībīn, see Le Strange, *Lands*, 94–95; Yāqūt, *Muʿjam*, IV, 787–89.

663. *Lam yuqhriḍu gharaḍahum* is difficult; see a parallel passage in Ṭabarī, I, 2500 l. 13: *lam yadrū al-Jazīrah yurīdūna am Ḥimṣ* "they did not know whether they [i.e., the Muslim troops from al-Kūfah] were heading for al-Jazīrah or for Ḥimṣ." A possible emendation of the text could be *lam yaʿrifū gharaḍahum*.

664. Ṭabarī's text of the last two sentences is dubious, and our translation is based on comparison with some parallel passages. Ibn al-ʿAdīm (*Zubdat al-ḥalab*, I, 31) says that the Byzantine troops besieging Ḥimṣ were reinforced by 30,000 men from the Jazīrah, belonging to Tanūkh and other tribes. They inflicted heavy losses on the Muslims. Anxious to alleviate the pressure on the town, ʿUmar instructed Saʿd b. Abī Waqqāṣ to dispatch Muslim troops into the Jazīrah in order to divert the attention of the Jazīrah contingent in the Byzantine army from the people of Ḥimṣ. When information about this troop movement reached Ḥimṣ, the men from the Jazīrah left Ḥimṣ and returned to defend their hometowns. See also Ṭabarī, I, 2500; (ʿI.) Ibn al-Athīr, *Kāmil*, II, 381; Yāqūt, *Muʿjam*, II, 73; Donner, *Conquests*, 150. This interpretation of our passage necessitates an emendation of the text; see notes 659, 663, above.

665. Bathaniyyah was a place in Syria, known for its wheat. See Yāqūt, *Muʿjam*, I, 493–94; Blachère *et al.*, *Dictionnaire*, s.v. *b-th-n*. An extensive discussion of *ḥattā*

Then Heraclius set out for Constantinople. There is disagreement concerning the date of his arrival there and of his departure from Syria; Ibn Isḥāq said that it had been in the year 15/636–37 whereas Sayf said that it had been in the year 16/637–38.

The Departure of Heraclius for Constantinople

[2395]

According to Sayf—Abū al-Zahrāʾ al-Qushayrī—a man from Qushayr: When Heraclius set out from al-Ruhāʾ and asked its inhabitants to follow him, they said: "We are better off here than with you," and they refused to follow him and separated themselves both from him and from the Muslims.

The first man to cause the dogs of al-Ruhāʾ to bark and its fowls to be scared[666] was Ziyād b. Ḥanẓalah,[667] who was a Companion of the Prophet. [In this expedition?] he was with ʿUmar b. Mālik; they were taking turns in commanding the troops.[668] Ziyād was a confederate of Banū ʿAbd b. Quṣayy.

Before [this incursion] Heraclius set out for Shimshāṭ.[669] When the Muslims reached al-Ruhāʾ, he entered the Byzantine territory and moved toward Constantinople.[670]

A man of the Byzantines who had been a prisoner of the Muslims caught up with Heraclius. Heraclius said to him: "Inform me about these people." The man said: "I shall tell you, and it will be as if you yourself were looking at them. They are horsemen during the day and monks at night.[671] In the area under their responsibility they do not eat except for a price and do not enter a house except with a greeting of peace. They stand up to those who fight them until they

---

idhā ṣārat bathaniyyatan wa ʿasalan can be found in Ibn Manẓūr, *Lisān al-ʿArab,* s.v. *b-th-n.*

666. Meaning the first Muslim to make an incursion into this region.

667. Ziyād b. Ḥanẓalah of the tribe of Tamīm was a Companion of the Prophet. Muḥammad sent him to fight against Musaylimah and al-Aswad al-ʿAnsī, the prophetic claimants in al-Yamāmah and the Yemen. Later he participated in the battle of Yarmūk, in the incursions into Syria, and in the battles waged by ʿAlī b. Abī Ṭālib. He is also known for several poems in which he described the wars against the *ahl al-riddah* and against the Byzantines. See (ʿI.) Ibn al-Athīr, *Usd,* II, 213; Ibn Ḥajar, *Iṣābah,* II, 583; Yāqūt, *Muʿjam,* I, 83, 137; II, 525.

668. Cf. note 173, above.

669. A city on the Arsanas, or eastern Euphrates. See Le Strange, *Lands,* 116–17; Yāqūt, *Muʿjam,* III, 319–20.

670. See Donner, *Conquests,* 150.

671. Meaning that they fight during the day and pray at night.

destroy them." Heraclius said: "If you have spoken the truth, they will, indeed, inherit the land on which I stand."

According to ʿUbādah and Khālid: Whenever Heraclius made the pilgrimage to Jerusalem, left Syria behind [on his way back], and entered into the land of the Byzantines, he used to turn back and to say: "Peace be upon you, O Syria! This is the farewell of a man who takes leave of you without fulfilling his desire and will return." When the Muslims moved on Ḥimṣ, he crossed the Euphrates and camped at al-Ruhā'. He remained there until the people of al-Kūfah appeared, Qinnasrīn was conquered, and Mīnās was killed. When this happened, he retreated to Shimshāṭ. When he left Shimshāṭ in order to cross into the Byzantine territory, he ascended to an elevated place,
[2396] turned back, looked in the direction of Syria, and said: "Peace be upon you, O Syria! This is a farewell after which there will be no reunion. No Byzantine man will ever return to you except in fear until the ill-fated one is born; would that he would not be born! How sweet will be his deeds and how bitter will be their outcome with regard to the Byzantines."[672]

According to Abū al-Zahrā' and ʿAmr b. Maymūn: When Heraclius left Shimshāṭ and entered the Byzantine territory, he turned back toward Syria and said: "I used to greet you in the manner of a traveler. Today I am greeting you in the manner of one who departs. No Byzantine man will ever return to you except in fear until the ill-fated one is born; would that he would not be born!" Heraclius moved onward and reached Constantinople, taking with him the people of the fortresses located between Alexandretta and Tarsus so that the Muslims should not be able to move within any populated territory between Antioch and the Byzantine land. He laid the fortresses waste[673] so that the Muslims would not be able to find any-

---

672. The "ill-fated one" (*al-mash'ūm*) is the eschatological figure al-Dajjāl, the false Messiah. His appearance is one of the miraculous events expected in the Muslim tradition to take place before the Day of Judgment (*ashrāṭ al-sāʿah*). In some traditions it is related to the defeat of the Byzantines. See, for instance, Ibn Mājah, *Sunan*, II, 1370 (*Kitāb al-fitan, bāb 35* no. 4091): "The Dajjāl will not emerge until the Byzantines are defeated (*fa-mā yakhruju al-dajjāl ḥattā tuftaḥa al-Rūm*). On al-Dajjāl in general see *EI*[2], s.v. "al-Dadjdjāl" (A. Abel).

The Dajjāl's deeds will be sweet with regard to the Byzantines because he will fight the Muslims; their outcome will be bitter because he will lose the fight.

673. For this meaning of *shaʿʿatha*, see de Goeje's *Glossary* to Balādhurī, *Futūḥ*, s.v. *sh-ʿ-th*. See also a similar description of these events in Balādhurī, *Futūḥ*, 163–64.

one there. At times Byzantines lay in ambush near the fortresses and launched surprise attacks on those who were lagging behind, and the Muslims had to take precautions against this.

The Conquest of Caesarea[674] *and the Siege of Gaza*[675]

According to Sayf—Abū ʿUthmān and Abū Ḥārithah—Khālid and ʿUbādah: When Abū ʿUbaydah and Khālid departed from Fiḥl on their way to Ḥimṣ, ʿAmr (b. al-ʿĀṣ)[676] and Shuraḥbīl (b. Ḥasanah)[677] [2397] camped at Baysān and conquered it. The province of Jordan (*al-Urdunn*)[678] made peace with them. The Byzantine army gathered at Ajnādayn,[679] Baysān, and Gaza. ʿAmr and Shuraḥbīl wrote to ʿUmar that the Byzantines had divided their forces, and ʿUmar wrote to Yazīd (b. Abī Sufyān) asking him to send them reinforcements[680] and to dispatch Muʿāwiyah to Caesarea. He also wrote to ʿAmr commanding him to confront Arṭabūn,[681] and he wrote to ʿAlqamah b. Mujazziz[682] to confront al-Fīqār.[683] The following is the text of the letter of ʿUmar to Muʿāwiyah:

674. See *EI²*, s.v. "Ḳaysāriyya" (M. Sharon).
675. See *EI²*, s.v. "Ghazza" (D. Sourdel).
676. For ʿAmr b. al-ʿĀs, whose fame is based mainly on his conquest for Egypt, see *EI²*, s.v. "ʿAmr b. al-ʿĀṣ" (A. J. Wensinck).
677. Shuraḥbīl b. Ḥasanah belonged to the tribe of Kindah and was a confederate of the Qurashī clan of Banū Zuhrah in Mecca. He was an early convert to Islam and took part in the early battles of the Prophet. He served as governor over a part of Syria on behalf of ʿUmar. According to one tradition, he had been sent by the Prophet as his envoy to Egypt, where he died. According to another, he died in the plague of "ʿAmwās in 18/639–40. See Ibn Saʿd, *Ṭabaqāt*, VII/ii, 118; (ʿI.) Ibn al-Athīr, *Usd*, II, 390–91; Ibn Ḥajar, *Iṣābah*, III, 328–29; Ibn Ḥajar, *Tahdhīb*, IV, 324–25.
678. For the province of al-Urdunn, roughly corresponding to northern Palestine, see *EI¹*, s.v. "al-Urdunn, ii" (Fr. Buhl).
679. For a discussion of the possible location of Ajnādayn, see *EI²*, s.v. "Adjnādayn" (H. A. R. Gibb).
680. Literally "to warm their backs with men"; cf. de Goeje's *Glossary*, s.v. *d-f-ʾ*.
681. A commander in the Byzantine army. For the derivation of Arṭabūn from *tribunus*, see de Goeje, *Mémoire*, 62; and Jawālīqī, Muʿarrab, ed. Sachau, 11; see also ed. Shākir, 74, where *arṭabūn* is glossed with *al-muqaddam fī al-ḥarb*. Butler (*Arab Conquest*, 195, 215) maintains that the correct reading is Aretion.
682. In addition to his role in the conquest of Palestine, ʿAlqamah b. Mujazziz was sent by ʿUmar on a naval expedition to Abyssinia, an expedition that ended in disaster. Other traditions maintain that it was the Prophet who had ordered ʿAlqamah to raid Abyssinia in 9/630–1 and describe the raid as successful. See Wāqidī, *Maghāzī*, III, 983; Ibn Saʿd, *Ṭabaqāt*, II/i, 117–18; (ʿI.) Ibn al-Athīr, *Usd*, IV, 14; Ibn Ḥajar, *Iṣābah*, IV, 559–61.
683. For the derivation of *al-fīqār* from *vicarius*, see de Goeje, *Mémoire*, 62.

> Now, then, I have appointed you to govern Caesarea. Go there and ask God's help against them. Say frequently 'There is no power nor strength except in God.' God is our Lord, our trust, our hope, and our Master; how excellent is the Master and how excellent is the Helper!

The two men reached the places where they were commanded to go. Muʿāwiyah with his soldiers established camp near the people of Caesarea, who were led by A—B—N—Y.[684] He defeated the latter and besieged him in Caesarea. Then the people of Caesarea began to fight Muʿāwiyah, but whenever they fought him he defeated them and compelled them to retreat into their fortress. Finally they attacked him again, emerged from their fortifications, and fought with zeal and self-sacrifice. The number of their fallen during the fighting reached eighty thousand; at the time of their defeat Muʿāwiyah increased the total to one hundred thousand. He sent the news of victory [to ʿUmar] with two men from the Banū al-Ḍubayb, but then he became apprehensive that they would be weak[685] and sent ʿAbdallāh b. ʿAlqamah al-Firāsī and Zuhayr b. al-Ḥilāb al-Khathʿamī to follow the first two and to overtake them. [Ibn ʿAlqamah and Zuhayr] caught up with them and passed them while they were asleep. Ibn ʿAlqamah repeatedly recited the following verses:

The two Judhāmīs have made my eye sleepless;
 how can I sleep while they are ahead of me,
Traveling in the heat of midday,
 the brother of Ḥushaym and the brother of Ḥarām?[686]

[2398] ʿAlqamah b. Mujazziz set out and laid siege to al-Fīqār in Gaza. He began corresponding with him but received no satisfaction. Eventually ʿAlqamah came to al-Fīqār pretending to be ʿAlqamah's messenger. Al-Fīqār ordered a man to wait for him on the way and to kill him when he passed by, but ʿAlqamah became aware of it and said: "I have with me a number of men who share my view. I shall go and bring them to you." Al-Fīqār sent a message to that man in-

---

684. I am unable to vocalize this name.

685. And unable to make the trip to Medina.

686. These verses are quoted in a slightly different—and better—arrangement in Balādhurī, *Futūḥ*, 142. See also Hitti, *Origins*, 218. According to Balādhurī's version, the first two messengers belonged to the tribe of Judhām, which tallies better with the first verse.

structing him not to attack ʿAlqamah. ʿAlqamah departed and did not return, doing the same thing which ʿAmr did with al-Arṭabūn.[687]

The messengers (*al-barīd*) of Muʿāwiyah brought the news to ʿUmar, who assembled the people and made them spend the night joyfully. He praised God and said to them: "Praise God for the conquest of Caesarea!" Muʿāwiyah kept the Byzantine prisoners with him before the conquest and after it and said: "Whatever Mikhāʾīl[688] does to our prisoners, we shall do to theirs." He thereby dissuaded Mikhāʾīl from molesting the Muslim prisoners until Caesarea was conquered.

The Conquest of Baysān[689] and the Battle of Ajnādayn[690]

When ʿAlqamah moved to Gaza and Muʿāwiyah to Caesarea, ʿAmr b. al-ʿĀs went to confront al-Arṭabūn and passed in front of him. Shuraḥbīl b. Ḥasanah set out with him, commanding the vanguard. ʿAmr b. al-ʿĀṣ appointed Abū al-Aʿwar to govern [the province of] Jordan in his stead. He put the two wings of his army in charge of ʿAbdallāh b. ʿAmr and Junādah b. Tamīm al-Mālikī [of the tribe of Mālik b. Kinānah]. He set out and camped near the Byzantines at Ajnādayn. The Byzantines were in their fortifications and trenches, with al-Arṭabūn, the most cunning of the Byzantines, the most farsighted, and the most harmful, as their commander. He placed a large army in al-Ramlah[691] and a large army in Jerusalem. ʿAmr (b. al-ʿĀṣ) informed ʿUmar of the news. When ʿAmr's letter reached him, he said: "We have sent the Arṭabūn of the Arabs to confront the [2399]
Arṭabūn of the Byzantines. Let us see what the outcome will be!"

At this time, ʿUmar began to dispatch the amīrs of Syria and to provide each commander with reinforcements. When he received ʿAmr's letter informing him that the Byzantines had divided their

---

687. See p. 2400, below.

688. For a discussion of Mikhāʾīl's identity, see de Goeje, *Mémoire*, 168.

689. See *EI*², s.v. "Baysān" (J. Sourdel-Thomine).

690. See *EI*², s.v. "Adjnādayn" (H. A. R. Gibb).

691. Al-Ramlah was founded only at the beginning of the eighth century C. E. by Sulaymān b. ʿAbd al-Malik, and the statement in our passage is anachronistic.

forces,[692] he wrote to Yazīd (b. Abī Sufyān) to send Muʿāwiyah with his cavalry to Caesarea. He wrote to Muʿāwiyah, appointing him to lead the fighting against the people of Caesarea, and to tie down their forces in order to prevent them from fighting ʿAmr. ʿAmr appointed ʿAlqamah b. Ḥakīm al-Firāsī and Masrūq b. so-and-so al-ʿAkkī[693] to fight the people of Jerusalem. They confronted the people of Jerusalem and prevented them from fighting ʿAmr. ʿUmar sent Abū Ayyūb al-Mālikī[694] to al-Ramlah, which was ruled by al-Tadhāriq. He confronted the two of them.[695]

When the reinforcements reached ʿAmr one after the other, he sent Muḥammad b. ʿAmr to reinforce ʿAlqamah and Masrūq and sent ʿUmārah b. ʿAmr b. Umayyah al-Ḍamrī[696] to reinforce Abū Ayyūb. ʿAmr stayed in Ajnādayn, without being able to cause al-Arṭabūn to make a mistake. Nor did the envoys bring him satisfaction (either), so he took the matter upon himself and entered upon al-Arṭabūn as if he were an envoy. He told al-Arṭabūn what he wanted, listened to what he said, and looked at his fortifications until he knew what he wanted to know. Arṭabūn said to himself: "By God, it is ʿAmr or a man whose advice ʿAmr follows. Nothing I could do would harm the Muslims more grievously than killing this man." Then he called in a member of his guard and secretly spoke to him about killing ʿAmr. He said: "Go out and stand in such-and-such a place, and when he passes near you, kill him." ʿAmr became aware of this and said:

> You have heard from me and I have heard from you, and I have been impressed by what you have said. I am one of ten men whom ʿUmar b. al-Khaṭṭāb sent with this governor in

---

692. Meaning that the Byzantine army was divided between Ajnādayn, Baysān, and Gaza. See p. 2397, above.

693. See Ibn Ḥajar, *Iṣābah*, VI, 92–93 no. 7940.

694. Abū Ayyūb al-Mālikī, better known as al-Anṣārī, was a Companion of the Prophet from the Medinan tribe of Khazraj. His fame is based mainly on his participation in the siege of Constantinople during the reign of Muʿāwiyah and on his reported burial there. See *EI*², s.v. "Abū Ayyūb . . . al-Anṣārī" (E. Lévi-Provençal et al.).

695. Al-Tadhāriq is said to have been the brother of the emperor Heraclius. See Ṭabarī, I, 2086, 2107.

It is not clear who the two men whom al-Tadhāriq confronts are. One is clearly Abū Ayyūb al-Mālikī; the other may be ʿUmārah b. ʿAmr b. Umayyah al-Ḍamrī, who is mentioned in the following paragraph.

696. See Ibn Ḥajar, *Iṣābah*, IV, 586 no. 5730.

order that we might assist him and he might make us aware of his affairs. I shall return and bring them to you forthwith. [2400]
If they view what you suggested as I do, then the members of the army and the amīr will view it in the same way. If they do not view it so, you will allow them to return to safety and you will be able to start your affair.[697]

Al-Arṭabūn said: "Agreed." He called a man, spoke to him secretly, and said: "Go to so-and-so and send him back to me." The man came back, and al-Arṭabūn said to ʿAmr: "Go and bring your companions." ʿAmr went away and decided not to come back. The Byzantine understood that ʿAmr had deceived him and said: "The man has deceived me; he is the most cunning of creatures." ʿUmar came to know about it and said: "ʿAmr got the better of him! How excellent is ʿAmr!"

ʿAmr moved against al-Arṭabūn after he came to know where he could be attacked and what would be his end. They confronted each other, and al-Arṭabūn did not have any other choice. The confrontation took place at Ajnādayn, and the two armies fought a heavy battle, like the battle of Yarmūk, in which many were killed. Arṭabūn was defeated with his men and took refuge in Jerusalem, while ʿAmr camped at Ajnādayn. When Arṭabūn came to Jerusalem, the Muslims did not stand in his way and enabled him to enter the city. Then ʿAmr moved the Muslims to Ajnādayn, and ʿAlqamah, Masrūq, Muḥammad b. ʿAmr, and Abū Ayyūb joined ʿAmr at Ajnādayn.

Arṭabūn wrote to ʿAmr saying: "You are my friend and opposite number; the position you hold among your people is comparable to my position among mine. By God, you will not conquer any part of Palestine after Ajnādayn. Go back and do not be deceived, lest you be defeated like those before you." ʿAmr summoned a man who spoke Greek, sent him to Arṭabūn, and ordered him to behave like a stranger and to disguise himself. He instructed him: "Listen to what he says so that you can give me the information about it when you come back, God willing," and he wrote to Arṭabūn, saying: "I have received your letter. You are my opposite number among your people. If you were not in possession of excellent qualities, you would not be aware of my virtues; but you do know that I am the

697. Probably meaning that he will be able to start the battle, having exhausted all other options.

man destined to conquer this land. I am seeking against you the help of so-and-so and so-and-so and so-and-so (he mentioned some of Arṭabūn's aides); read my letter to them and let them look into what is between me and you."

[2401] The envoy set out in accordance with ʿAmr's orders. He came to Arṭabūn and gave him the letter in the presence of some people, and Arṭabūn read the letter aloud. They laughed and wondered; then they approached Arṭabūn, saying: "From what source do you know that he is not the man destined to conquer this land?" Arṭabūn said: "The name of the man destined to do it is ʿUmar. It is written with three letters."[698] The envoy returned to ʿAmr, who understood now that the man was ʿUmar. He wrote to ʿUmar, asking his help and saying: "I am conducting a difficult and fierce war and [struggling for] a land that has been held and preserved for you. I desire your opinion." When ʿAmr wrote to ʿUmar about this, ʿUmar knew that he was speaking out of knowledge. He summoned the people, set out with them, and camped at al-Jābiyah.[699]

All in all ʿUmar went to Syria four times. The first time he rode a horse; the second time he rode a camel; the third time he failed to reach Syria because the plague was raging, and the fourth time he entered Syria on a donkey.

ʿUmar appointed [ʿAlī to govern Medina in his stead].[700] At the
[2402] time of his departure [from Medina] for the first time he wrote to the amīrs of the provinces and instructed them to meet him at al-Jābiyah on a day which he specified for them. He instructed them to come with light cavalry (*mujarradah*)[701] and to appoint deputies to govern their provinces. They met him where al-Jābiyah came into view. The first man to meet him was Yazīd, then Abū ʿUbaydah, and then Khālid. They were riding on horses and were clad in brocade and silk. ʿUmar dismounted, took stones in his hand, and pelted them. He said: "How quickly were you turned away from your senses! Is it me that you are coming to meet in this attire?[702] You

698. The name ʿUmar consists of three letters in the Arabic script, whereas the name ʿAmr consists of four.

699. See note 487, above.

700. I have augmented Ṭabarī's cryptic text here, in light of (ʿI.) Ibn al-Athīr, *Kāmil*, II, 389, and the tradition adduced in note g to this page in the Leiden edition.

701. See note 63, above.

702. Knowing ʿUmar's austere demeanor. For a different description of ʿUmar's meeting with his silk-clad commanders, see Kūfī, *Futūḥ*, I, 295.

have been eating well for two years. How quickly has gluttony led you astray! By God, if you did this at the head of two hundred men, I would have replaced you with others." They replied: "O Commander of the Faithful, these are coats, and we have our weapons with us." ʿUmar said: "It is all right, then," and he rode on till he entered al-Jābiyah. ʿAmr and Shuraḥbīl were at that time in Ajnādayn and did not move from their place.

The Conquest of Jerusalem

According to Sālim b. ʿAbdallāh: When ʿUmar reached al-Jābiyah, a [2403]
Jew said to him: "O Commander of the Faithful, you will not return to your country before God has granted you victory over Jerusalem." While in al-Jābiyah ʿUmar b. al-Khaṭṭāb saw an approaching detachment of horsemen. When they came close, they drew their swords, but ʿUmar said: "These are people who are coming to seek an assurance of safety. Grant it to them." They drew near and it became clear that they were people from Jerusalem. They made peace with ʿUmar on the condition that they would pay the poll tax and opened up Jerusalem for him. When ʿUmar was granted victory over Jerusalem, he summoned that same Jew, and it was said to him: "He is, indeed, in possession of knowledge." ʿUmar asked the Jew about the false Messiah, for he was wont to ask about him a great deal. The Jew said to him: "What are you asking about him, O Commander of the Faithful? You, the Arabs, will kill him ten odd cubits in front of the gate of Lydda."[703]

According to Sālim: When ʿUmar entered Syria, a Jew from Damascus met him and said: "Peace be upon you, O Fārūq! You are the master of Jerusalem. By God, you will not return before God conquers Jerusalem!"[704]

---

703. For the killing of al-Dajjāl in the eschatological struggle between him and the true Messiah near the gate of Lydda, see Ibn Mājah, *Sunan*, II, 1361 (*Kitāb al-fitan*, *bāb* 36).

704. For a very different version of the prediction of the conquest of Palestine by the Muslims, see Kūfī, *Futūḥ*, I, 296–97. For an analysis of the differences between the two versions, see Crone, *Slaves*, 207–8 n. 60.

Regarding ʿUmar's epithet al-Fārūq, the Sunni Muslim tradition maintains that ʿUmar was so named because he knew the distinction between truth and falsehood (*farraqa bayna al-ḥaqq wa al-bāṭil*). See Ibn al-Jawzī, *Manāqib*, 19. See also now S. Bashear, "The Title 'Fārūq.'"

[The people of Jerusalem] caused distress to ʿAmr and he caused distress to them, but he could not conquer Jerusalem, nor could he conquer al-Ramlah.

While ʿUmar was camping in al-Jābiyah, the Muslims seized their weapons in alarm. ʿUmar asked: "What is it?", and they replied: "Do you not see the horsemen and the swords?" ʿUmar looked and saw a detachment of horsemen brandishing their swords. He said: "They are seeking an assurance of safety. Do not be afraid, but grant it to them." They granted them an assurance of safety and [it became clear that] these were people from Jerusalem. They gave to ʿUmar ... [705] and asked him to give them in writing [the peace terms] for Jerusalem and its region and for al-Ramlah and its region. Palestine was divided into two parts: one part was with the people of Jerusalem, and the other with the people of al-Ramlah. The people of Palestine were [organized in] ten provinces, and Palestine was equal to Syria in its entirety.

The Jew witnessed the conclusion of the peace treaty. ʿUmar asked him about the false Messiah. The Jew said: "He is from the sons of Benjamin. By God, you Arabs will kill him ten odd cubits from the gate of Lydda."

[2404] According to Khālid and ʿUbādah: The peace treaty concerning Palestine was concluded by the populace of Jerusalem and al-Ramlah. The reason for this was that Arṭabūn and al-Tadhāriq had left for Egypt when ʿUmar came to al-Jābiyah; they were subsequently killed in one of the summer expeditions.

It was said that the reason for ʿUmar's coming to Syria was the following: Abū ʿUbaydah besieged Jerusalem. Its people asked him to conclude peace with them on the conditions of the Syrian cities and asked that ʿUmar b. al-Khaṭṭāb be responsible for the treaty. Abū ʿUbaydah wrote to ʿUmar about it, and ʿUmar made the journey from Medina.

According to ʿAdī b. Sahl: When the Muslims of Syria asked ʿUmar to help them against the people of Palestine, he appointed ʿAlī as his deputy and set out to reinforce them. ʿAlī said: "Where
[2405] are going by yourself? You are heading toward a rabid enemy." ʿUmar said: "I hasten to fight the enemy before the death of al-ʿAbbās. If

705. The object of the verb is missing. The Leiden editor's suggestion is that a word like "obedience" (*ṭāʿah*) or "poll tax" (*jizyah*) was omitted.

you lose al-ʿAbbās, evil will untwist you like the ends of a rope." ʿAmr and Shuraḥbīl joined ʿUmar in al-Jābiyah when the peace [with the people of Palestine] was concluded. They witnessed the writing [of the treaty].

According to Khālid and ʿUbādah: ʿUmar made peace with the people of Jerusalem in al-Jābiyah. He wrote for them the peace conditions. He wrote one[706] letter to all the provinces (of Palestine) except to the people of Jerusalem:[707]

> In the name of God, the Merciful, the Compassionate. This is the assurance of safety (*amān*) which the servant of God, ʿUmar, the Commander of the Faithful, has granted to the people of Jerusalem. He has given them an assurance of safety for themselves, for their property, their churches, their crosses, the sick and the healthy of the city,[708] and for all the rituals that belong to their religion. Their churches will not be inhabited [by Muslims] and will not be destroyed. Neither they, nor the land on which they stand, nor their cross,[709] nor their property will be damaged. They will not be forcibly converted. No Jew will live with them in Jerusalem. The people of Jerusalem must pay the poll tax like the people of the [other] cities, and they must expel the Byz- [2406]
> antines and the robbers.[710] As for those who will leave the city, their lives and property will be safe until they reach their place of safety; and as for those who remain, they will be safe. They will have to pay the poll tax like the people of Jerusalem. Those of the people of Jerusalem who want to leave with the Byzantines, take their property, and abandon

706. In the sense of "identical"; see the phrase introducing the letter to the people of Lydda, p. 2406, below.

707. The people of Jerusalem received a different letter, which follows here.

708. See note 225, above.

709. Busse ("ʿOmar b. al-Khaṭṭāb," 114–15) suggests that this is a reference to the "true cross," taken by the Persians during their invasion of 614 and returned to Jerusalem by Heraclius in 629; cf. Ostrogorsky, *History*, 95, 104; de Goeje (*Mémoire*, 153) and Fattal (*Le status*, 45) translate as if *ṣalīb* were in the plural, like *ṣulbān* above.

710. Ṭabarī has *luṣūt* (sg. *liṣt*) for the usual Arabic *luṣūṣ* (sg. *liṣṣ*). According to Ibn Manẓūr (*Lisān al-ʿArab*, s.v. *l-s-t*), this is the form of the word in the dialect of Ṭayyiʾ. For the connection between *liṣṣ* and the Aramaic *lisṭim*, see Fraenkel, *Fremdwörter*, 284.

their churches and their crosses will be safe[711] until they reach their place of safety. Those villagers (*ahl al-arḍ*) who were in Jerusalem before the killing of so-and-so[712] may remain in the city if they wish, but they must pay the poll tax like the people of Jerusalem. Those who wish may go with the Byzantines, and and those who wish may return to their families. Nothing will be taken from them before their harvest is reaped. If they pay the poll tax according to their obligations, then the contents of this letter are under the covenant of God, are the responsibility of His Prophet, of the caliphs, and of the faithful. The persons who attest to it are Khālid b. al-Walīd, ʿAmr b. al-ʿĀṣī, ʿAbd al-Raḥmān b. ʿAwf,[713] and Muʿāwiyah b. Abī Sufyān. This letter was written and prepared in the year 15/636–37.

The rest of the letters were identical to the letter of Lydda [which follows]:

In the name of God, the Merciful, the Compassionate. This is what the servant of God, ʿUmar, the Commander of the
[2407] Faithful, awarded to the people of Lydda and to all the people of Palestine who are in the same category. He gave them an assurance of safety for themselves, for their property, their churches, their crosses, their sick and their healthy, and all their rites. Their churches will not be inhabited [by the Muslims] and will not be destroyed. Neither their churches, nor the land where they stand, nor their rituals, nor their crosses, nor their property will be damaged. They will not be forcibly converted, and none of them will be harmed. The people of Lydda and those of the people of Palestine who are in the same category must pay the poll tax like the people of the Syrian cities. The same conditions, in their entirety, apply to them if they leave (Lydda).

He then sent to them [an army] and divided Palestine between two

711. I have omitted here the words *ʿalā biyaʿihim wa-ṣulubihim*, "their churches and crosses [will be safe]"; this does not make sense in this place. Cf. de Goeje, *Mémoire*, 153 n. 2.

712. The meaning of these words is not clear; cf. de Goeje, *Mémoire*, 153 n. 3. They are missing in the text of the letter included in Suyūṭī, *Itḥāf*, I, 233.

713. See note 4, above.

men; he put ʿAlqamah b. Ḥakīm in charge of one half and stationed him in al-Ramlah, and he put ʿAlqamah b. Mujazziz in charge of the other half and stationed him in Jerusalem. Each of them stayed in his province with the soldiers who were with him.

According to Sālim: [ʿUmar] appointed ʿAlqamah b. Mujazziz governor of Jerusalem and appointed ʿAlqamah b. al-Ḥakīm governor of al-Ramlah. He placed the soldiers who were with ʿAmr (b. al-ʿĀsī) at their disposal. He ordered ʿAmr and Shuraḥbīl to join him in al-Jābiyah. When they reached al-Jābiyah, they found ʿUmar riding. They kissed his knee, and ʿUmar embraced them, holding them to his chest.

According to ʿUbādah and Khālid: Having sent the assurance of safety to the people of Jerusalem and having stationed the army there, ʿUmar set out from al-Jābiyah to Jerusalem. He saw that his horse had injuries on its hooves. So he dismounted, and a jade was brought to him and he rode it. The jade shook him, however, so ʿUmar dismounted, hit the jade's face with his mantle, and said: "May God make ugly him who taught you this!" Then he called for his horse to be brought to him, after he had left him unridden for a few days, and treated his hooves. He mounted his horse and rode until he reached Jerusalem.

According to Abū Ṣafiyyah, an elder from Banū Shaybān: When ʿUmar came to Syria, he was brought a jade and rode it. The jade moved in an unstable manner, inclining from side to side. ʿUmar dismounted, hit the jade's face, and said: "May God not teach him [2408] who taught you this sort of pride!" He had not ridden a jade before that or after that.

Jerusalem and its entire region were conquered by ʿUmar, except for Ajnādayn, which was conquered by ʿAmr (b. al-ʿĀṣi), and Caesarea, which was conquered by Muʿāwiyah (b. Abī Sufyān).

According to Abū ʿUthmān and Abū Ḥārithah: Jerusalem and its region were conquered in the month of Rabīʿ al-Ākhir of the year 16/May 637.

According to Abū Maryam, the client of Salāmah, who said: I witnessed the conquest of Jerusalem with ʿUmar: He set out from al-Jābiyah, leaving it behind until he came to Jerusalem. He then went on and entered the mosque.[714] Then he went on toward the *miḥrāb*

714. *Al-masjid* refers in this context to the Temple Mount, in keeping with the

of David,[715] while we were with him; he entered it, recited the prostration of David,[716] and prostrated himself, and we prostrated ourselves with him.

According to Rajāʾ b. Ḥaywah—persons who were present at the event: When ʿUmar came from al-Jābiyah to Jerusalem and drew near the gate of the mosque,[717] he said: "Watch out for Kaʿb on my behalf!"[718] When the gate was opened for him, he said: "O God, I am ready to serve you in what you love most." Then he turned to the *miḥrāb*, the *miḥrāb* of David, peace be upon him. It was at night, and he prayed there.[719] It was not long before dawn broke, and then ʿUmar ordered the *muʾadhdhin* to sound the call for prayer.[720] Then he moved forward, led the prayer, and recited Sūrat Ṣād[721] with the people. During the prayer he prostrated himself. Then he stood up and read with them in the second (*rakʿah*) the beginning of Sūrat Banī Isrāʾīl.[722] Then he prayed another *rakʿah* and went away. He said: "Bring Kaʿb to me." Kaʿb was brought to him. ʿUmar said: "Where do you think we should establish the place of prayer?" Kaʿb

---

most current interpretation of Qurʾān 17:1, which identifies *al-masjid al-aqṣā*, "the farthest mosque," with Jerusalem. Cf. Busse, "ʿOmar b. al-Khaṭṭāb," 83.

715. For a discussion of the possible meanings of *miḥrāb Dāwūd*, the citadel of David near the Jaffa gate, on the northwestern corner of the old city of Jerusalem or a place on the Temple Mount itself, see Busse, "ʿOmar b. al-Khaṭṭāb," 79–83; Busse, "ʿOmar's Image," 165–66.

716. Qurʾān 38:21–25, where David prostrates himself, repents, and asks God to forgive him.

717. *Masjid* is used here in the sense of the whole *ḥaram* area; a mosque was not yet in existence. I am indebted to my colleague Dr. A. Elʿad for this note.

718. Kaʿb al-Aḥbār was a Yemenite Jew who converted to Islam during the reign of Abū Bakr or ʿUmar and was considered an important transmitter of Jewish traditions into Islamic lore. See Wolfensohn, *Kaʿb al-Aḥbār*. Numerous traditions transmitted by him have been assembled and analyzed in Kister, "Ḥaddithū ʿan banī Isrāʾīl." See also *EI*², s.v. "Kaʿb al-Aḥbār" (M. Schmitz).

719. Busse maintains that, in this tradition, *miḥrāb Dāwūd* refers to the citadel of David. He suggests that ʿUmar's night prayer is a reflection of a Christian custom of praying there at night. See "ʿOmar b. al-Khaṭṭāb," 84; Busse, "ʿOmar's Image," 166.

720. The tradition uses the word *iqāmah*, which signifies the second call to prayer, pronounced in the mosque immediately before the service begins. See *EI*², s.vv. "Adhān" (Th. W. Juynboll), "Iḳāma" (Th. W. Juynboll).

721. Qurʾān 38.

722. Qurʾān 17, known also as *Sūrat al-isrāʾ*, "the nocturnal journey." The "further mosque" in the first verse of this sūrah is usually understood as referring to Jerusalem. The verse reads "Glory be to Him, Who carried His servant by night from the Holy Mosque to the Further Mosque the precincts of which We have blessed, that We may show him some of Our signs." (Arberry's translation)

said: "Toward the Rock."[723] ʿUmar said: "O Kaʿb, you are imitating the Jewish religion! I have seen you taking off your shoes." Kaʿb said: "I wanted to touch this ground with my feet." ʿUmar said: "I have seen you. Nay, we shall place the *qiblah* in the front of it; the Messenger of God likewise made the front part of our mosques the *qiblah*.[724] Take care of your own affairs; we were not commanded to venerate the Rock, but we were commanded to venerate the Kaʿbah."

ʿUmar made the front part of the mosque its *qiblah*. Then he stood up from his place of prayer and went to the rubbish in which [2409] the Romans buried the temple (*bayt al-maqdis*) at the time of the sons of Israel. (When he came to the Byzantines, they had uncovered a part but left the rest [under the rubbish].) He said: "O people, do what I am doing."[725] He knelt in the midst of the rubbish and put it by the handful into the lower part of his mantle.[726] He heard behind him the proclamation "God is most great!" He disliked improper behavior[727] in any matter and said: "What is this?" The people said:

---

723. The tradition as it appears in Ṭabarī is not very clear and has to be understood in light of a fuller version which can be found in Suyūṭī, *Itḥāf*, I, 236–37. It reads: "ʿUmar said to Kaʿb: 'Where do you think we should place the mosque?' Or he said: '... the direction of prayer?' Kaʿb said: 'Place the mosque behind the Rock, so that the two directions of prayer—that of Moses and that of Muḥammad—merge with one another'" (*fa-qāla ʿUmar li-Kaʿb: ayna tarā an najʿala al-masjida? aw qāla: al-qiblata. fa-qāla: ijʿalhu khalfa al-ṣakhrati fa-tajtamiʿu al-qiblatāni qiblatu Mūsā wa-qiblatu Muḥammad* ...) In our version Kaʿb responds to ʿUmar's question about the direction of prayer, which is not mentioned in Ṭabarī's text.

See additional sources for this tradition in Wāsiṭī, *Faḍāʾil*, 45–46. See also Kister, "Three Mosques," 194, for another tradition forbidding the combination of the two directions of prayer. It has to be kept in mind, however, that Muslim tradition has also preserved material that treats the Rock in a much more positive way; see, for instance, Wāsiṭī, *Faḍāʾil*, 67ff.

It is noteworthy that the idea of combining the *qiblah* of Jerusalem with that of Mecca can be found also in the traditions describing the customs of the Prophet himself. While still in Mecca, before the *hijrah*, he is said to have prayed "facing Syria, placing the Kaʿbah between himself and Syria" (*wa-kāna idhā ṣallā istaqbala al-Shām wa-jaʿala al Kaʿbah baynahu wa-bayna al-Shām*). See Ibn Hishām, *Sīrat*, 228 (= Guillaume, *Life of Muḥammad*, 157–58), Maqdisī, *Faḍāʾil*, 54. For the *qiblah* in general, see *EI*², s.v. "Ḳibla. i" (A. J. Wensinck).

724. The front part of the mosque seems to mean here the southern part of the Temple Mount. The believers pray facing the south, with their backs toward the Rock.

725. Cf. Busse, "ʿOmar b. al-Khaṭṭāb," 87–88.

726. For this meaning of *farj*, see de Goeje's *Glossary*, s.vv. *farj*, *birka*. Al-Wāsiṭī (*Faḍāʾil*, 78) has *malaʾa asfala thawbihi min al-mazbalah*.

727. The impropriety seems to lie in proclaiming God's greatness while dealing with rubbish.

"Kaʿb proclaimed 'God is most great!' and the people proclaimed it following him." ʿUmar said: "Bring him to me!" Kaʿb said: "O Commander of the Faithful, five hundred years ago a prophet predicted what you have done today." ʿUmar asked: "In what way?" Kaʿb said:

> The Byzantines (*Rūm*) attacked the sons of Israel, were given victory over them, and buried the temple. Then they were given another victory, but they did not attend to the temple until the Persians attacked them. The Persians oppressed the sons of Israel. Later the Byzantines were given victory over the Persians. Then you came to rule. God sent a prophet to the [city buried in] rubbish and said: "Rejoice O Jerusalem (*Ūrī shalam*)![728] Al-Fārūq[729] will come to you and cleanse you." Another prophet was sent to Constantinople. He stood on a hill belonging to the city and said: "O Constantinople, what did your people do to My House? They ruined it, presented you as if you were similar to My throne and made interpretations contrary to My purpose.[730] I have determined to make you one day unfortified (and defenseless).[731] Nobody will seek shelter from you, nor rest in your shade. [I shall make you unfortified] at the hands of Banū al-Qādhir, Sabā, and Waddān."[732]

By the time it was evening nothing remained of the rubbish.

An identical tradition was transmitted according to Rabīʿah al-Shāmī. He added: "Al-Fārūq came to you with my obedient army. They will take revenge upon the Byzantines on behalf of your people." Regarding Constantinople he said: "I shall leave you unforti-

728. The use of this unusual form, rather than the common Iliyā or Bayt al-Maqdis, is intended to enhance the air of authenticity that the tradition seeks to infuse into this prophecy.

729. See note 704, above.

730. This meaning of *ta'awwalū ʿalayya*, which is close to that suggested by Busse ("ʿOmar b. al-Khaṭṭab," 92), seems better than that in Blachère *et al.*, *Dictionnaire*, I, 307b.

731. Ibn Manẓūr (*Lisān al-ʿArab*, s.v. *j-l-ḥ*) quotes a different version of this tradition and explains *jalḥā'* as "having no fort." The basic significance of the root is baldness; hence it came to mean a bull without horns that he can use to defend himself, thus *qaryah jalḥā'*, a city without a fort as means of defense.

732. See Ezekiel 27:19–22. Busse ("ʿOmar b. al-Khaṭṭāb," 92 n. 72) suggests reading Dedan, mentioned in Ezekiel together with Qedar and Sheva, instead of Waddān.

fied and exposed to the sun; nobody will seek shelter from you, and you will not cast your shade on anyone."[733]

According to Anas b. Mālik:

> I was present in Jerusalem with ʿUmar. While he was giving food to the people one day, a monk from Jerusalem came to him without knowing that wine had been prohibited. The monk said: "Do you want a drink which will be permissible according to our books [even] when wine is prohibited?" [2410]

ʿUmar asked him to bring it and said: "From what has it been prepared?" The monk informed him that he had cooked it from juice until only one-third of it remained. ʿUmar dipped his finger into it, then stirred it in the vessel, divided it into two halves, and said: "This is syrup (*ṭilā*ʾ)." He likened it to resin (*qaṭirān*), drank from it, and ordered the amīrs of the Syrian provinces to prepare it. He wrote to the newly established garrison towns (*amṣār*), saying: "I have been brought a beverage cooked from juice until two-thirds of it were gone and one-third remained. It is like syrup. Cook it and provide it to the Muslims."[734]

According to Abū ʿUthmān and Abū Ḥārithah: Arṭabūn went to Egypt when ʿUmar came to al-Jābiyah. Those who rejected the peace agreement and wanted [to go with him] joined him. Then, when the people of Egypt made a peace agreement [with the Muslims] and defeated the Byzantines, he took to the sea and survived afterward. He commanded the summer expeditions of the Byzantines and con-

---

733. Cf. Wolfensohn, *Kaʿb al-Aḥbār*, 27–28.

734. In this tradition ʿUmar is described as giving legitimacy to a beverage that may be problematic because of its affinity with wine. Although the method of preparation does not indicate that the beverage contained alcohol, it is noteworthy that the Muslim tradition preserved prophetic utterances in which *ṭilā*ʾ is understood as a euphemism for wine. See Abū Dāwūd, *Sunan*, III, 450 (and Ibn Ḥanbal, *Musnad*, V, 342): "ʿAbd al-Raḥmān b. Ghanm entered upon us, and we discussed *ṭilā*ʾ. He said: Abū Mālik al-Ashʿarī told me that he had heard the Prophet saying: 'People from my community will drink wine, calling it by another name.'" For a more outspoken version, see Ibn Manẓūr, *Lisān al-ʿArab*, s.v. *ṭ-l-y*: "'People from my community will drink wine and call it by another name,' meaning that they will drink intoxicating cooked date wine (*nabīdh*) and call it a 'syrup' (*ṭilā*ʾ), because of their unwillingness to call it 'wine' (*khamr*)."

For traditions stating that two-thirds of the juice must evaporate in cooking before it becomes permissible for the Muslims, see Nasāʾī, *Sunan*, VIII, 328–31, Kūfī, *Futūḥ*, I, 298. See also Mālik b. Anas, *Muwaṭṭa*ʾ, II, 847 (*Kitāb al-ashribah*, 14), for a tradition very similar to that reported by Ṭabarī.

fronted the commander of the Muslim summer expeditions. Arṭabūn and a man from the tribe of Qays, whose name was Ḍurays, exchanged blows,[735] and Arṭabūn cut the Qaysī's hand.[736] The Qaysī killed him and recited:

Though Arṭabūn of the Byzantines maimed my hand,
there is still some use to it, praise be to God.
Two fingers and a stump,[737] with which I hold straight
the front part of the spear when people are struck with fear.[738]
Though Arṭabūn of the Byzantines cut my hand,
I left his limbs cut to pieces, in return.

Ziyād b. Ḥanẓalah recited:

I remembered the long wars against the Byzantines,
when we spent a year full of journeys.
[2411] When we were in the land of Ḥijāz and
a month's journey separated us,[739] with anxieties in between;
When Arṭabūn of the Byzantines defended his country,
a noble chieftain tackled him here and struggled with him;
When al-Fārūq saw that the time [was right] for the conquest of Arṭabūn's land,
he brought forward God's soldiers to attack him.
When they became aware of al-Fārūq and feared his assault,
they came to him and said: "You are of those whom we shall befriend."
Syria threw its buried treasures at his feet,[740]

---

735. Ṭabarī has *fa-yakhtalifu huwa wa-rajulun mim Qays*. I have translated according to a parallel version of the story in Tibrīzī's commentary on Abū Tammām, *Ḥamāsah*, I, 239, where the Muslim warrior is ʿAbdallāh b. Ṣabrah and the text reads: *fa-ʾkhtalafa huwa wa-ʿAbdallāh ḍarbatayni*. See also Ibn Ḥajar, *Iṣābah*, V, 11–12 no. 6177, 89 no. 6327. For another occurrence of this idiom, see Sarakhsī, *Sharḥ al-siyar*, I, 174.

736. The rest of the story and the following poem indicate that he cut off only three fingers.

737. Reading *judhmūr* instead of *jurmūz*. This version of the verse, attributed to ʿAbdallāh b. Ṣabrah, can be found in Tibrīzī's commentary on Abū Tammām, *Ḥamāsah*, I, 239. See also Ibn Manẓūr, *Lisān al-ʿArab*, s.v. *j-dh-m-r*. On ʿAbdallāh b. Ṣabrah, who is counted among the "brigands" (*futtāk*) of Islam, see Ibn Ḥajar, *Iṣābah*, V, 89; Ibn Ḥabīb, *Muḥabbar*, 222–26.

738. Meaning that he is still capable of defending his people despite the injury that Arṭabūn inflicted upon him.

739. Presumably from the Byzantines.

740. It is noteworthy that similar descriptions of the earth's throwing up its buried

as well as a life of abundance with countless gains.[741]
He put whatever was between east and west at our disposal,
as inheritance for posterity, gathered by his two-humped camels.[742]
Many a beast of burden that had been unable to carry its load,
[now] carried a burden while being well into pregnancy.[743]

Ziyād b. Ḥanẓalah also recited:

When ʿUmar received the letters,[744] he rose
like a proud, young chieftain defending the property of the tribe.
The land of Syria was bursting with people,
desiring the most courageous of men.
When he received (the information) that he received, he responded
with an army to which dissensions bowed their heads.[745]
Spacious Syria brought what
Abū Ḥafṣ[746] wanted, and even more.
He allotted among them the poll tax,
and every pleasant and commendable gift.

The Introduction of the Pay System (ʿaṭāʾ)[747] *and of the Military Register* (dīwān)[748]

In this year ʿUmar assigned payments to the Muslims and established the [military] registers. He determined the payments accord-

---

treasures can be found in the chapters of Muslim tradition dealing with the miraculous events expected to occur immediately before the Day of Judgment: "Earth will throw up oblong pieces of gold and silver, having the size of a column" (*taqīʾu al-arḍ aflādha kabidihā amthāl al-usṭuwān min al-dhahab wa al-fiḍḍah*). See Muslim, *Ṣaḥīḥ*, II, 701 (*Kitāb al-zakāt, bāb* 18:62); Tirmidhī, *Sunan*, IV, 362 (*Kitāb al-fitan, bāb* 36:2209). See also Ibn Manẓūr, *Lisān al-ʿArab*, s.v. *th-q-l*, where *aflādh kabidihā* is glossed by *kunūz*. Although one should not read too much into this similarity, it is an indication of the tremendous impression that the newly acquired wealth made on the early Muslims.

741. For this meaning of *maʾkal*, pl. *maʾākil*, see Jawharī, *Tāj al-lughah*, III, 1365, who glosses *maʾkal* by *kasb*.

742. I am translating according to de Goeje's suggestion in *Glossary*, s.v. *qarmal*: *thabathā* instead of *banathā*.

743. The translation of this verse is tentative and uncertain.

744. Probably meaning letters that bear the news of victory.

745. While de Goeje's suggestion in *Glossary* (s.v. *sh-b-k*), on which my translation is based, is not very convincing, I am at present not able to provide a better one.

746. This is ʿUmar's *kunyah*; cf. Ibn al-Jawzī, *Manāqib*, 9.

747. See *EI*², s.v. "ʿAṭā" (Cl. Cahen).

748. See *EI*², s.v. "Dīwān i" (A. A. Duri).

ing to seniority [in Islam].[749] He gave to Ṣafwān b. Umayyah,[750] al-
[2412] Ḥārith b. Hishām,[751] and Suhayl b. ʿAmr[752] with the people of the conquest (*ahl al-fatḥ*)[753] less than what those who had preceded them received. They refused to accept it, saying: "We do not acknowledge that anybody is more noble than we are." ʿUmar replied: "I have given to you according to your seniority in Islam, not according to your ancestral nobility." They said: "It is all right, then," and they accepted the payment. Al-Ḥārith and Suhayl left for Syria with their families and continued to wage *jihād* until they were killed in one of the frontier points there; but according to another tradition, they died in the plague of ʿAmwās.[754]

---

749. Meaning that the payments were determined according to the date on which the person in question embraced the new religion: Those who joined Islam at the earliest date received the largest amount.

750. Ṣafwān b. Umayyah was a prominent member of Quraysh. His father was killed in the battle of Badr, fighting on the side of the Meccans. Ṣafwān also fought in skirmishes against the Muslims and embraced Islam only after the conquest of Mecca. He was given a share in the spoils of the battle of Ḥunayn and became one of the *mu'allafah qulūbuhum* "those whose hearts have been reconciled" (i.e., to Islam, by means of gifts). According to some traditions, Ṣafwān participated in the battle of Yarmūk; according to others, there is no evidence that he ever took part in any battle on the side of the Muslims. He died in Shawwāl 36/March–April 657 (or in 41/661–62, or 42/662–63). See Ibn Saʿd, *Ṭabaqāt*, V, 332 and index; (ʿI.) Ibn al-Athīr, *Usd*, III, 22–23; Ibn Ḥajar, *Iṣābah*, III, 432–34; Ibn Ḥajar, *Tahdhīb*, IV, 424–25.

751. Al-Ḥārith b. Hishām was a prominent member of the Qurashī clan of Makhzūm. He fought against the Muslims in the battles of Badr and Uḥud. He embraced Islam after the conquest of Mecca, participated in the battle of Ḥunayn, and received a share in the spoils. Later he took part in the battles of Fiḥl and Ajnādayn against the Byzantines. According to some traditions, he was killed in the battle of Yarmūk; according to others, he died in the plague of ʿAmwās in 18/639–40. See Ibn Saʿd, *Ṭabaqāt*, V, 329; VII/ii, 126; (ʿI.) Ibn al-Athīr, *Usd*, I, 351–52; Ibn Ḥajar, *Iṣābah*, I, 605–8 no. 1506; Ibn Ḥajar, *Tahdhīb*, II, 161–62.

752. Suhayl b. ʿAmr was a leading member of Quraysh. He fought against the Muslims in the battle of Badr, was taken prisoner, and was ransomed by his tribe. He was the person who negotiated the treaty of Ḥudaybiyyah with the Prophet. After the conquest of Mecca he switched sides; he took part in the battle of Ḥunayn on the side of the Prophet, though he was still a polytheist. He embraced Islam after this battle and became one of the *mu'allafah qulūbuhum*. After the Prophet's death he urged Quraysh to embrace Islam. Despite his late conversion, he became a pious and devout Muslim; he fought against the Byzantines in Syria and died in the plague of ʿAmwās (or in the battle of Yarmūk). See Ibn Saʿd, *Ṭabaqāt*, V, 335 and index; (ʿI.) Ibn al-Athīr, *Usd*, II, 371–73; Ibn Ḥajar, *Iṣābah*, III, 212–15 no. 3575; Ibn Ḥajar, *Tahdhīb*, IV, 264–5.

753. Those who embraced Islam only after the conquest of Mecca in 8/630 and did not join the Prophet in the earliest and most difficult period of his activity.

754. A notorious plague that struck Syria and Palestine in the year 18/639–40. See *EI*², s.v. "ʿAmwās" (J. Sourdel-Thomine); Balādhurī, *Futūḥ*, 139; Donner, *Conquests*, 152.

When ʿUmar intended to establish the military register, ʿAlī and ʿAbd al-Raḥmān b. ʿAwf[755] said to him: "Begin with yourself!" He said: "No, I shall rather begin with the uncle of the messenger of God, then the next and the next."[756] First he determined the share of al-ʿAbbās. Then he allotted to the participants in the battle of Badr[757] five thousand [dirhams] each. Then he allotted to those [who embraced Islam] after the battle of Badr and till al-Ḥudaybiyyah[758] four thousand each. Then he allotted to those [who embraced Islam] after al-Ḥudaybiyyah and up to the time when Abū Bakr finished the war with the people of apostasy (*ahl al-riddah*) three thousand each. Among them were those who participated in the conquest of Mecca, those who fought for Abū Bakr, and those who participated in the battles (of Iraq and Syria) before al-Qādisiyyah. All these received three thousand each. Then he allotted to the people of al-Qādisiyyah and to those who fought in Syria [after the battle of al-Qādisiyyah] two thousand each. To the people of outstanding bravery from among them he allotted two thousand and five hundred each. It was said to him: "Would you make the people of al-Qādisiyyah equal to those who had fought in the previous battles?"[759] He replied: "I am not in a position to make them equal with those whose rank they had not attained." It was also said to him: "But you have already made those who live far [from the battlefield] equal to those who live close and fought in defense of their homes." He replied: "Those who live close deserve more because they provided assistance in pursuit and constituted an obstruction for the enemy. And did the Emigrants not say the same when we made them equal with the Helpers? [2413] The assistance provided by the Helpers was near their homes, and the Emigrants came to them from far away."

ʿUmar allotted to those [who embraced Islam and joined the Muslim army] after al-Qādisiyyah and al-Yarmūk[760] one thousand [dirhams] each. Then he allotted to the second group of latecomers[761]

755. See note 4, above.

756. In kinship with the Prophet.

757. The first and victorious battle of the Prophet against the Meccans in 2/634. See *EI*², s.v. "Badr" (W. Montgomery Watt).

758. A famous treaty that the Prophet concluded with the Meccans in 6/628. See *EI*², s.v. "al-Ḥudaybiyya" (W. Montgomery Watt).

759. See p. 2343, above.

760. For the battle of Yarmūk, see Donner, *Conquests*, 129ff.

761. *Rawādif*, sg. *rādifah*. For a discussion of this concept, see Donner, *Conquests*, 231ff.

five hundred each; and to the third group[762] three hundred each. Members of each group received equal payment, whether they were strong or weak, Arabs or non-Arabs. To the fourth group he allotted two hundred and fifty dirhams. He allotted to those who came after them, i.e., the people of Hajar[763] and the Christians of al-Ḥīrah (*al-ʿIbād*),[764] two hundred dirhams. He made four persons who had not participated in the battle of Badr equal to the participants: al-Ḥasan and al-Ḥusayn,[765] Abū Dharr,[766] and Salmān. He allotted to al-ʿAbbās twenty-five thousand dirhams, but according to another tradition, twelve thousand.

He gave to the wives of the Prophet ten thousand dirhams each, except those who were slave girls.[767] The Prophet's wives said: "The Prophet did not prefer us to them in the division of his time; make us all equal!"[768] ʿUmar agreed. He gave ʿĀʾishah two thousand dirhams more than to the others because the Prophet loved her,[769] but she did not accept that. He allotted to the wives of the participants in the battle of Badr five hundred dirhams each; to the wives of those who came after them, till al-Ḥudaybiyyah, four hundred each; to the wives of those who came after them, till the battles of Iraq and Syria,

---

762. Omitting *baʿdahum* "who came after them."

763. Hajar was a town in Baḥrayn, in eastern Arabia. See *EI*[1], s.v. "Hadjar" (Fr. Buhl); *EI*[2], s.v. "al-Ḥasā" (F. S. Vidal). For the emigration from Hajar to Iraq, see *EI*[2], s.v. "ʿAbd al-Ḳays" (W. Caskel); Morony, *Iraq*, 241.

764. Presumably after they embraced Islam. For another interpretation of *al-ʿibād*, see Donner, *Conquests*, 233 n. 65.

765. Al-Ḥasan and al-Ḥusayn were the sons of Fāṭimah and ʿAlī b. Abī Ṭālib and grandsons of the Prophet.

766. Abū Dharr al-Ghifārī was a Companion of the Prophet and is considered in the tradition to be one of the first believers. See *EI*[2], s.v. "Abū Dharr" (J. Robson).

767. *Man jarā ʿalayhā al-milk* has to be understood in light of Qurʾān 4:4: "Marry such women as seem good to you, two, three, four; but, if you fear you will not be equitable, then only one or what your right hand owns" (*aw man malakat aymānukum*). This phrase is normally understood as a reference to slave girls taken captive in war. Balādhurī (*Futūḥ*, 455) records a tradition according to which ʿUmar allotted to Juwayriyyah (bt. al-Ḥārith) and Ṣafiyyah bt. Ḥuyayy b. Akhṭab only 6,000 dirhams (as against 12,000 for the free wives) because they were "part of the booty that God had restored to His prophet" (*mimmā afāʾa Allāh ʿalā rasūlihi*). Cf. Ibn Saʿd, *Ṭabaqāt*, VIII, 83 l. 22, 153 l. 14, 158 l. 3, where these and other slave girls whom the Prophet married are described in similar terms.

768. The question of how the Prophet divided his time among his wives is discussed in Ibn Saʿd, *Ṭabaqāt*, VIII, 121–24.

769. Cf. Balādhurī, *Futūḥ*, 454; on the Prophet's relationship with ʿĀʾishah, see Ibn Saʿd, *Ṭabaqāt*, VIII, 39ff.

three hundred each; to the wives of the people of al-Qādisiyyah two hundred each. He made the women after that equal, and he allotted to the boys one hundred dirhams each, equally.[770] Then he gathered sixty poor people and gave them bread to eat; they calculated what they ate and found that it was more than two *jarības*.[771] ʿUmar [2414] allotted to each of them and to his family two *jarības* per month. ʿUmar said before his death: "I planned to make the payments four thousand dirhams each: a man would give one thousand to his family; one thousand he would take with him [while traveling]; for one thousand he would equip himself;[772] and for one thousand he would equip his home (*yataraffaqu bihā*)."[773] But ʿUmar died before he could implement this.

Abū Jaʿfar al-Ṭabarī has said: According to al-Sarī — Shuʿayb — Sayf—Muḥammad, Ṭalḥah, al-Muhallab, Ziyād, Mujālid, and ʿAmr — al-Shaʿbī; and Ismāʿīl — al-Ḥasan and Abū Ḍamrah — ʿAbdallāh b. al-Mustawrid—Muḥammad b. Sīrīn and Yaḥyā b. Saʿīd—Saʿīd b. al-Musayyab and al-Mustanīr b. Yazīd—Ibrāhīm and Zuhrah—Abū Salamah: When ʿUmar allotted the payments, he allotted them to the people entitled to share in the immovable booty (*ahl al-fayʾ*) to whom God had restored it. These were the people of al-Madāʾin who moved to al-Kūfah, al-Baṣrah, Damascus, Ḥimṣ, Jordan, Palestine, and Egypt. He said: "The booty belongs to the people of the newly established garrison towns (*amṣār*) and to those who joined them, gave them assistance and stayed with them. It was not allotted to others. Is it not true that the cities and the villages were populated by them, that the peace treaties were administered by them, the poll tax was paid to them, that they made the frontier safe and that they subdued the enemy?" Then ʿUmar wrote a letter instructing that the payments be given to those who were entitled to them in one sum, in the year 15/636–37. Somebody said: "O Commander of the Faithful, would you leave in the treasury provisions for some [unexpected] eventuality?" ʿUmar said: "This is a sentence which Satan

770. Probably meaning that the allottment for the boys was determined without regard to the time when their fathers had embraced Islam and joined the Muslim army.

771. See Hinz, *Masse*, 38.

772. Presumably with military equipment.

773. Cf. Balādhurī, *Futūḥ*, 451, where the 4,000 dirhams are divided as follows: for traveling, for weapons, for the family, and for the horse and the shoes.

threw into your mouth. May God protect me from its wickedness! It
[2415] would be a temptation to those who will come after me. Nay, I shall prepare for them[774] what God and His Messenger have commanded us [to prepare]: obedience to God and to His Messenger. These are our provisions, and by virtue of these we attained to what you see. If this money is the price of your religion, you will perish."[775]

According to al-Sarī—Shuʿayb—Sayf—Muḥammad, al-Muhallab, Ṭalḥah, ʿAmr, and Saʿīd: When God granted victory to the Muslims, Rustam was killed, and the news of the victory in Syria reached ʿUmar, he assembled the Muslims and said: "How much of this property can the leader legally keep?" All of them said:

> As for his private needs, his livelihood, and the livelihood of his family, neither more nor less; their garments and his garments for the winter and the summer; two riding beasts for his *jihād*, for attending to his needs, and for carrying him to his pilgrimage (*ḥajj*) and to his *ʿumrah*. Equitable distribution means giving to the valiant people according to their bravery. He will put the people's affairs right, and he will take care of the people at the time of misfortunes and calamities, until these are over. He will deal with those entitled to the immovable booty[776] first.

According to al-Sarī—Shuʿayb—Sayf—Muḥammad—ʿUbaydallāh b. ʿUmar: When ʿUmar received the news about the conquest of al-Qādisiyyah and Damascus, he assembled the people in Medina and said: "I was formerly a merchant, and God provided sufficiently for my family by means of my commerce. Now you have made me preoccupied with your affair. What do you think, how much of this property can I legally keep?" The people suggested a large amount, while ʿAlī (b. Abī Ṭālib) remained silent. ʿUmar said: "What do you say, O ʿAlī?", and ʿAlī replied, "[You can have] what will keep you and your family in a moderately good condition,[777] but you have no
[2416] right to this property beyond that." The people said: "The [right] words are the words of Ibn Abī Ṭālib."

---

774. Meaning his successors in the leadership of the community.

775. If your religion is so weak that it depends on leaving this money in the treasury, you will perish.

776. *Ahl al-fayʾ*, meaning the warriors who seized enemy property in battle.

777. Cf. Ṭabarī, I, 2142–43, where Abū Bakr's income is discussed in similar terms.

According to al-Sarī—Shuʿayb—Sayf—Muḥammad—ʿUbaydallāh—Nāfiʿ—Aslam: A man approached ʿUmar b. al-Khaṭṭāb and said: "How much of this property can you legally keep?" ʿUmar replied: "What will keep me in a moderately good condition: a garment for the summer and a garment for the winter, a riding beast to take ʿUmar for his pilgrimage and the *ʿumrah*, and a riding beast for his needs and his *jihād*."[778]

According to al-Sarī—Shuʿayb—Sayf—Mubashshir b. al-Fuḍayl—Sālim b. ʿAbdallāh: When ʿUmar assumed power, he was receiving the living allowance which had been allotted to Abū Bakr. He lived in this condition, but his needs kept increasing. A group of Emigrants, which included ʿUthmān, ʿAlī, Ṭalḥah, and al-Zubayr got together, and al-Zubayr said: "We should speak to ʿUmar about increasing his income." ʿAlī said: "We have wanted to do it before. Let us go." ʿUthmān said: "This is ʿUmar.[779] Let us try hard to find out what he really thinks. Let us go to Ḥafṣah[780] and ask her in confidence." They entered into her presence and ordered her to inform ʿUmar [of the proposal] in the name of the group, but not to identify anyone of them to ʿUmar until he should agree. Then they left the house. Ḥafṣah met ʿUmar concerning this matter and discerned anger in his face. He said: "Who are they?" She said: "You have no way to know it before I know what you think." ʿUmar said: "If I knew who they were, I would harm them. You stand between me and them. I implore you by God, what was the best garment which the Messenger of God acquired for himself in your house?" Ḥafṣah said: "Two dyed garments in which he used to meet delegations[781] and deliver sermons to the assembled people." ʿUmar said: "And what was the most sumptuous food which he received in your house?" She said: "We baked barley bread. While it was hot, we poured over it [the contents of] the humblest skin,[782] and we made it soft and [2417]

778. The tradition shifts from direct speech by ʿUmar to wording in which ʿUmar is referred to in the third person.

779. Meaning, probably, that, in view of ʿUmar's austere way of life, one cannot speak to him directly about the proposed increase.

780. Ḥafṣah was the daughter of ʿUmar and one of the wives of the Prophet. See Ibn Saʿd, *Ṭabaqāt*, VIII, 56–60.

781. The reference is to delegations of tribal groups that came to meet the Prophet and embrace Islam, especially in the year 9/630–31, which came to be known as "year of the delegations," *sanat al-wufūd*.

782. *ʿUkkah* is a small skin used to hold clarified butter or honey. See Ibn Manẓūr, *Lisān al-ʿArab*, s.v. *ʿ-k-k*.

fatty. He tasted it and found it good." ʿUmar said: "And what blanket which he used to spread in your house was the softest?" Ḥafṣah said: "We had a coarse cover which we used to spread in the summer and put under us. When winter came, we spread half of it, and covered ourselves with the other half." ʿUmar said:

> O Ḥafṣah, tell them on my behalf that the Messenger of God was frugal, put the surplus in its proper place, and contented himself with the bare necessities. By God, I am (also) frugal; I shall put the surplus in its proper place and shall content myself with the bare necessities. I and my two companions[783] are like three men who traveled on a road. The first one set out, took his provisions, and reached his destination. The second one followed him, traveled the same road, and reached him. Then the third one went in his footsteps. If he sticks to their road and is content with their provisions, he will reach them and be in their company; but if he travels another road, he will not [be able to] join them.

According to al-Sarī—Shuʿayb—Sayf—ʿAṭiyyah—his companions and al-Ḍaḥḥāk—Ibn ʿAbbās: When al-Qādisiyyah was conquered and certain people of the *sawād* entered into peace agreements, and when Damascus was conquered and the people of Damascus entered into peace agreements, ʿUmar said to the Muslims: "Assemble and let me know your views on the spoils which God has restored to those who fought in al-Qādisiyyah and in Syria." ʿUmar and ʿAlī agreed to follow the Qur'ān and said: "'Whatever God has given to His Messenger from the people of the cities' (meaning the fifth) 'belongs to God and His Messenger' ... *li-Allāhi wa-li-al-rasūli* means *ilā Allāhi wa-ilā al-rasūli*; this means that God commands and the messenger is obliged to divide [the spoils] '... and to the near kinsman, the orphans, the needy [and the traveler, so that it may not be a thing taken in turns among the rich of
[2418] you ...].'"[784] Then they interpreted this in the light of the verse that follows: "It is for the poor Emigrants [who were expelled from their habitations and their possessions, seeking bounty from God and good pleasure]."[785] They took the four-fifths [and divided them] in

783. Meaning the Prophet and Abū Bakr, the first caliph.

784. Qur'ān 59:7.

785. For interpretations of these verses, see Ṭabarī, *Tafsīr*, XXVIII, 25.

the same way as the fifth had been divided among those who received it in the first three divisions. The four-fifths belong to those to whom God gave the spoils. They found proof of this in the verse "Know that, whatever booty you take, the fifth of it is God's and the messenger's."[786] The [four] fifths were divided according to this. ʿUmar and ʿAlī agreed upon this and the Muslims after them implemented it [as well]. ʿUmar began with the Emigrants, then with the Helpers, then with those who followed them, and with those who participated with them in battles and helped them.

ʿUmar then allotted the stipends from the poll tax which was imposed on those who entered [willingly] into peace agreements or were called upon to do so. The poll tax was restored to the Muslims in moderate sums. The poll tax is not to be divided into fifths. It belongs to those who protect the *ahl al-dhimmah,* fulfill the obligations toward them, and to those who join them and assist them, unless they willingly share the surplus [of the poll tax] with others who were not eligible to receive from it what they themselves had received.

Al-Ṭabarī has said: In this year, meaning the year 15/636–37, there were battles according to the report of Sayf b. ʿUmar. According to the report of Ibn Isḥāq, this was in the year 16. We have already mentioned the account of this on his authority. The report of al-Wāqidī is the same.

---

786. Qur'ān 8:42.

Bibliography of Cited Works

ʿAbd al-Razzāq b. Hammām al-Ṣanʿānī, *al-Muṣannaf*. Edited by Ḥ. al-Aʿẓamī. Beirut, 1971.

Abel, L., *Abû Miḥjan poetae Arabici carmina*. Leiden, 1887.

Abū Dāwūd Sulaymān b. al-Ashʿath al-Sijistānī al-Azdī, *Sunan Abī Dāwūd*. Edited by M. M. ʿAbd al-Ḥamīd. Cairo, n.d.

Abū Tammām Ḥabīb b. Aws al-Ṭāʾī, *Kitāb ... al-Ḥamāsah ... maʿa sharḥ al-Tibrīzī*. Edited by G. W. Freytag. Bonn, 1828.

———, *Naqāʾiḍ Jarīr wa-al-Akhṭal*. Edited by A. Ṣāliḥānī. Beirut, 1922.

Abū Yūsuf, *Kitāb al-kharāj*. Edited by M. I. al-Bannā. Cairo, n.d.

ʿAlī, J., *al-Mufaṣṣal fī taʾrīkh al-ʿArab qabl al-Islām*. Beirut and Baghdad, 1969.

al-ʿAlī, Ṣ. A., "Khiṭaṭ al-Baṣrah," *Sumer* VII (1952), 282–86.

———, "al-Madāʾin fī al-maṣādir al-ʿarabiyyah," *Sumer* XXIII (1967), 47–65.

———, "Minṭaqat al-Kūfah: Dirāsah jughrāfiyyah mustanidah ilā al-maṣādir al-ʿarabiyyah," *Sumer* XXI (1965), 229–53.

al-Anbārī, Abū Bakr Muḥammad b. al-Qāsim, *Sharḥ al-qaṣāʾid al-sabʿ al-ṭiwāl al-jāhiliyyāt*. Edited by ʿA. S. M. Hārūn. Cairo, 1963.

al-Aʿrābī, Muḥammad b. Ziyād, *Kitāb asmāʾ al-khayl wa fursānihā*. Edited by ʿA. Aḥmad. Cairo, 1984.

Arazi, A., *La réalité et la fiction dans la poésie arabe ancienne*. Paris, 1989.

Arberry, A. J., *The Koran Interpreted*. London, 1955.

Ashtor, E., *Histoire des prix et des salaires dans l'Orient médiéval*. Paris, 1969.

al-Aṣmaʿī, ʿAbd al-Malik b. Qurayb, *Kitāb al-nabāt*, I. Ed. ʿA. Y. al-Ghunaym. Cairo, 1972.

al-ʿAynī, Badr al-Dīn Maḥmūd b. Ahmad, *ʿUmdat al-qārī sharḥ Ṣaḥīḥ al-Bukhārī*. Beirut, n.d.

al-Azharī, Abū Manṣūr Muḥammad b. Aḥmad, *Tahdhīb al-lughah*. Edited by M. ʿA. al-Najjār and Y. ʿAbd al-Nabī. Cairo, n.d.

al-Baghdādī, Muḥammad b. al-Ḥasan b. Muḥammad al-Kātib, *Kitāb al-ṭabīkh*. Edited by F. al-Bārūdī. Beirut, 1964.

al-Balādhurī, Aḥmad b. Yaḥyā b. Jābir, *Futūḥ al-buldān*. Edited by M. J. de Goeje. Leiden, 1868.

Bashear, S. "The Title 'Fārūq' and Its Association with ʿUmar I," *SI* LXXII (1990), 47–78.

al-Bayḍāwī, ʿAbdallāh b. ʿUmar b. Muḥammad al-Shīrāzī, *Anwār al-tanzīl wa asrār al-taʾwīl*. Cairo, 1330/1912.

Bevan, A. A., ed., *The Naqāʾiḍ of Jarīr and al-Farazdaq*. Leiden, 1905.

Blachère, R., M. Chouemi, and C. Denizeau, *Dictionnaire arabe-française-anglaise*. Paris, 1967.

Bosworth, C. E., "Iran and the Arabs before Islam." *CHI*, III/i, 593–612.

al-Bukhārī, Muḥammad b. Ismāʿīl, *Kitāb al-taʾrīkh al-kabīr*. Hyderabad, 1363/1944.

———, *Ṣaḥīḥ*. Edited by L. Krehl. 4 vols. Leiden, 1864.

Busse, H., "ʿOmar b. al-Khaṭṭāb in Jerusalem," *JSAI* V (1984), 73–119.

———, "ʿOmar's Image as the Conqueror of Jerusalem," *JSAI* VIII (1986), 149–68.

Butler, A. J., *The Arab Conquest of Egypt*. 2nd ed. Oxford, 1978.

Caskel, W., and G. Strenziok, *Ǧamharat an-nasab: Das genealogische Werk des Hišām ibn Muḥammad al-Kalbī*. 2 vols. Leiden, 1966.

Christensen, A., *L'Iran sous les Sassanides*. Copenhagen, 1936.

Crone, P., *Slaves on Horses: The Evolution of the Islamic Polity*. Cambridge, 1980.

——— and M. A. Cook, *Hagarism: The Making of the Islamic World*. Cambridge, 1977.

al-Damīrī, *Ḥayāt al-ḥayawān al-kubrā*. Cairo, 1958.

al-Dīnawarī, *Al-Akhbār al-ṭiwāl*. Tehran, 1960.

Donner, F. M., *The Early Islamic Conquests*. Princeton, 1981.

Dozy, R., *Dictionnaire détaillé des noms des vêtements chez les Arabes*. Amsterdam, 1845.

———, *Supplément aux dictionnaires arabes*. Leiden, 1881.

Duri, A., "Notes on Taxation in Early Islam," *JESHO* XVII (1974), 135–44.

———, *The Rise of Historical Writing among the Arabs*. Princeton, 1983.

Elad, A., "'And He Who Seeks His Leg . . . ': An Interpretation of a Verse," *JSAI* XI (1988), 240–47.

Fahd, T., *La divination arabe: Études religieuses, sociologiques et folkloriques sur le milieu natif de l'Islam*. Leiden, 1966.

———, "Les présages par le corbeau." *Arabica* VIII (1961), 30–58.

Fattal, A., *Le statut légal des non-musulmanes en pays d'Islam*. Beirut, 1958.
al-Fayrūzābādī, *al-Qāmūs al-muḥīṭ*. 4 vols. Beirut, n.d.
Forand, P. G., "The Status of the Land and Inhabitants of the *Sawād* during the First Two Centuries of Islam," *JESHO* XIV (1971), 25–37.
Fraenkel, S., *Die aramäischen Fremdwörter im Arabischen*. Leiden, 1886.
Friedmann, Y., "Minor Problems in al-Balādhurī's Account of the Conquest of Sind," *RSO* XLV (1970), 253–60.
Fries, N., *Das Heereswesen der Araber zur Zeit der omaijaden nach Ṭabarī*. Tübingen, 1921.
al-Ghundijānī, Muḥammad al-Aʿrābī, *Kitāb asmāʾ khayl al-ʿarab wa-ansābihā wa-fursānihā*. Edited by M. ʿA. Sulṭānī. Damascus, n.d.
de Goeje, M. J., *Mémoire sur la conquête de la Syrie*. Leiden, 1900.
Goldziher, I., *Introduction to Islamic Theology and Law*. Translated by Andras and Ruth Hamori. Princeton, 1981.
———, *Muslim Studies (Muḥammedanische Studien)*. Edited by S. M. Stern. 2 vols. London, 1967–71.
———, "Ueber den Ausdruck *sakîna*," in *Abhandlungen zur arabischen Philologie*. Leiden, 1896. Pp. 177–204.
Guillaume, A., *The Life of Muhammad*. London, 1957.
Heyd, W., *Histoire du commerce du levant au moyen âge*. Leipzig, 1886.
Hill, D. R., *The Termination of Hostilities in the Early Arab Conquests*. London, 1971.
Hinz, W., *Islamische Masse und Gewichte*. Leiden, 1955.
Hitti, P. K., *Origins of the Islamic State*. New York, 1916.
Ibn ʿAbd al-Barr al-Namarī, Yūsuf b. ʿAbdallāh, *Kitāb al-istīʿāb fī maʿrifat al-aṣḥāb*. Hyderabad, 1336/1918.
Ibn Abī al-Dunyā, *Kitāb dhamm al-dunyā*. Edited by E. Almagor. Jerusalem, 1984.
Ibn Abī Ḥātim al-Rāzī, *Kitāb al-jarḥ wa-al-taʿdīl*. Hyderabad, 1952.
Ibn al-ʿAdīm, Kamāl al-Dīn, *Zubdat al-ḥalab min taʾrīkh Ḥalab*. Damascus, 1951.
Ibn al-Athīr, ʿIzz al-Dīn, *Al-Kāmil fī al-taʾrīkh*. Edited by C. J. Tornberg. Leiden, 1868.
———, *Usd al-ghābah fī maʿrifat al-ṣaḥābah*. n.p., n.d.
Ibn al-Athīr, Majd al-Dīn, *Al-Nihāyah fī gharīb al-ḥadīth wa-al-athar*. Edited by Ṭ. A. al-Zāwī and M. M. al-Tanājī. Cairo, 1963.
Ibn Durayd, Muḥammad b. al-Ḥasan, *Kitāb al-ishtiqāq*. Cairo, Beirut, and Baghdad, 1958.
———, *Kitāb jamharat al-lughah*. Hyderabad, 1345/1926–27. Repr. Beirut, n.d.
Ibn Ḥabīb b. Umayyah b. Hāshim al-Baghdādī, Muḥammad, *Kitāb al-muḥabbar*. Edited by I. Lichtenstaedter. Hyderabad, 1942.

Ibn Ḥajar al-ʿAsqalānī, *al-Iṣābah fī tamyīz al-ṣaḥābah*. Edited by ʿA. M. al-Bajāwī. Cairo, n.d.

———, *Tahdhīb al-tahdhīb*. Beirut, 1968.

Ibn Ḥanbal al-Shaybānī al-Marwazī, Aḥmad b. Muḥammad, *Musnad*. n.p., n.d.

———, *Kitāb al-zuhd*. Beirut, 1976.

Ibn Hishām, ʿAbd al-Malik, *Sīrat... Muḥammad rasūl Allāh*. Edited by F. Wüstenfeld. Göttingen, 1858.

Ibn al-Jawzī, Abū al-Faraj ʿAbd al-Raḥmān b. ʿAlī, *Manāqib Amīr al-Mu'minīn ʿUmar b. al-Khaṭṭāb*. Edited by Z. I. al-Qārūt. Beirut, 1980.

Ibn Juzayy al-Kalbī al-Gharnāṭī, ʿAbdallāh b. Muḥammad, *Kitāb al-khayl*. Edited by M. al-ʿArabī al-Khaṭṭābī. Beirut, 1986.

Ibn Kathīr, Ismāʿīl b. ʿUmar, *Kitāb al-bidāyah wa-al-nihāyah*. Cairo, 1383/1963–64.

Ibn Khaldūn, *Muqaddimah*. Beirut, 1900. Translated as *The Muqaddimah* by F. Rosenthal. 3 vols. New York, 1958.

Ibn Khurradādhbih, Abū al-Qāsim ʿUbaydallāh, *Kitab al-masālik wa-al-mamālik*. Edited by M. J. de Goeje. BGA VI. Leiden, 1889.

Ibn Mājah, Muḥammad b. Yazīd al-Qazwīnī, *Sunan*. Cairo, 1954.

Ibn Manẓūr, Muḥammad b. Mukarram, *Lisān al-ʿArab*. Qumm, 1405/1984–85.

Ibn al-Mubārak, ʿAbdallāh, *Kitāb al-zuhd wa-al-raqā'iq*. Edited by Ḥ. al-Aʿẓamī. Malegaon, India, 1966.

Ibn Munabbih, *Kitāb al-tījān*. Hyderabad, 1348/1929–30.

Ibn Qutaybah, *Kitāb al-maʿārif*. Edited by Th. ʿUkkāshah. Cairo, 1960.

———, *Kitāb al-shiʿr wa-al-shuʿarā'*. Edited by M. J. de Goeje. Leiden, 1902.

———, *ʿUyūn al-akhbār*. Cairo, 1925.

Ibn Saʿd, Muḥammad, *Kitāb al-ṭabaqāt al-kabīr*. Edited by E. Sachau et al. 9 vols. Leiden, 1904–40.

Ibn Sallām, Abū ʿUbayd al-Qāsim, *Kitāb al-amwāl*. Edited by M. Ḥ. al-Fiqqī. Cairo, n.d.

al-Iṣfahānī, Abū al-Faraj, *Kitāb al-aghānī*. Edited by I. al-Ābyārī. 30 vols. Cairo, 1969–79.

al-Jabūrī, Y., *Shiʿr ʿAmr b. Shās*. Najaf, 1976.

al-Jāḥiẓ, *Kitāb al-bukhalā'*. Edited by C. van Vloten. Leiden, 1900.

———, *Kitāb al-ḥayawān*. Edited by ʿA. Hārūn. Cairo, 1965.

al-Jawālīqī, Abū Manṣūr, *al-Muʿarrab min al-kalām al-aʿjamī ʿalā ḥurūf al-muʿjam*. Edited by E. Sachau as *Ĝawālīqī's al-Muʿarrab*. Leipzig, 1867. Edited by A. M. Shākir. Cairo, 1969.

Jawharī, *Tāj al-lughah wa-ṣiḥāḥ al-ʿarabiyyah*. Cairo, n.d.

al-Jumaḥī, Muḥammad b. Sallām, *Ṭabaqāt fuḥūl al-shuʿarā'*. Edited by J. Hell. Leiden, 1916. Reprinted Beirut, n.d.

Juynboll, G. H. A., trans., *The Conquest of Iraq, Southwestern Persia, and Egypt: The Middle Years of ʿUmar's Caliphate*. The History of al-Ṭabarī XIII. Albany, 1989.
Kinberg, L., "What Is Meant by al-Zuhd?" *SI* LXI (1985), 17–44.
Kister, M. J., "ʿAn Yadin" (Qurʾān IX, 29): An Attempt at Interpretation." *Arabica* XI (1964), 272–78.
"Haddithū ʿan banī Isrāʾīla wa-lā ḥaraja. A study of an Early Tradition," *IOS* II (1972), 215–39.
______, "On 'Concessions' and Conduct: A Study of an Early Ḥadīth," In G. H. A. Juynboll, ed. *Studies on the First Century of Islamic Society*. Carbondale, Ill., 1982.
______, "Some Reports Concerning al-Ṭāʾif," *JSAI* I (1979), 1–18.
______, "'You Shall Only Set Out for Three Mosques': A Study of an Early Tradition," *Muséon* LXXXII (1969), 173–96. Reprinted in *Studies in Jāhiliyya and Early Islam*. Variorum Reprints XIII. London, 1980.
al-Kūfī, Aḥmad b. Aʿtham, *Kitāb al-futūḥ*. Hyderabad, 1968.
Landau-Tasseron, E., "Sayf b. ʿUmar in Medieval and Modern Scholarship." *Der Islam* LXVII (1990), 1–26.
Lane, E. W., *An Arabic-English Lexicon*. 8 vols. London, 1863–93.
M. Lecker, *The Banū Sulaym: A Contribution to the Study of Early Islam*. Jerusalem, 1989.
Le Strange, G., *The Lands of the Eastern Caliphate*. Cambridge, 1930.
Lichtenstaedter, I., "A Note on the *Gharānīq* and Related Qurʾānic Problems." *IOS* V (1975), 54–61.
Løkkegaard, F., *Islamic Taxation in the Classical Period with Special Reference to Circumstances in Iraq*. Copenhagen, 1950.
al-Makkī, Abū Ṭālib, *Qūt al-qulūb*. Cairo, 1936.
Mālik b. Anas, *al-Muwaṭṭaʾ*. Edited by M. F. ʿAbd al-Bāqī. 2 vols. Cairo, 1951.
al-Maqdisī al-Ḥanbalī, Ḍiyāʾ al-Dīn Muḥammad b. ʿAbd al-Wāḥid, *Faḍāʾil bayt al-maqdis*. Edited by M. M. al-Ḥāfiẓ. Damascus, 1985.
al-Masʿūdī, *Kitāb al-tanbīh wa-al-ishrāf*. *BGA* VIII. Leiden, 1894.
______, *Murūj al-dhahab wa-maʿādin al-jawhar*. Edited by Barbier de Meynard. 9 vols. Paris, 1861–77. Edited by C. Pellat. 7 vols. Beirut, 1966–79.
al-Maydānī, Aḥmad b. Muḥammad b. Aḥmad b. Ibrāhīm, *Majmaʿ al-amthāl*. Edited by M. A. Ibrāhīm. 4 vols. Cairo, 1977–79.
Mayer, L. A., *Mamluk Costume*. Geneva, 1952.
Morony, M. G., *Iraq after the Muslim Conquest*. Princeton, 1984.
Mubārak Shāh, Muḥammad b. Manṣūr, *Ādāb al-ḥarb wa-al-shajāʿah*. Edited by A. Suhaylī Khwānsārī. Tehran, 1346 Sh./1967.
al-Muqaddasī, Muḥammad b. Abī Bakr, *Aḥsan al-taqāsīm fī maʿrifat al-aqālīm*. *BGA* III. Leiden, 1877.

Musil, A., *The Middle Euphrates: A Topographical Itinerary*. New York, 1927.

Muslim b. al-Ḥajjāj al-Qushayrī al-Naysābūrī, Abū al-Ḥusayn, *Ṣaḥīḥ*. Cairo, 1955.

al-Nasā'ī, Aḥmad b. Shuʿayb, *Sunan*. Cairo, n.d.

Noth, A., *Quellenkritische Studien zu Themen, Formen und Tendenzen frühislamischer Überlieferung*. Bonn, 1973.

———, "Zum Verhältnis von kalifaler Zentralgewalt und Provinzen in umayyadischer Zeit. Die 'Sulh-ʿAnwa' Traditionen für Ägypten und den Iraq," *WI* XIV (1973), 150–62.

al-Nuwayrī, Aḥmad b. ʿAbd al-Wahhāb, *Nihāyat al-arab fī funūn al-adab*. Cairo, 1975.

Oppenheimer, A., B. Isaac, and M. Lecker, *Babylonia Judaica in the Talmudic Period*. Wiesbaden, 1983.

Ostrogorsky, G., *History of the Byzantine State*. New Brunswick, N.J., 1969.

al-Qasṭallānī, Shihāb al-Dīn Aḥmad b. Muḥammad, *Irshād al-sārī sharḥ Ṣaḥīḥ al-Bukhārī*. Būlāq (Cairo), 1304/1886 – 87. 10 vols. Reprinted Baghdad, n.d.

Qudāmah b. Jaʿfar, *Nubadh min Kitāb al-kharāj wa-ṣanʿat al-kitābah*. *BGA* VI. Leiden, 1889.

Reckendorf, H., *Arabische Syntax*. Heidelberg, 1921.

Rodinson, M., "Recherches sur les documents arabes relatifs à la cuisine," *REI* (1949), 95–165.

Rosenthal, F., *A History of Muslim Historiography*. Leiden,. 1952.

Rowson, E. K., tr., *The Marwānid Restoration: The Caliphate of ʿAbd al-Malik*. The History of al-Ṭabarī XXII. Albany, 1989.

Rufus of Ephesus, *Krankenjournale*. Edited and translated by M. Ullmann. Wiesbaden, 1978.

Sadan, J., *Le mobilier au proche orient médiéval*. Leiden, 1976.

al-Sarakhsī, Muḥammad b. Aḥmad, *Sharḥ al-siyar al-kabīr*. Edited by Ṣ. al-Munajjid. Cairo, 1957.

al-Sarrāj, *Kitāb al-lumaʿ fī al-taṣawwuf*. Edited by R. A. Nicholson. Leiden and London, 1914.

Sauvaire, H. M., "Matériaux pour servir à l'histoire de la numismatique et de la métrologie musulmanes," *Journal asiatique*, 8th series, VII (1886), 124–77, 394–468, VIII (1886) 113–65, 272–97.

Schmucker, W., *Zu einigen wichtigen bodenrechtlichen Konsequenzen der islamischen Eroberungsbewegung*. Bonn, 1972.

Schwarzlose, F. W., *Die Waffen der alten Araber aus ihren Dichter dargestellt*. Leipzig, 1886.

Shaban, M. A., *Islamic History* A.D. *600–750. A New Interpretation*. Cambridge, 1971.
Spitaler, A., "Was bedeutet baqija im Koran?" in F. Meier, ed., *Westöstliche Abhandlungen Rudolf Tschudi*... Wiesbaden, 1954. Pp. 137–46.
al-Suyūṭī, Muḥammad b. Shihāb al-Dīn, *al-Aḥādīth al-ḥisān fī faḍl al-ṭaylasān*. Edited by A. Arazī. Jerusalem, 1983.
______, *Itḥāf al-akhiṣṣā' fī faḍā'il al-masjid al-aqṣā*. Edited by A. R. Aḥmad. Cairo, 1982.
al-Ṭa''ān, H., ed., *Dīwān ʿAmr b. Maʿdīkarib al-Zubaydī*. N.p., n.d.
Al-Ṭabarī, Abū Jaʿfar Muḥammad b. Jarīr, *Jāmiʿ al-bayān fī tafsīr al-Qu'rān*. Cairo 1325/1907. Reprinted Beirut, 1986.
______, *Kitāb al-jihād wa-kitāb al-jizyah wa-aḥkām al-muḥāribīn min kitāb ikhtilāf al-fuqahā'*. Edited by J. Schacht. Leiden, 1933.
______, *Ta'rīkh al-rusul wa-al-mulūk*. Edited by M. J. de Goeje. 13 vols. plus 2 vols. *Indices* and *Introductio, glossarium, addenda et emendanda*. Leiden, 1879–1901.
al-Tarābīshī, M., *Shiʿr ʿAmr b. Maʿdīkarib al-Zubaydī*. Damascus, 1974.
al-Thaʿālibī, Abū Manṣūr ʿAbd al-Malik, *Ghurar akhbār mulūk al-furs wa-siyarihim*. Paris, 1900.
Thilo, U., *Die Ortsnamen in der altarabischen Poesie*. Wiesbaden, 1958.
al-Tirmidhī, Abū ʿĪsā Muḥammad b. ʿIsā b. Sawrah, *Sunan*. 10 vols. in 5. Ḥimṣ, 1965–68.
Ullmann, M., *Die Medizin im Islam*. Leiden und Cologne, 1970.
al-Wāqidī, Muḥammad b. ʿUmar, *Kitāb al-maghāzī*. Edited by M. Jones. London, 1966.
al-Wāsiṭī, Abū Bakr Muḥammad b. Aḥmad, *Faḍā'il al-bayt al-muqaddas*. Edited by I. Hasson. Jerusalem, 1979.
Watt, W. M., *Muḥammad at Medina*. Oxford, 1977.
Wellhausen, J., *Skizzen und Vorarbeiten*. Berlin, 1899. Reprinted Berlin, 1985.
Wensinck, A. J., et al., *Concordance et indices de la tradition musulmane*. 8 vols. Leiden, 1936–88.
Wolfensohn, I. (Ben Zeev), *Kaʿb al-Aḥbār und seine Stellung im Ḥadīth und in der islamischen Legendenliteratur*. Frankfurt, 1933.
Yaʿqūbī, *Ta'rīkh*. Edited by M. T. Houtsma. Leiden, 1888.
Yāqūt, *Muʿjam al-buldān*. Edited by F. Wüstenfeld. Leipzig, 1868.
S. M. Yusuf, "The Battle of al-Qadisiyya," *IC* XIX (1945), 1–28.

Index

Included are names of persons, groups, and places, as well as Arabic terms that recur often in the text or are discussed in the footnotes. An asterisk (*) indicates a figure who is mentioned in the text only as a transmitter. Entries that are mentioned in both text and footnotes on the same page are listed by page number only. Finally, the Arabic definite article al-, *the abbreviation* b. *(for* ibn*), and all material in parentheses have been disregarded in the alphabetizing of entries.*

E

F

G

H

I

L

M

T

U

Printed in the United States
25332LVS00002B/594